In the same

INTERNATIONAL

FILM GUIDE SERIES

edited by Peter Cowie

Parallel with this volume:
Hollywood in the Twenties *by David Robinson*
Hollywood in the Thirties *by John Baxter*

Previously published:
The Cinema of Orson Welles *by Peter Cowie*
Hitchcock's Films *by Robin Wood*
The Marx Brothers
Their World of Comedy *by Allen Eyles*
French Cinema since 1946
(Vol. 1: The Great Tradition
Vol. 2: The Personal Style) *by Roy Armes*
Swedish Cinema *by Peter Cowie*
The Musical Film *by Douglas McVay*
Buster Keaton *by J.-P. Lebel*
Animation in the Cinema *by Ralph Stephenson*
The Horror Film *by Ivan Butler*
The Cinema of Joseph Losey *by James Leahy*
The Western
An Illustrated Guide *by Allen Eyles*
Suspense in the Cinema *by Gordon Gow*
The Cinema of Alain Resnais *by Roy Armes*
A Dictionary of the Cinema *by Peter Graham*
4 Great Comedians
Chaplin, Lloyd, Keaton, Langdon *by Donald W. McCaffrey*

HOLLYWOOD IN THE FORTIES

by
CHARLES HIGHAM
and
JOEL GREENBERG

A. ZWEMMER LIMITED, LONDON
A. S. BARNES & CO., NEW YORK

Acknowledgements

WE should like to express our thanks to the following for their help in preparing this volume:

In Hollywood Louis Blaine (Universal); Ely Levy (Columbia); Milton and Gitta Luboviski; Geoffrey Shurlock and Albert van Schmus (Production Code Administration of the Motion Picture Association of America); Bob Vogel (Metro-Goldwyn-Mayer); Robert Aldrich, Curtis Bernhardt, Henry Blanke, David Bradley, John Brahm, George Cukor, William Daniels, Bette Davis, John Ford, William Frye, Lee Garmes, Curtis Harrington, Alfred Hitchcock, James Wong Howe, Christopher Isherwood, Fritz Lang, Ranald MacDougall, Rouben Mamoulian, Lewis Milestone, Vincente Minnelli, Jean Negulesco, Gerd Oswald, Irving Rapper, Mark Robson, Barbara Stanwyck, Joe Stefano, Jacques Tourneur, King Vidor, Billy Wilder; and especially Don Prince of 20th Century Fox, whose kindness and encouragement were at all times indispensable. *And in Sydney* Bill Collins (TCN-Channel 9); and the staff of the Public Library of New South Wales.

Stills courtesy of Bill Collins, also Barrie Pattison.

Front Cover: Ingrid Bergman and Humphrey Bogart in *Casablanca*.
Back Cover: (Forties) Joan Crawford in *Mildred Pierce*; (Twenties) Rudolph Valentino practises the tango; (Thirties) Spencer Tracy in *Twenty Thousand Years in Sing Sing*.

Contents

1 INTRODUCTION .. .. *page* 7

2 BLACK CINEMA 19

3 MELODRAMA 36

4 FANTASY AND HORROR 50

5 PROBLEM AND SOCIOLOGICAL FILMS 68

6 WAR PROPAGANDA 86

7 PRESTIGE PICTURES: BIOGRAPHIES AND
   LITERARY ADAPTATIONS 104

8 ACTION, OUTDOOR AND PASTORAL FILMS .. 124

9 WOMEN'S PICTURES 139

10 COMEDY 154

11 MUSICALS 170

INDEX 182

TO DUSTY AND JEAN NEGULESCO

1. Introduction

1940 LOOKED LIKE an inauspicious year for Hollywood. After the gigantic bonanza of the late Thirties, ending with the supreme box-office triumph of *Gone With the Wind*, clouds began to darken the air. The outbreak of war in Europe caused the closure of the rich Continental market. Currency restrictions meant a drastic reduction of potential in the Commonwealth and the United Kingdom. The Far Eastern markets shrivelled as well. Almost overnight, the reckless extravagance of the previous decade stopped dead. Hollywood pulled its purse-strings tight, studio staffs were laid off, and all but the biggest stars had to take heavy cuts in salary.

By the end of the year, losses were as much as one-third on the figures of 1939. To make matters worse, the old system whereby theatres were compelled to book "blind" a studio's entire annual product was broken by government action. From now on, pictures were to be sold only in blocks of five, and exhibitors had to see them first. And from the Attorney General's Department came a threat that had begun to gather force as early as 1937: that the theatre chains might be detached from the studios that owned them, that the old, powerful monopolies would be broken down.

But a year of strain was followed by a wonderful burst of Hollywood vitality. Rigid economy drives and a sharp increase in first-class scripts resulted in the beginnings of an upsurge in 1941. Technical qualities underwent a vast improvement: first, special lacquers were developed to give film prints an unprecedented sheen, processing now reduced grain, and sound recording underwent major changes. It now became possible to use more subtle and varied lighting in colour films. At Warners, new fog machines were constructed, along with a battery of special effects devices, and Anatole Litvak's *Out of the Fog* became a show-case for this new development. A leaner, tougher and more expert industry emerged, and at the same time the intelligence and wit of the American cinema surged to a peak.

By mid-1941, box-office receipts had begun to mount. And it was a brilliant year for creative achievement: Welles directed *Citizen Kane*, von Sternberg *The Shanghai Gesture*, John Ford *How Green Was My Valley*, Cukor *A Woman's Face*, Sturges *The Lady Eve*, René Clair *The Flame of New Orleans*, Hawks *Sergeant York*. These directors were at the top of their form; and of them two — Sturges and Welles — were never to achieve quite that level again.

Each of the studios, when the U.S.A. entered the war after Pearl Harbor, settled down to an individual policy that was pursued almost to the end of the decade. Under Louis B. Mayer, M-G-M had the biggest array of top box-office stars: Mickey Rooney was the first favourite, followed by Clark Gable and Spencer Tracy. Later, Greer Garson joined their company. At Metro, the idea was to concentrate on stories of nice people involved in heartbreak, finding their happiness at last in each other's arms, and all in settings of an idealised and antiseptic beauty: an England full of sunshine and chintz and doves, an America of white fences and rambler roses round the door. Hagiographies of scientists or reformers glowed with optimistic charm, Herbert Stothart's violin scores oozed sentimental grace, and the photographers and art directors conspired to create a beautiful synthetic world. The formula worked, and the M-G-M stable of stars remained supreme for many years. But it took a Vincente Minnelli to take the candied artifice of Mayerland and turn it into an expression of his own bright vision. His best musicals, charming, elegant, civilised, remained the summits of the studio's work at the time until Stanley Donen and Gene Kelly's *On The Town* eclipsed them with a far more virile exuberance at the very end of the decade.

Warners was run with an iron hand: writers, directors and players had to clock in early in the morning, working hours often stretched far into the night. If a star refused to act a role, he or she could be suspended for months. Directors were on long-term contract and were shuffled relentlessly from script to script. Only Bette Davis, queen of the lot, was sacrosanct. She could summon her own directors and writers, and not even Jack Warner could out-argue her. Other players — Barbara Stanwyck, even Joan Crawford — often had to battle to avoid appearing in inferior films.

Yet West Point, Sing Sing and San Quentin — as Warners was variously known — benefited greatly from the ruthless economising enforced by its bosses, and in Steve Trilling, its production chief, it had a brilliant administrator. Films there were made swiftly and expertly, and the studio word was that nothing must lag. Hal Wallis and Henry Blanke, production geniuses of the period, cut every film for speed, ensuring the tremendous drive and pace of the Warners pictures, the melodramas and war pictures of the era. A distinctive low-key Warners style was developed with the aid of cameramen like Sol Polito and Ernest Haller: murky and sombre, with every cocktail bar seemingly full of cigarette smoke, streets and piers gleaming with rain, and heroines mink-clad and ready with convenient pistols to be produced at moments of stress to the strains of rich scores by Steiner, Waxman or Korngold. Bogart, laconic and dry-voiced, Bacall, sultry and sexy, Stanwyck, tough and energetic in tweeds and sensible shoes, Davis, huge-eyed and clip-voiced, Crawford, massive and dominating, broadshouldered and ankle-strapped: these were the definitive figures of this Warner period, and directors like Negulesco, Rapper, Sherman, Bernhardt and above all Michael Curtiz set its emotional tone.

At Paramount, the influence of Lubitsch remained strong: high-key comedies like *Going My Way* were popular, and in Preston Sturges — sophisticated master of film repartee and the double-take — the studio found a prodigy at skilled farce. The cynical talents of Billy Wilder and Charles Brackett enjoyed free expression under the extraordinarily enlightened directorship of the studio head Buddy de Sylva, and Mitchell Leisen was able to indulge his charming lightweight talent in films like *Kitty*, most elegant of period comedies. Ray Milland, relaxed and unassuming, Alan Ladd, diminutive and tough in trench-coats and Fedoras, Paulette Goddard, Veronica Lake, with her wing of peek-a-boo hair and tiny, child-like face gave the studio its individual acting look, until at the end of the decade Hal Wallis imported his brand of steamy melodrama from Warners, and created a group of powerful new stars: Lizabeth Scott, growling huskily, Burt Lancaster, Wendell Corey and Kirk Douglas.

Columbia's tight-fisted and hard-bitten policy under Harry Cohn

9

ensured a rash of slick B-pictures, and at A-level chiefly concentrated on wringing every drop out of Rita Hayworth, its only major female star and sex symbol; the studio's chief achievement of the decade was *Gilda*, a masterpiece of *Kitsch* under the direction of Charles Vidor with at least one quintessential Forties sequence: Rita singing "Put the Blame on Mame, Boys" in black satin, an apotheosis of G.I. dreams.

Twentieth Century-Fox went all out for a hard, brassy and relentlessly professional approach, using the cleanest and sharpest photography in the business. Betty Grable was the studio's leading female attraction, the G.I.'s favourite pin-up girl, and her sparkling and irresistibly charming personality was well displayed in half-a-dozen musicals, beginning with the best of them all, Walter Lang's *Moon over Miami*.

To attract Latin America, the only strong foreign market left following the closure of Europe, Carmen Miranda was imported to Hollywood and musical after musical was set in Brazil or Argentina or Costa Rica. Miranda's superbly vulgar personality was cleverly exploited by directors like Busby Berkeley, Walter Lang and Irving Cummings: in fruit hats, frilly sleeves and swinging skirts, her eyes popping with excitement, the Brazilian Bombshell epitomised the period's energy perhaps more than any other star.

Fox's black-and-white films of the period also had a polish, a suave and accomplished air of elegance which reflected the showman's flair of Darryl F. Zanuck, and in *The Razor's Edge* the apotheosis of the Fox style was achieved. The photography of Arthur Miller ensured an incomparable pictorial richness, the writing of Lamar Trotti matched the skill of Maugham's own, and the direction by Edmund Goulding of the starry cast — Clifton Webb, Anne Baxter, Gene Tierney, Herbert Marshall, Tyrone Power — had a perfectly realised skill and balance.

Universal concentrated on Deanna Durbin musicals and yashmak operas and created in Maria Montez a fabulous symbol of the decade's more glorious absurdities: Sabu, Montez, Jon Hall and Turhan Bey riding out to some strange Arabian Nights adventure in the desert sands sent a generation of children into ecstasies of pleasure, and turbans became an international female fashion. At R.K.O. (despite such flings at culture as *Citizen Kane*, the Val Lewton pictures, *Crossfire*), Eagle Lion and Republic, the B-picture melodrama was the staple product, and Republic could offer in Vera Hruba Ralston a perfect Forties figure for the addict.

Through all the studios, it was often the minor players who set the tone of the period more than the top contract stars like Rooney, Flynn, Power, Faye, Davis, Cagney. Peggy Ryan and Donald O'Connor, spunky kids of Universal's hayseed musical comedies, Judy Canova, whose pigtails stood on end with fright in a spook picture, Laird Cregar, dead at 28 from a crash diet, huge, glowing-eyed and silken voiced, Ella Raines, fresh, brisk, pageboy-haired friend of troubled men, Eve Arden, witty and pointed bachelor girl and heroine's adviser, Claude Rains, suave and ironical in smoking jackets, Lucile Watson, dignified epitome of diplomatic society ladies, Ian Wolfe, prim and discreet hoverer in the background of innumerable films as butler, attorney, doctor or reliable family friend, Albert Bassermann, octogenarian refugee from the Berlin stage, equally adept as torture victim or Von Papen-like diplomat, Mary Wickes, angular and hilarious nurse or housemaid, Doris Lloyd, doing her British bit as tart or wardress, or going up the social scale all the way to duchess, and a host of other players whose names can only be mentioned: Mary Beth Hughes, the Andrews Sisters, Lynn Bari (called by *Variety* the Paulette Goddard of B-pictures), Evelyn Ankers, Vera Vague, Veda Ann Borg, Marion Marshall, Gloria Jean, Audrey Totter, Frances Rafferty, Brenda Joyce, Belita, Louise Allbritton, Joan Davis, Spring Byington, Porter Hall, Fritz Feld, Franklin Pangborn, Lee Patrick. It is the population of Forties films that still creates a world of its own, a world of snappy secretaries, bright factory girls, wide-eyed chorines, ice-skaters involved in murder cases and hotel switchboard operators who, more often than not, were likely to hear something really lethal over the telephone. And the fashions of the period still spell nostalgia: hairdos upswept or shoulder-length, eyebrows well plucked, knee-length skirts, heroines often tending to be chubby.

★ ★ ★

The animated film enjoyed a boom during the decade. Mostly featuring crudely comic animal characters like Bugs Bunny, Heckle and Jeckle the Talking Magpies, and Tom and Jerry, they allowed little scope for subtlety or experimentation but often achieved a fantastic audacious surreal humour that pulled the laws of physics and gravity spectacularly awry. Disney still led the field with Donald Duck, Mickey Mouse, Pluto and Goofy, but others were making rapid gains: Terrytoons, George Pal with his Puppetoons and Madcap Models, Warners' Merrie Melodies and Looney Tunes, Columbia's Jolly Frolics and Color Rhapsodies. The last-named series produced possibly the decade's most brilliant cartoon short, *The Herring Murder Mystery* (1944), an inspired piece of craziness in which a manufacturer of marinated herring is given a deserved underwater trial by fish judge and jury and a creature in a bowl murmurs, "I'm just a silver fish among the gold."

Where Disney was almost without rival was in the field of the full-length animated feature. He began the decade with *Fantasia* (1940), an ill-advised, costly excursion into "culture" which — apart from the evolution sequence accompanying Stravinsky's *Rite of Spring* and the wonderful animation in *Night on Bald Mountain* — was an unhappy misfire, arch, sentimental, self-conscious, a monument to Midcult tastelessness. *Pinocchio* (1940), more modest and less inventive, contained a scene recalling *The Island Of Lost Souls* that children (and not a few adults) must have found terrifying: the moment when the youth Lampwick suddenly realises he is turning into a jackass. *Dumbo* (1941) was the story of a circus elephant, while *Bambi* (1942), adapted from Felix Salten's novel, represented Disney at his peak: with his Multiplane technique permitting a hitherto impossible realism, this had superbly managed animation and a minimum of saccharine cuteness.

His other Forties features — *The Reluctant Dragon* (1941), *The Three Caballeros* (1944), *Make Mine Music* (1946), *Melody Time* and *So Dear To My Heart* (both 1948) — tended to use live-action as well as animated footage, presaging the time when Disney would virtually forsake feature animation for conventional production. The only challenge he received in this period as a feature-film animator was from

12

Paramount's Max Fleischer, who, with *Gulliver's Travels* (1940) and *Mr. Bug Goes To Town* (1941), provided a welcome relief from Disney's near-monopoly.

Shorts of the 1940s were perhaps even more characteristic of the period than features. The leading short-subject studio was M-G-M, which wisely followed a policy of using its shorts department as a training ground for developing talent (Zinnemann, George Sidney and Dassin, among others, are alumni). Fledgling directors could show their paces in John Nesbitt's *Passing Parade* series of historical semi-documentaries, or in *Crime Does Not Pay*, a collection of crisply made, modestly budgeted quasi-realistic pieces foreshadowing the post-World War Two "realism" vogue. More stereotyped fare was provided in the *Pete Smith Specialties*, with Dave O'Brien as a harassed and hen-pecked husband, battler against sundry comic domestic setbacks, and in the celebrated James A. Fitzpatrick Traveltalks, tuppence-coloured moving postcards accompanied by the ubiquitous producer's unctuous voice.

Warners' answer to Pete Smith was Joe McDoakes, a character shown perennially "behind the eight-ball" as he vainly tries various occupations ("So You Want to Be a . . . ?"). Further comic capers were indulged in by the underrated Three Stooges, Larry, Curly and Moe, whose brand of insolent, anarchic, outrageous farce survived well into the Fifties and beyond. Nor must we forget the "singalong" shorts, with their bouncing white balls picking out the lyrics of community songs to which audiences were expected to respond lustily, or the "novelty" shorts often featuring real animals "singing" with the aid of animated mouths ("Doing the Cow-Cow Boogie in the *strangest* way . . .").

As for serious documentaries, only Louis de Rochemont's The March of Time, a survival from the 1930s, appeared with any regularity. Covering such diverse subjects as the break-up of Holland's colonial empire, the history of gramophone records, new medical discoveries and Australia at war, the series, for all its Luce-inspired attitudes, was nevertheless the only way many people in movie theatre audiences were ever made aware of certain major social, political and international problems. Intelligently written and edited, The March of Time two-reelers performed a valuable service, one that has since been largely taken over by television.

Hollywood's assistance to the war effort earned it the highest praise: not only were stars called up for distinguished service — Robert Montgomery, James Stewart, Douglas Fairbanks and Clark Gable particularly shone — but the stars at home worked washing dishes and serving meals in the Hollywood Canteen, and performers like Bob Hope, Abbott and Costello, Joe E. Brown, Al Jolson, Martha Raye, Mitzi Mayfair and Kay Francis made enormously popular tours of the battle areas. In 1943, 630,000 men in the armed services were seeing Hollywood films each night, and many had seen the stars in person as well. Four thousand Hollywood personnel and personalities were in uniform that year, and many movie entertainers appeared on the famous Stars Over America tours, raising 838,025,000 dollars in cash, visiting 151 hospitals, 254 army camps, and 41 cities. By war's end, celebrities had made 122 overseas tours, the Hollywood Canteen had entertained an estimated three million Service personnel, and the troops had watched 43,306 prints of 16mm feature films donated by the industry's War Activities Committee. In *Stage Door Canteen* (1943) and *Hollywood Canteen* (1945) ordinary doughboys could be seen dancing with Joan Crawford or being served food by Katharine Cornell: proof that the stars yielded to no one in their allegiance to democracy.

The cessation of hostilities seemed to create more problems than it solved. True, major male stars — among them James Stewart, Clark Gable, Tyrone Power and Henry Fonda — did return to sound-stage duty, but Hollywood had still to put itself on a stable peace-time basis. Despite record box-office earnings, it was plagued by strikes, increasing production costs and the problem of recapturing its markets in formerly enemy or enemy-occupied countries. And in the U.S. district court of New York, eight major companies went on trial in 1945 on charges of monopolistic practices, chiefly involving multiple ownership of the means of production, distribution and exhibition.

But amid the boom years it was hard to discern decline and disaster ahead: 1946, with its gross takings of $1750-million, was the most profitable year in the industry's history. Who could have foreseen that by 1949 this figure would have dropped to $1375-million, that crippling British taxes on overseas companies' film earnings would drastically slash Hollywood's income, that government investigations of alleged industry Communists would dramatically divide its personnel, create a clandestine blacklist and severely — perhaps irreparably — damage its prestige and drive many talented people into obscurity?

Yet to have prognosticated these things would not have required undue prescience or pessimism, since for several years they had formed real if hitherto negligible threats. Labour troubles, which resulted in an eight-month studio union strike in 1945, a 25% pay rise for studio employees in 1946, and print hold-ups in laboratories the same year, intensified as the decade neared its end. In 1947, everything seemed to hit the industry at once: Britain announced a 75% tax on foreign film earnings, which threatened to reduce Hollywood's major source of foreign revenue from an annual $68 million to $17 million; other sterling countries followed suit; and the results swiftly made themselves felt in the studios.

Sudden economy waves threw thousands out of work. Budgets were trimmed, crowd scenes minimised, epics involving large and expensive sets abandoned in favour of pictures emphasising "story" and "realism" rather than lavish production values. Independent companies decreased production, one or two — Rainbow and Liberty, for example — ceasing to exist altogether. Efficiency was the keynote everywhere: more careful planning and preparation meant that script difficulties that were formerly worked out on the set were now solved beforehand, that numerous takes for the one scene were now obviated by increased rehearsals.

Despite all this, income still continued to decline, until by 1948 studio employment fell by about 25%, an estimated 50% of the Publicists Guild was unemployed, and the purchase of story material was severely curtailed. At the close of the year, Warner Brothers and Eagle Lion studios were both shut down, but expected to reopen early in 1949.

This was the period of the relatively inexpensive "quality" picture, the psychological melodrama in black-and-white with mainly indoor sets and small casts, the "sociological" dramas often shot on location with ordinary people as extras. In 1947, 28% of films given a Motion Picture Association Code seal had a "problem" content, and their styles — a felicitous amalgam of studio craftsmanship and actuality — represented a departure from the almost unrelieved studio-bound glossiness of the past.

By far the biggest bombshell of 1947, however, was the House Committee on Un-American Activities' Washington hearings to investigate alleged Communists in Hollywood and alleged communist content of some of its pictures. When a group of ten "unfriendly" witnesses invoked the Fifth Amendment to the U.S. Constitution and refused to state whether they were or ever had been Communists, a meeting of top film executives in New York under the chairmanship of Eric Johnston, a former president of the U.S. Chamber of Commerce and since 1945 president of the Motion Picture Association of America, issued what came to be called the Waldorf Statement, declaring that henceforth known Communists would not be employed in Hollywood and reiterating the industry's longstanding opposition to government censorship, a possibility which it was feared the committee hearings might ultimately presage.

The effect of this on film production was twofold: it resulted, firstly, in the making of a number of overtly anti-Communist features (*The Iron Curtain, The Red Menace, The Red Danube*) which were designed not so much to make money (they didn't make money anyhow) as to establish Hollywood's political *bona fides*; and it meant the creation of an unofficial but tacitly acknowledged "blacklist" of unemployables and a consequent departure from Hollywood of many prominent talents — writers, directors, actors — no longer politically acceptable. To some observers this represented a long overdue house-cleaning process; to others, it meant the beginning of an era of fear, betrayal and witch-hunting hysteria. What is certain is that Communist influence in Hollywood, if it ever existed, was driven out, and that the ranks of key contributors to the movie-making process were appreciably thinned. It was easy enough for those remaining to applaud the departure of Left-oriented creators and interpreters; less easy to make films as good, or as profitable, as some of those for which the departed had been responsible.

The big corporations, in this second half of the decade, began to lose some of the stability that had characterised them for years: in 1948, Howard Hughes obtained control of the financially shaky R.K.O., and Dore Schary left that studio to assume under Louis B. Mayer the post of head of production at M-G-M. In 1946, Universal merged with International, and in 1949 both Eagle Lion and the David O. Selznick organisation ceased production. February, 1949, was Hollywood's lowest point for some time: with only 22 features in production, about half the normal amount, it began to seem as if the old days of vast grosses, with Hollywood movies supplying most of the world's entertainment, were gone for good. The rise of television, the departure of still more talent, and the failure to develop new creators and performers of comparable calibre to the old, hastened the trend. Also, the climax of four years' court action in 1949 when Paramount and R.K.O. arrived at a consent decree divorcing their exhibition from their producer-distributor interests foreshadowed similar action with regard to other studios in the 1950s, and the consequent additional weakening of the Hollywood financial empire.

The picture was not altogether gloomy, however. Mechanically, movies were constantly improving. The introduction of tri-acetate safety film for 35mm stock in 1948, and the departure of cellulose nitrate base, meant greater ease and less hazard in the handling and transport of motion pictures. Magnetic recording, one of the Allied victors' spoils from Nazi Germany, yielded better quality sound as it was gradually integrated into U.S. film production. Low-cost plastic set materials, improved colour stock and other devices made movies look and sound better than ever.

Yet at the decade's end something vital seemed ebbing away ever more swiftly from the films of Hollywood, a process accelerating in the early Fifties and reaching a climax with the introduction of Cinema-Scope, the loss of guaranteed markets when the government finally took away the theatre chains from the studios, and a failure of nerve, a subsequent deadening and flattening from which American movies have never recovered. The Forties may now be seen as the apotheosis of the U.S. feature film, its last great show of confidence and skill before it virtually succumbed artistically to the paralysing effects of bigger and bigger screens, the collapse of the star system.

This book is an attempt to chart and evaluate that marvellous lost era, to evoke it both for those who lived through it and those too young to have done so. Sufficiently distant in time to have become historic, yet not so distant that many of us cannot still remember it, the decade has so far resisted — except perhaps sporadically — most efforts at analysis. Our aim here has not been simply to produce an exercise in nostalgia, a sentimental backward look at the *mores* and pre-occupations of twenty years ago; it has been, rather, to arrive at a valid judgement of the decade's films, which, viewed as a whole, constitute in our opinion an output of unrivalled richness and excellence.

Inevitably, much has been omitted for reasons of space: nearly all B-pictures, which deserve a special history of their own; shorts, serials, documentaries; no mention here of the "Why We Fight" series, or of M-G-M's Passing Parades. Some features have been crowded out: Julien Duvivier's *Tales of Manhattan,* for instance, an elegantly polished story of the adventures of a tail coat, which embraced many categories; John Ford's *How Green was my Valley,* not quite melodrama or prestige picture, in an area outside any satisfactory category; or, in the B or minor-A category such oddities as *The Outlaw*, *High Wall*, *The Dark Past*, *Crack-Up*, *The Locket*, *Guest in the House*, *Gun Crazy*, *Sunday Dinner for a Soldier*, *The Window* and Nicholas Ray's widely admired *They Live By Night*. Some other book, some other time must do justice to the rich melodramatic substratum of the Forties and early Fifties.

We have tried, despite the omissions, to draw attention to the work of directors long overdue for proper study, too often dismissed as impersonal and efficient hacks, but in fact *hommes du cinéma* with marked styles of their own: Jean Negulesco, romantic artificer, investing melodramas and women's pictures with his flamboyant painter's visual sense, reminding one that he studied in Modigliani's *atelier*; Edmund Goulding, Negulesco's antithesis in his corrosive *Nightmare Alley*, that masterly portrait of evil ambition and human gullibility, creator, too, of suave melodrama in *The Razor's Edge*, of comedy in the brilliant *Everybody Does It*; Mitchell Leisen, brittle but exact light comedy director; Vincent Sherman, a fine craftsman rivalled only by the precise and meticulous Curtis Bernhardt in the second echelon of the Warner team; John Cromwell, versatile technician, creator of the beautifully made *Since You Went Away* and *Victory*, best version to date of a Conrad novel, and, greatest of all, Michael Curtiz, the Forties' magnifico whose films embraced almost all genres, whose style — florid, romantically U.F.A.-esque, sombrely low-key — brought to life a nocturnal America of the imagination, and whose wholly American drive, energy and flair expressed themselves in the Forties' most characteristic single film, the unforgettable *Casablanca*.

2. Black Cinema

A DARK STREET in the early morning hours, splashed with a sudden downpour. Lamps form haloes in the murk. In a walk-up room, filled with the intermittent flashing of a neon sign from across the street, a man is waiting to murder or be murdered . . . the specific ambience of *film noir*, a world of darkness and violence, with a central figure whose motives are usually greed, lust and ambition, whose world is filled with fear, reached its fullest realisation in the Forties. A *genre* deeply rooted in the nineteenth century's vein of grim romanticism, developed through U.F.A. and the murky, fog-filled atmosphere of pre-war French movies, flowered in Hollywood as the great German or Austrian expatriates — Lang, Siodmak, Preminger and Wilder —

arrived there and were allowed more and more freedom to unleash their fantasies on the captive audience.

To that scene of night streets, recurring again and again in the films of the period, most notably in Michael Curtiz's *The Unsuspected*, can be added images of trains: clanking and swaying through storm-swept darkness, their arrival at remote stations signalled by the presence of mysterious raincoated figures, while in the narrow corridors, the antiseptic cramped compartments, assignations are made and, more often than not, a murder is planned. . . . Elevators often figure as well, most notably in *Dark Passage*, where the lift gives an entrance, for the fugitive central figure, to an enclosed world of luxury and safety, haunted by the San Francisco foghorns, and in *The Maltese Falcon*, where the gates clanging shut on the tear-stained face of the defeated villainess forebode her own incarceration in Tehachapi. Cocktail bars, too, exercise a special fascination: mirrors, stretching to the ceiling, reflect the stew of faces, each one predatory, doomed or afraid, and the glasses are piled in pyramids, often — this was an especial passion of Curtiz's — to be smashed by one of the principals in an outburst of rage. Standard lamps fallen on pile carpets, spilling a fan of light about the face of a corpse; interrogation rooms filled with nervous police, the witness framed at their centre under a spotlight; heels clicking along subway or elevated platforms at midnight; cars spanking along canyon roads, with anguished faces beyond the rain-splashed windscreen . . . here is a world where it is always night, always foggy or wet, filled with gunshots and sobs, where men wear turned-down brims on their hats and women loom in fur coats, guns thrust deep into pockets.

The soundtracks, laced by the minatory scores of Franz Waxman, Max Steiner, Miklos Rozsa or Erich Wolfgang Korngold, also create the flavour: one remembers the whine of Dan Duryea in Fritz Lang's *Woman in the Window* and *Scarlet Street*, the breathlessness and the faked sob in the voice of Mary Astor in *The Maltese Falcon*, the scream of the elevated across the luxurious self-contained world of the threatened woman in *Sorry, Wrong Number* and the cold hard voices on the telephone switchboard; the cry of the train in *The Strange Love of Martha Ivers*, carrying away, in the rain of course, the escaping adolescents to a lifetime of suffering; the rapping of Ella Raines's heels on the platform and the hysterical jangle of the jazz-band in *Phantom Lady*, the shuffle of the husband's feet on the ceiling in *Gaslight* and the dissonant wood-wind of Bronislau Kaper's score as the gaslights dim; the sound of *Tangerine* floating from a radio down the street as the lovers enter their death-clinch in the shuttered room in *Double Indemnity*.

And above all, shadow upon shadow upon shadow . . . Lee Garmes, Tony Gaudio, Lucien Ballard, Sol Polito, Ernest Haller, James Wong Howe, John F. Seitz and the other great cameramen of the era pitched every shot in glistening low-key, so that rain always glittered across windows or windscreens like quicksilver, furs shone with a faint halo, faces were barred deeply with those shadows that usually symbolised some imprisonment of body or soul. The visual mode was intensely romantic, and its precise matching to the stories of fatal women and desperate men — straight out of *The Romantic Agony* — gave Forties *film noir* its completeness as a *genre*. A world was created, as sealed off from reality as the world of musicals and of Paramount sophisticated comedies, yet in its way more delectable than either.

Hitchcock's notable *film noir* of the period, *Shadow of a Doubt* (1943), was pitched in a calm world, its darkness suggested rather than stated. The opening takes place on a sunny, dusty day, Charlie, the widow-murderer, dodging the police, lying wearily back in his walk-up room or standing looking at his pursuers, puffing proudly at a cigar. Later, as he enters the chintzy little world of his small-town Californian relatives, he shows himself a genuine occupant of *film noir*: in a café, he tells his niece that the universe is a "foul sty", and over dinner he discloses something of his neurotic, perhaps basically homosexual loathing of women. Joseph Cotten's performance cleverly suggests the psychotic tension under the bland generous front; here is a creature of the darkness blinking against the light of a very American innocence.

Rope (1948) and *The Paradine Case* (1948) are more firmly centred on a world of evil. In *Rope* two homosexuals murder a "straight" youth, serving his father, aunt and *fiancée* dinner from the chest he is en-tombed in; while in *The Paradine Case* "une belle dame sans merci", the heartless Maddelena Paradine, murders her blind husband and shows complete contempt for the defence counsel engaged to save her. Hitchcock and his writers here delineate lives lived without conscience and without love. In *Rope*, the homosexual ambience is ably suggested: the slightly over-decorated apartment, the "understanding" housekeeper, the elliptical, wounding and sharp-witted exchanges between the killers, played by Farley Granger and John Dall, and their mutually suspicious and resentful relationship with the dead boy's girl-friend. The gradual breakdown from smooth party badinage to nerves and finally dissolution of the psyche, arrest and ruin, is charted with precision, and the endlessly gliding takes, moving from death-chest to window spangled with New York lights to shifting trays of food, create an atmosphere as stifling as the interior of a coffin.

The Paradine Case has as its centre a fatal woman of whom Wedekind would have been proud: as played by Alida Valli, she is a leprous madonna, her lips permanently twisted into a smile of contempt, her hair tightly drawn back, her skin stretched on the delicate skull. The prison scenes are pure *film noir*: echoing corridors, barred with Lee Garmes's famous shadows, enclose her in a world of stone; the shadows deepen in her face as her foolish, infatuated counsel drones on and on. No less sinister, in Hitchcock's black vision, the judge Lord Horfield (Charles Laughton) smacks his lips over Mrs. Paradine's forthcoming hanging while gobbling a meal, dwelling on the convolutions of a walnut ("they resemble the human brain") while framed through a silver candelabra in his mansion, the reward of a lifetime of judicial murder.

Closely allied to Hitchcock, Robert Siodmak — a colleague of Billy Wilder and Fred Zinnemann at U.F.A. in the early 1930's — expresses a more detached, urbane and less cynical observation of the dark side of human nature. Nevertheless, his Germanic pessimism and fascination with cruelty and violence are not in doubt.

Phantom Lady (1944), produced by Joan Harrison (who had also worked with Hitchcock) created, with the aid of John Goodman's art direction and Woody Bredell's nocturnal camerawork, a powerful *mise en scène* of squalor and violence. The story — from a pulp novelette about a search for an accused murderer's alibis, most notably a mysterious woman in a bizarre hat met in a bar to the strains of "I Remember April" — becomes an excuse for the exploration of the underworld, for a series of descending spirals into hell.

New York is evoked during the toxic heat of midsummer: menace and poetry come together in images of pursuit, as the accused's girl (Ella Raines) tries to break down the bribed witnesses to her lover's innocence. A bartender is tracked across an elevated platform: heels tap on stone, a turnstile groans, a train shrieks to a stop. A tap-drummer sweats through a fog of cigarettes and alcohol in a dive rocking to the sounds of a jazz-band. Behind the suave apartment blocks, Siodmak is telling us, there is a world waiting to pounce in: at the gates of the respectable, the jungle is already thrusting upwards.

Christmas Holiday (1944) is no less black: after an opening of gaiety — Robert and Abigail are idyllic newlyweds — Robert is gradually exposed as a crook, squandering the family fortune in gambling. One morning he burns a pair of blood-stained trousers: Abigail finds that he has murdered a bookmaker, hiding the body with his mother's help. Moreover, his relationship with his mother is depicted as incestuous, and his manner suggests homosexual tendencies. Siodmak's elliptical direction and the cleverly off-beat casting of Deanna Durbin and Gene Kelly help to create an atmosphere of lightly suggested menace, of wickedness just an inch below the suburban surface.

The Suspect (1945), based on the Crippen case and set in late Victorian London, is equally merciless about human nature: a tobacconist (Charles Laughton), flabby and dominated by a vicious wife (Rosalind Ivan), murders her, but he is made to seem less evil than the inquisitive neighbour (brilliantly played by Henry Daniell) and the cruelly observant detective (Stanley Ridges) who brings about his downfall. In thickly cluttered, stifling sets, full of aspidistras, wax fruit and gewgaws, Siodmak discloses the horror of breakdown, a lifetime of genteelly endured misery collapsing into moral disintegration, ruin and death.

Again, in *Conflict* (1945), from a Siodmak story but not directed by him, a husband is dominated by a vicious wife whom he murders, and is destroyed by a detective — here once more the genteel suburban world is shown to contain cracks which at any moment can bring about its destruction. *The Strange Affair of Uncle Harry* (1945) shows a "nice" New England family: celibate, careful Harry (George Sanders) and his two sisters (Geraldine Fitzgerald and Moyna MacGill). When Harry falls in love, his younger sister Lettie, insane with incestuous jealousy, tries to destroy the relationship and finally goes to the gallows for her pains. The bickering, despair and repressed sexual longing of this tight little clan are exposed in shadows as black as those which blanket the characters' psyches. And in *The Spiral Staircase* (1946), the story of a mute terrified girl in a town haunted by a killer of maimed women, the darkness closes in. A murder in a room above a flickering bioscope display; an eye lurking deep in a cupboard; a face that swims out of focus as the dumb mouth blurs into a hole, watched by the killer: here is direction of the boldest Gothic flair.

The Dark Mirror (1946), about twins, one evil, one good, *The Killers* (1946) and *Criss Cross* (1949) were less successful, although patches of technique — the grim first sequence of *The Killers*, based on Hemingway's story, a robbery sequence in *Criss Cross* — are justly remembered. But in *Cry of the City* (1948), Siodmak returned strongly to form. In this story about a conflict between a sanctimonious policeman (Victor Mature) and an accused killer (Richard Conte), the director evokes a fine range of low-life locales: the sense of a lived-in night city is admirably managed. The gross, six-foot masseuse (Hope Emerson) is a memorable monster, gobbling her breakfast or striding through her house to receive a nocturnal guest, observed by the camera through a glass-topped doorway as she switches on the lights in successive rooms. And so is the furtive shyster of Berry Kroeger, white and plump as a slug. Little scenes like a police interview with abortionists — mostly European refugees — show Siodmak's talent for observing squalor in full display. A tense prison hospital escape matched to an almost imperceptibly swelling drum-beat; a murder in a swinging, creaking office chair — the film is crammed with sequences like these, powerfully realised and charged with an oppressive coldness.

Fritz Lang's *Woman in the Window* (1944), and *Scarlet Street* (1945) were equally rancid portraits of darkness and the city. In both, a weakling played by Edward G. Robinson, sexually unfulfilled, lonely and depressed, becomes the victim of a pretty and ruthless seductress played by Joan Bennett. Lang and his writers disclose without mercy how the beautiful can feed on the ugly, and the films — set in classic surroundings of wet, dark streets, rooms full of hideous knick-knacks, shimmering street lamps — remain memorable for the viciousness of the characterisations, notably Dan Duryea's stripe-suited pimps, and the unblinking look at middle-class life: a retirement party with bawdy jokes accompanying the presentation of a watch, a quarrel across a cluttered flat, a close-up of a clerk's embarrassed face as his fly-by-night asks him for money in a public place.

In *Laura* (1944) and *Fallen Angel* (1945) Otto Preminger made two remarkable contributions to the *genre*. On the surface, *Laura* looks atypical: from the first shot, a slow left to right pan across a series of shelves filled with *objets d'art*, the world we are shown is cool, sunlit or filled with the soft light of standard lamps: a world of apartments in the highest brackets of New York. But the characters cast their own shadows: Waldo Lydecker, played expertly by Clifton Webb, is a brittle jealous killer behind the front of a Woollcott-like columnist; Shelby Carpenter (Vincent Price) is a parasite feeding on rich women; his mistress (Judith Anderson) is a purchaser of male flesh. Only Laura herself, played as the Eternal Woman by Gene Tierney, remains beyond reach of the mire. Preminger's direction, calm and detached, and Jay Dratler's and Samuel Hoffenstein's sophisticated dialogue, turn the women's magazine conventions of the story inside out, so that at the end we are given a portrait of the utmost corrosiveness. Elegance and taste are balanced by greed and cruelty, and these endlessly bright rooms, these soft carpets and clocks and screens and china figures express a menace not reduced by the high-key handling.

Conversely, *Fallen Angel* (1945), is set in the lower rungs of the American *milieu*: this story of a man who marries for money in a small town so he can afford a floozie has an admirable *mise en scène*, evoking the contrast between suburban house and end-of-the-road hotel, a fine

Forties range of seedy rooms, neons flashing in the dark, doors opening from dark streets into the cosy vibrant warmth of a café or bar.

Much the same atmosphere pervades Michael Curtiz's *Mildred Pierce* (1945) and *The Unsuspected* (1947). *Mildred Pierce*, wittily adapted by Ranald MacDougall from the novel by James M. Cain, charts the rise of a housewife (Joan Crawford) from waitress to owner of a chain of restaurants on the Californian coast, with mayhem along the way. No film has caught so completely the feel of Southern California, and it is not surprising that a restaurant commemorates it in Hollywood, with dishes named after Cain's characters. The coast roads, the plush taut atmosphere of restaurants, and the endless jostling greed of the environment are conveyed with an *aficionado's* knowledge. The opening is typical Curtiz: a series of shots fired into a mirror, following distant views of a beach-house at night, the murdered lover (Zachary Scott) lurching past his reflected face, gasping a last word "Mildred." The film conveys Curtiz's love of the American night world, of piers shining under rain, dark beaches, the Pacific moonlight seen through a bar's windows, and the tough direction of the players at all times pays dividends. In their respective portrayals of ambition, sisterly humour and brainless lust, Joan Crawford, Eve Arden and Zachary Scott are in splendid form.

The Unsuspected is even more beguiling: here Curtiz surpassed himself with U.F.A.-esque camera effects. As Victor Grandison, superbly hammed by Claude Rains, moves from harmless Waldo Lydecker-like crime story-telling on radio to committing murder himself, Curtiz charts a vivid course of greed and heartlessness. In order to satisfy his desire for possessions, for control of a fortune and his niece's mansion, Grandison murders and risks his life: he is finally arrested while broadcasting to America on a particularly violent murder case.

The images have an unusually massive opulence: the huge house, with its tables covered in black mirrors, pyramids of glasses in the cocktail bar, and record library which plays a complex role in the action, is a triumph of the Warners art department. A girl's poisoning is seen through the bubbles of a glass of champagne, as though she were drowning in alcohol. A chest containing a body that has to be got rid of in a hurry is lifted high on a crane above a disposal-ground, watched desperately by the murderer's accomplice. And one sequence remains the quintessence of Forties *film noir*. The camera moves out of a train window, across a narrow street filled with neon signs, and up to a room where a killer lies smoking, terrified in the dark, listening to the story of his crimes related by Victor Grandison on the radio.

Lewis Milestone, in *The Strange Love of Martha Ivers* (1946), also created a striking addition to the lists. An aunt murdered and a getaway on a freight-car at night; the rise of an ambitious woman, definitively played by Barbara Stanwyck, and her no less ruthless mate, the attorney O'Neill; with the aid of her childhood companion Martha plans her husband's murder. Replete with impressive images of cruelty and destructiveness, this *chef d'oeuvre* could not have been more persuasively directed. Nor could the similar Joan Crawford vehicle *The Damned Don't Cry* (1949-50) of Vincent Sherman's, made at the very end of the period. Here, the sense of an enclosed world of criminals is masterfully suggested, as the pushing girl played by Crawford moves from a ravishingly photographed Tobacco Road setting to furs, luxury, guns and the company of murderers and thieves.

Still more black a portrait of the underworld — but this time of a different kind — is Edmund Goulding's *Nightmare Alley* (1947), based by Jules Furthman on the novel by William Lindsay Gresham. This is the story of a small-town carnival operator, Stanton Carlisle (Tyrone Power) who obtains the secrets of a fake mind-reader and climbs to the big time in Chicago by setting himself up as a spiritualist. On the way, he acquires a partner in crime, Zeena, a sideshow fortune teller, and a remarkably clever accomplice, the psychologist Dr. Lilith Ritter, played brilliantly, with icy, calculating intelligence by Helen Walker. Huge-eyed, sly as a cat, Dr. Ritter's gestures suggest a soulless ambition; the web of hair, the smoothly disciplined face are unforgettable.

Nightmare Alley is a work of great daring, even risking a few shots at human belief in immortality. People are shown as venal, gullible, and hell-bent on success at any cost. Memorable are the portraits of Ezra Grindle (Taylor Holmes), the millionaire determined to materialise his dead mistress Addie so that he can again make love to her; of the alcoholic ex-mind reader (Ian Keith); and of the shrewd and wealthy Mrs. Peabody bamboozled by spiritualism. Joan Blondell is perfect as Zeena, the warm, fleshy, blowsy carny queen out of the sticks; Lee Garmes's photography effectively evokes the circus settings; but the film's greatest triumph lies in its uncompromising portrait of American corruption. As Carlisle rises from hick to ace charlatan and crashes to become a "geek" — a creature tearing the heads off live chickens in a bran-pit — we see a frightening glimpse of life without money or hope in a society that lives by both. Scenes like the one in the cheap hotel when a waiter asks the now stricken Carlisle if he would "like anything else" convey, with the aid of sleazy sets, an ambience of almost unbearable squalor, achieved through the bitter, heartless writing, and through direction of an unusually cutting edge.

Only one director could exceed Goulding in sophisticated observation of greed: Billy Wilder. But whereas Goulding's was an honest understanding, Wilder's was a cynical and corrosive criticism. *Double Indemnity* (1944), one of the highest summits of *film noir*, is a film without a single trace of pity or love.

A blonde, Phyllis Dietrichson (Barbara Stanwyck) sets out to seduce an insurance man, Walter Neff (Fred MacMurray) so she can dispose of her unwanted husband for the death money. Infatuated, he succumbs, and helps her work out a complicated scheme; this misfires, the couple meet desperately after the killing in supermarkets or risk telephone calls; finally, they shoot each other in a shuttered room, with *Tangerine*, most haunting of numbers, floating through the windows. As in *Mildred Pierce*, the Californian ambience is all important: winding roads through the hills leading to tall stuccoed villas in a Spanish style 30 years out of date, cold tea drunk out of tall glasses on hot afternoons, dusty downtown streets, a huge and echoing insurance office, Chinese Checkers played on long pre-television evenings by people who hate each other's guts. The film reverberates with the forlorn poetry of late sunny afternoons; the script is as tart as a lemon; and Stanwyck's white rat-like smoothness, MacMurray's bluff duplicity, are beautifully contrasted. A notable scene is when the car stalls after the husband's murder, the killing conveyed in a single close-up of the wife's face, underlined by the menacing strings of Miklos Rozsa's score.

Lana Turner impersonated a *femme fatale* not unlike Stanwyck's in a similar story, *The Postman Always Rings Twice* (1946), directed by Tay Garnett, based by Harry Ruskin and Niven Busch on the novel by James M. Cain, already adapted for the screen twice before: as *Le Dernier Tournant* (Pierre Chenal, 1939), and *Ossessione* (Visconti, 1942). Cold and hard in brilliant high-key lighting, Garnett's film captured Cain's atmosphere as perfectly as Curtiz's *Mildred Pierce*: in this story of a girl in a roadside cafe (Lana Turner) who seduces a ne'er do well (John Garfield) and induces him to murder her husband (the estimable Cecil Kellaway) the tension is drawn very tight. Lana Turner, almost always dressed in ironical white, introduced when she drops her lipstick case to the floor in a memorable sequence, is cleverly directed to suggest a soulless American ambition; and Garfield, tense, nervous, unwillingly drawn into the web of crime, makes an excellent foil. This is the perfect *film noir*, harsh and heartless in its delineation of character, disclosing a rancid evil beyond the antiseptic atmosphere of the roadside dinery.

But one should accord an even greater accolade to Welles's *The Lady from Shanghai* (1948); here is a film Shakespearian in the complexity of its response to an evil society. Rita Hayworth, sex symbol of the Forties, is made to play a deadly preying mantis, Elsa Bannister; her husband, Arthur Bannister, the great criminal lawyer, is, as interpreted by Everett Sloane, an impotent and crippled monster whose eyelids are like the freckled hoods of a snake's.

The Fatal Woman theme is reworked in brilliant detail; the fake sex symbol that beamed down from the hoardings along American highways and glittered from the period's front-of-house is stripped bare, while the husband becomes a no less striking symbol of the emasculated American male. Only Michael, played by Welles himself, the sailor trapped into a charge of murder by his love of Elsa, is made to seem decent and free. At the end of the film, when Elsa and her husband shoot each other to death in a hall of mirrors, Michael walks across a wharf sparkling with early morning sunlight, released from an evil civilisation to the clean life of the sea.

Physically, the film is Welles's most mesmerising achievement. It conjures up the "feel" of the tropics, of the lazy movement of a yacht at sea, of the beauty of marshes and palms, and the misty calm of remote ports-of-call. In the film's most beautiful sequence, when Elsa Bannister lies on her back on deck singing, and Bannister and his partner Grisby exchange wisecracks ("That's *good*, Arthur!" —"That's good, George!") Welles's love of luxury, of relaxation and pleasure, flash through the bitter social comment and show him to be essentially a poet of the flesh.

The soundtrack is no less exhilarating than the images of Charles Lawton, Jr. Heinz Roemheld's menacing arrangements of Latin American themes match the tensions of the yachting holiday, the journey through Mexican backwaters. Woodwinds and castanets echo throughout the preparations for a mammoth party near Acapulco, a commercial jingle on the yacht's radio mockingly underlines the sailor's seduction; and while the wife in a white dress runs through the pillars of an Acapulco street a male chorus sings a primitive song, followed by two startlingly harsh chords from the brass section. Throughout the film, the feral shrieks and neurotic whispers or giggles of the cast, the sneezes, coughs and chatter of the trial scene extras, give the listener the impression of being trapped in a cage full of animals and birds.

From a film loaded with detail, baroque and sumptuous, one can pick out a handful of memorable scenes. The picnic party, lights strung out across an inlet, men wading through water, and the sailor emerging from the darkness to tell his sweating, hammocked employers a symbolic tale about a pack of sharks which tore each other to pieces off the Brazilian coast. A talk about murder high on a parapet above the fiords of Acapulco harbour, interrupted by a gigolo's shrill "Darling, of course you pay me!" A conversation in the San Francisco Aquarium, the wife's fake passion breathed in silhouette against the mindless pouting of a groper fish. The trial, and the final shoot-out in the mirror hall, the lawyer firing at his wife through layers and layers of deceiving glass panes.

Closely allied to the "pure" black cinema of Hitchcock, Siodmak, Lang, Wilder and Welles, though not quite in the same category, are the series of period melodramas made in the Forties; a rich group, they reflect the proper ambience but for the most part fail to disclose the kind of strong personal attitude which could have raised them to the level of works of art.

Of these, *Kings Row* (1941) was among the most accomplished. Henry Bellaman's novel dealt with the wickednesses that go on in a small town: operations unnecessarily performed by sadistic doctors, the venality and greed of business people contrasted with the dash and vitality of the provincial American young. Sam Wood's direction and Casey Robinson's script recreate the earlier part of the chronicle with skill: a birthday party over which hangs the pall of madness and death, youngsters skipping along a street or swinging from the rings of an icehouse while just round the corner a man is having his legs scraped of their ulcers without chloroform. James Wong Howe's sun-dappled photography, rich as a succession of oil paintings of Americana, and Erich Wolfgang Korngold's minatory score, create a powerful contrast between innocence and horror. The second half, tracing the career of Parris Mitchell (Robert Cummings) from eager young medical student to psychoanalyst under Freud in Vienna, is less well managed, but the film contains some extraordinary performances: Claude Rains as the once idealistic Dr. Tower haunted by fear of madness in his family, Betty Field as his pathetic unbalanced daughter Cassie, Ann Sheridan as the warm and eager small-town girl who grows into womanhood through suffering. The massiveness of the film, its powerful structure and strength, bear testimony to the rich resources of Warners at the time.

John Brahm, a European expatriate slightly older than Billy Wilder and Robert Siodmak, who had begun his career with a remake of *Broken Blossoms* in England, made two striking period films from scripts by Barré Lyndon: *The Lodger* (1944) and *Hangover Square* (1945). *The Lodger* is based on the story of Jack the Ripper already filmed by

Hitchcock in the silent period: in this version, and in the fine performance of Laird Cregar, he becomes a fat, liquid-eyed, Bible-quoting doctor with a manic hatred of women, who goes down to the Thames at night to bathe his bloodstained hands in its dark waters.

From the opening, which shows a blind beggar hearing word of the latest butchery, moving away into the darkness, the tap-tapping of his stick slowly fading away, this is a film of breathtaking intensity and skill. The murders are suggested rather than shown — a dark hole in a wall, the soundtrack filled with the victim's cries and the killer's heavy breathing; a prostitute starting back from the camera which moves forward subjectively, hand-held to suggest the murderer's last trembling glimpse of his prey. After each killing, the director and cameraman (Lucien Ballard) create fantastic chiaroscuro effects of fog, flashing torches, mounted police galloping through the streets, shot vertically from above or below, at one stage concentrating on a constable mounting a steep ladder, drawing nearer and nearer to the camera, and finally shining a torch straight into the lens.

The killer's psychotic isolation is cleverly conveyed: he is continually looking at passers-by from behind lace curtains whose crisscross patterns are like the meshes of a cage. When he is at last trapped in the flies of a theatre, Laird Cregar brilliantly suggests the tension, agony and fear of the character, a huge animal dodging like the Phantom of the Opera through a spider's web of steel ladders.

As he crawls along a catwalk, successive shadows of the rungs ripple across his face like the bars of a cell while he occupies one of the great close-ups of the screen, his eyes starting with terror. And at the climax, he is caught in the corner of a room, panting bestially, plunging through a glass pane into the dark river below, eyes black and shining as the water which carries him to his doom. It is a motif that has been beautifully sustained from the beginning, when a dead prostitute's hand trails in a water-filled gutter, through the Ripper's speech to his friends about the cleansing powers of dark waters to the crouching figure of the murderer on a pier, rinsing fresh blood from his hands. And underlined by Hugo Friedhofer's score, with its savage pouncing strings for the successive murders, its powerful suggestion of ever encroaching terror.

Joan Crawford and Jack Carson in MILDRED PIERCE, a film that conveyed director Michael Curtiz's love of the American night world.

A furtive meeting in a supermarket between the conspirators, Barbara Stanwyck and Fred MacMurray, in Billy Wilder's DOUBLE INDEMNITY.

Above left, the rise of an ambitious woman: Barbara Stanwyck with Van Heflin in THE STRANGE LOVE OF MARTHA IVERS, persuasively directed by Lewis Milestone.

Above right, Ingrid Bergman, victim of a plot to drive her insane, in George Cukor's GASLIGHT (THE MURDER IN THORNTON SQUARE).

The dash and vitality of the provincial American young: Ann Sheridan and Ronald Reagan in KINGS ROW, directed by Sam Wood.

Hangover Square is less well scripted — an over-elaborate re-working of Patrick Hamilton's novel, it becomes the story of an insane pianist (Cregar again) in a no less weird London setting — but even more fantastically mounted. A murder of a pawnbroker in the first reel, a lamp smashed, a window broken through, flames leaping down a flight of stairs, is electrifyingly shot and recorded. And so, too, the climax with the pianist playing his obligatory concerto in a room full of fire and falling plaster, each swooping crane shot cut to the precise dictates of the score.

The Fatal Woman theme recurs splendidly in Irving Pichel's *Temptation* (1946), based on the once celebrated novel *Belladonna* by Robert Hichens, already filmed before. The book's scented Edwardian plushness is skilfully recreated and Lucien Ballard's photography (he also shot the earlier Brahm film) is replete with compositions as complex as a pattern of Brussels lace. In this story of a woman (Merle Oberon) who poisons to satisfy her ambitions, the setting — Egypt in the early years of the century — is very fully realised. One remembers the arrival of a mysterious visitor at Belladonna's house in Cairo, bearing a box of poison which she must swallow to avoid ruin and disgrace; the discovery of a Pharaoh's tomb near the pyramids; and the death of the poisoned husband in the middle of a supper party to celebrate the disinterment in a desert marquee at night. An atmosphere of Middle-Eastern decadence, pervasive as incense, suffuses every frame of the film.

Sam Wood's *Ivy* (1947) made by the same studio, based like *The Lodger* on a story by Marie Belloc Lowndes, also deals with the activities of a poisoner in a series of period settings. Ivy Lexton (Joan Fontaine) is, like Merle Oberon in *Temptation*, an expressionless beauty driven by greed to commit murder; both figures glide, perfectly groomed, through men's lives, luring and destroying at every stage. And here again the period — also Edwardian, but this time English — is recreated with filigree precision: Ivy's visit to a fortune-teller, accompanied by the jangling of a harpsichord, is a *tour-de-force* of Russell Metty's photographic art; as the faces shift from shadow to light and back again, as tulle and lace and shabby hangings melt and refocus, the images achieve a rich beauty. The scenes on a millionaire's yacht, the flight of Blériot across the Channel watched by white parasol-carrying figures on the cliffs of Dover, the trial scene (foreshadowing David Lean's in *Madeleine*), all are neatly realised, but it is the final sequence one remembers most vividly. At last trapped in her guilt — the gradual closing in on this evil butterfly has been brilliantly charted by the writer, Charles Bennett — Ivy whirls round her rooms looking for a tell-tale poison phial she has left behind: it is concealed, like the gun in *Laura*, in a clock. She runs to the lift-shaft. In a shot from below eye level we see the figure in its foam of lace cling for a moment to the railings; the lift is not there. She falls down the shaft; the film — and her life — are over. It is a shocking climax to a *chef-d'oeuvre* in which the direction by Sam Wood and design by William Cameron Menzies, the writing and playing, have created an intensely civilised pleasure.

In the same group, Lewis Allen's *So Evil My Love* (1948), shot in England, is an equally impressive record of a woman's greed. Olivia Sacret (Ann Todd) is determined to leave her life of drudgery as missionary's widow and household companion for a career of luxury with an artist (Ray Milland). She attempts to extort money from her employer, betrays her friend and benefactress, and finally stands outwitted and exposed, murdering her lover in a carriage and walking up the steps of the police station to face trial and death.

The chief fascination of this film, full of fog, ferns and plush, drawn from a novel by Joseph Shearing, lies in its portrait of will. Behind the discreet Victorian front of Olivia Sacret we are made to feel a psyche of refined steel. As we follow her into her employer's house, as we see her conflict with his mother and finally poison him, sending (like Ivy Lexton) her friend to the gallows, we watch her every move with the fascination of a chess audience. Each gambit is plotted with care, each tiny victory marked up, until we are totally involved in her fate, and Ann Todd's portrait of the character is a masterpiece of the actress's art.

George Cukor's *Gaslight* (1944) also recreates a picture of greed in a Victorian setting: Alice Alquist, a celebrated soprano, is murdered by her jewel-addicted lover, who seduces her niece into marriage and tries to drive the girl mad in order to obtain possession of the Alquist diamonds. Like the central figures of *Temptation, Ivy* and *So Evil My Love*, Gregory Anton is driven by a dominating obsession.

Much of the interest of *Gaslight* results from its sense of the dead singer's presence in the house, suggested by a perfumed glove signed by Gounod in a cabinet, her portrait over the fireplace, the words of the killer on the soundtrack as the camera probes into the fireplace's cavernous darkness: "She had been strangled." Behind the credits, a flickering gas-jet accompanies the wordless main theme of "The Last Rose of Summer", sung by Alice Alquist, and the opening sequence is staged in soft focus as the bereaved niece leaves the murder house and moves by carriage down a foggy street.

The honeymoon with the seducer in Italy has a nice irony: a romantic abstraction of Victorian literary dreams, the villa by the water, vines trailing from a trellis and the bride rising happily from her bed while ahead lie madness, attempted murder and the prison cell. And when the couple enter the house with its endlessly sliding claustrophobic doors and stifling bric-à-brac, when the patient, cruel husband torments his wife by day and searches the dead singer's belongings in the attic at night, the tension grows unbearably. As in the other period films of this group, the surface of discretion, of manners groomed to a fault, is made to contrast with sudden outbreaks of passion or fear: the wife's scream down the staircase when her nerves finally give, her breakdown at Lady Dalroy's musical *soirée*, all fans, whispers and discreet reproofs across the potted palms.

An especially fine sequence takes place at the Tower of London. Looking at the Crown Jewels, the husband gazes transfixed at a single item, his eyes flashing like the facets of a gem as he breathes the words "The Koh-i-Noor, or Lake of Light, is the largest diamond in the world. . . ." Later, his wife searches frantically for a brooch her husband has in fact stolen while the guide describes medieval tortures off-screen. Hypnotic, too, are the scenes when the husband scrapes across the attic while the wife lies on her bed in terror below, the camera gliding from the gaslit ceiling of one room into another, then down in a slow crane shot to her cowering figure.

Joseph Ruttenburg's supple camerawork, the complex period *mise en scène* and Bronislau Kaper's eerie, atonal woodwinds for the dimming gaslight combine with precision at every stage; although the subject matter is of the broadest melodrama, the treatment is at all times civilised, and Charles Boyer and Ingrid Bergman, cast against type as criminal and victim, give their performances of a lifetime. The final turning of the tables, when the wife has it within her power to save her now captive husband's life and refuses to do so, is a scene that sets the seal of triumph on the film. The jewels the husband has been seeking are sewn into the dress Alice Alquist wore as the Byzantine Empress Theodora represented in the portrait that hangs over the fireplace where the strangled woman lay: a clever original touch.

These period portraits of greed bridge the gap between the "pure" black cinema of *Nightmare Alley* and *Double Indemnity* and the excursions into "grey" melodrama of the adapters of Hammett, Chandler and Graham Greene in the Forties. "Grey" by virtue of a certain withdrawal of personality on the part of the directors, of an acrid humour about violence rather than a pessimistic judgment of life itself. If the "black" director tends to show humanity as totally amoral, grasping and prepared to sacrifice anything for material gain, it is from a viewpoint without mercy and without a sense of possible redemption. The "grey" directors merely laugh at their world of terror and cruelty, or decorate it with decadent trimmings. For this reason, theirs is the slighter achievement, but within their narrower range they have created some of the most pleasing diversions of the Forties cinema.

3. Melodrama

A WRY detachment, an amused view of the subject: these are the qualities of the best Forties melodramas. The films were made by hard-bitten men who knew city life inside out: they have the flavour of a neat Scotch-on-the-rocks. And of all the figures who walked through their half-world, Humphrey Bogart justly remains the most durable. His voice, throwaway and laconic, was meant to talk the dialogue of Chandler and Hammett; his manner, a combination of bitterness and amusement at a world of duplicity, exactly matched the edge of Dashiell Hammett's Sam Spade or Raymond Chandler's Philip Marlowe.

In *The Maltese Falcon* (1941), directed by John Huston, photographed by Arthur Edeson, he virtually ushered in an era. As Spade, hard-as-nails and ready with acts of violence ("When you're slapped you'll take it and like it"), he snarled his way through a film notable for its amusement at greed, its mocking portrait of a group of criminals in pursuit of a legendary jewel-studded bird. Almost the whole film takes place indoors, in cramped rooms, and the characters are put under a powerful microscope: Gutman (Sydney Greenstreet) is a fat pansy with waistcoat and watch-chain and a line of quasi-English banter ("By Gad, sir, you *are* a character!"; "I tell you right out, sir, I'm a man who likes talking to a man who likes to talk!"). Brigid O'Shaughnessy is the endlessly lying, fake-school-girlish Fatal Woman in the case, played with tearful beauty by the marvellous Mary Astor. Joel Cairo, crimp-haired, scented with gardenia, bursting into tears or screaming abuse at his colleagues, is classically embodied by Peter Lorre. The direction frames and re-frames these figures in a series of tightly-knit compositions: this is a film that preserves the unities without a blemish.

Perhaps the film's most striking feature is its insolent casualness, its deliberate lack of flourish. A fire aboard a ship in harbour, a man staggering into an office with the falcon wrapped in rags, a shooting at night following the murder victim's laconic reference to a planned date with a girl: these are rare touches of "cinema" in a film the technique of which is to suppress all show. The concentration is all on character, so that the end of the drama, when Brigid O'Shaughnessy is finally made to realise that she is going to gaol and probably death, is agonisingly painful. Repressing his desire to protect and save her, Spade abandons her to her fate. No one who saw it can forget Mary Astor's tear-stained face as the bars of the litt close on it, cutting her off forever from the world. It is an almost isolated moment of pain in a film of consistently cynical humour.

Bogart appeared also in *The Big Sleep* (1946), this time with Lauren Bacall, introduced in the sleazy studio Caribbean night of *To Have and Have Not* the year before. Their partnership was notable for its ironic and acid, but basically affectionate give-and-take: two sophisticated people deploring but not angered by the world.

The Big Sleep, like *The Maltese Falcon*, is distinguished by its wit. But it lacks the earlier film's cohesion, its perfect control of agony and violence. Confused and involved — has anyone fully understood the plot? — it nevertheless does express much of the flavour of Chandler's world: a bookshop with hints of pornography and a surprisingly sexy custodian; art collections humming with booby-traps; rooms full of palms and plush; a millionaire preserved in the heat of a conservatory like a bottled spider. Howard Hawks's direction creates a sense of claustrophobia, of a life lived as though under stones, and he observes the human insects who inhabit it — most notably, the nymphomaniac girl played by Martha Vickers and the typically furtive little guy of Elisha Cook, Jnr. — with a cold humour.

High Window, *The Blue Dahlia* (1946), the subjective camera *Lady in the Lake* (1947) and *Murder, My Sweet* (1944-5) were less successful versions of Chandler, as was *The Glass Key* of Hammett (1942). *High Window* was a partial misfire, relieved only by Florence Bates's performance as a rich bitch. Robert Montgomery's *Lady in the Lake* was even less satisfactory. In George Marshall's *The Blue Dahlia* — about an ex-serviceman (Alan Ladd) who throws his tramp wife and her no-good friends out of his bungalow apartment, and is suspected of her murder later — even Chandler's own script was insignificant. The best things in the picture are the credits unfolding against an elaborate neon flower, sign of the Blue Dahlia *boite*. Edward Dmytryk's *Murder, My Sweet* was an ambitiously arty misfire. Too self-consciously clever, lacking the throwaway excellence of *The Maltese Falcon*, it was notable mainly for Claire Trevor's sensual and sluttish villainess (a worthy cell-mate for Stanwyck's Phyllis Dietrichson) drooling over Philip Marlowe's biceps. A final showdown in a darkened room matches that in *Double Indemnity* (a co-Chandler script). Dick Powell as Marlowe, insolently striking a match on a cupid's marble bottom, is good, too.

Closely related to the Chandlers and Hammetts in style was Bruce Humberstone's *Hot Spot* (1941), with Laird Cregar as a psychotic cop. Delmer Daves' *Dark Passage* (1947) was in many ways superior to all of these films save *The Maltese Falcon*. In subjective camera, we follow an escaped criminal from San Quentin, concealed in a barrel, rolling down an embankment, hitching a ride from a petty crook and finally finding concealment with an artist in a flat filled with the sound of the San Francisco foghorns. Bogart as escapee and Bacall as artist guardian play with enchanting grace and humour, so that a dinner enjoyed across a candlelit table, the playing of a tinny gramophone record, the moment when she unwraps his operated-on face and sees him for the first time, achieve an unusually warm sense of intimacy.

The film is directed with a tense impressionist vividness, bringing to life within a fully realised San Franciscan ambience a whole small world of personal relationships. Agnes Moorehead's prying, vicious Madge Rapf is a definitive portrait of bitchery; Houseley Stevenson's plastic surgeon is a memorable gargoyle; and the minor parts — a taxi driver, a blackmailer, even the bystanders in a bus terminal — are brought before us with startling realism. Fluent cutting and Sid Hickox's subtle camerawork evoke the enclosed luxury of the apartment, a spiral staircase, a spinning record, a face pressed to a door-grille, a man nervously withdrawing into the shadows of an upstairs room. A bitter quarrel between friends in the flat late at night, punctuated by foghorns; an operation scene, developed in bizarre montage full of laughing faces and flashing cigarette-lighters; and the death of Madge from a high window: this is a film in which the images and sounds are orchestrated without flaw.

In two adaptations of Graham Greene, much the same atmosphere of a world within a world was created. Frank Tuttle's *This Gun For Hire* (1942) sacrificed Greene's story of a shabby English murderer for a story of a Mabuse-like figure (Tully Marshall) controlling a vast network of criminals in America; among those involved in the web are a hoodlum (Alan Ladd), fond of cats and children, mackintoshed and always alone, and a gross and epicene coward (Laird Cregar) who combines ordering murder with a habit of sitting up in bed in black silk pyjamas reading *Paris Nights* and gobbling boxes full of chocolate creams. Ladd's first major screen appearance, silky and schizophrenically cold, and Cregar's carefully observed performance, make memorable a film in which the emotional temperature was kept slightly too low to make a really strong impact.

Confidential Agent (1945), Greene's own favourite among versions of his work, was far more successful. A story of Spanish refugees in London during the Civil War of the Thirties, this remarkable work, directed by Herman Shumlin, written by Robert Buckner, achieved a strong sense of lives lived furtively and desperately under cover of night. The dialogue was unusually literate and mature, and some political discussions — between Victor Francen as an escaped aristocrat and Charles Boyer as a shabby intellectual, between the group of Fascist agents played by Katina Paxinou and Peter Lorre, among others — achieved a very high level of writing, direction and playing. Paxinou's portrait of animal greed and cunning was particularly striking.

Two films of Jean Negulesco belong in this group: *The Mask of Dimitrios* (1944), an Eric Ambler story that recalled *The Maltese Falcon* and reunited some of the cast, and, equally well realised, *Three Strangers* (1946). In this John Huston *conte* about three people who meet on the Chinese New Year, invoke the aid of Kwan-Yin, Chinese goddess of mercy, in winning the Irish Sweepstake, and finally lose everything they have, the direction is sharply sophisticated. Geraldine Fitzgerald's possessive wife Crystal Shackleford; Peter Lorre's pathetic drudge; Sydney Greenstreet's pampered lawyer Jerome K. Arbutny putting a prize carnation in his buttonhole before preparing an elaborate suicide attempt; Rosalind Ivan's spiritualist widow, recalling her husband from the grave to advise her against Arbutny's misappropriation of the family fortune: the players under Negulesco act these portraits of corruption with practised skill.

Anatole Litvak's *Blues in the Night* (1941), about a group of jazz musicians in the sticks, featured some notable surrealist montages; his *Out of the Fog* (1941), images of quays and mist reminiscent of *Quai des Brumes*; and his *Sorry, Wrong Number* (1948) was a masterpiece of technical bravura. In Lucille Fletcher's story of a woman who over-

hears a plan to kill her on the telephone, a powerful sense of imprisonment is built up: the bedridden hypochondriac in her lace in a Sutton
Place mansion, the elevated clattering across a bridge seen through the
windows; the camera circling and re-circling the room from dressing-
table to chair to bed; and finally the shadow of the killer on the stairs,
a leather gloved hand coldly replacing the receiver: here, and in the
handling of the impersonal voices on the phone, the direction is
masterly. And outside the confined action of the room, the film never
falters either: a visit to Staten Island, a boy digging clams, a house that
is the only one left in a long-vanished street; a frantic telephone conversation over the sound of a subway train on a platform at night.
Barbara Stanwyck as the victim, Burt Lancaster as her murderous
husband, Ann Richards as the one true friend: these are figures very
much in the round.

Seductive in a different way were two Max Ophüls melodramas of
the period: *Caught* and *The Reckless Moment* (both 1949). These were
more subdued and elegant than most of the melodramas of the decade,
the works of a civilised miniaturist. *Caught** deals with the way in which
a romantic girl, determined to marry for money, is infatuated with a
millionaire who, in Robert Ryan's powerful performance, is a megalo-
maniac of unusual viciousness, with a Xanadu-like mansion on Long
Island (the parallel with *Kane* is deliberately stressed: the wife's bored
imprisonment, the late-night home movie show, with the tycoon
bursting into rage when a joke at a bar makes the girl giggle at the back
of the room). In her relationship with her husband, and in her growing
affection for a doctor, the girl's character matures and changes, and
Barbara Bel Geddes plays her with a delightful open charm and
directness.

Lee Garmes's camera tracks constantly and with magical suppleness
and fluency, across a darkly shining cocktail bar and round a dance
band to rejoin a couple on the floor without a break, down a staircase
as the doctor makes a dash to a late-night telephone, across a desk as
two men talk in a room at night, the hum of an electric razor cutting
across their conversation. James Mason as the doctor, and Curt Bois

* John Berry is also said to have worked extensively on this film.

as the ex-head waiter turned millionaire's stooge calling everybody "darling," playing Chopin waltzes at a snowy 3 a.m. to the bored and frustrated Long Island grass widow, both act excellently, and Arthur Laurents's dialogue is very refined. Ophüls's romanticism suffuses the whole film, from the first scene when to Frederick Hollander's lilting waltz theme Barbara Bel Geddes and her room-mate turn over the pages of a magazine, their voices off-screen talking of the excitement of riches, furs and jewels to the last scene in the hospital when doctor and girl decide to share their future, and a nurse walks off with the girl's mink, symbol of the life she has rejected. It is a film shot almost entirely at night, quiet in tone, notable for its romantic softness and subtlety.

The Reckless Moment is just as adroit. A housewife (Joan Bennett) in a small Californian town drives home with the shopping, talks with her husband (who is abroad) on the telephone, struggles with the bills. Then suddenly her life of domestic calm is shattered by the attempt of a local rake to make love to her daughter, and his accidental death in a fall. She panics, trying to cover the tracks, as a smooth blackmailer (James Mason) does his best to pin her down. Once again, the direction at every stage raises the level of the material, and the growing involvement of the nervous woman and the blackmailer is treated with great sympathy and understanding. The light, clear small-town Californian locations, full of masts, sails and anchors; the sunny unpretentious house, explored with unusual fluency by Burnett Guffey's cameras; the conflicts between mother and rebellious nail-biting daughter (played with dark intensity by Geraldine Brooks): Ophüls has the ability to bring a detailed texture of personal suburban relationships to life.

So too does Welles, in another story of small-town tensions, *The Stranger* (1946). A war crimes commissioner (Edward G. Robinson, in a part originally intended for Agnes Moorehead), tracks down an escaped war criminal to a Connecticut village where he comes across bigger prey: the commandant of a Nazi prison camp, Franz Kindler, now disguised as a school-teacher (Orson Welles). This underrated film, exquisitely photographed by Russell Metty, is full of memorable things: a drugstore proprietor forever listening to the patter of a radio comedian; Kindler's murder of his old colleague, boys racing in a paper-chase through the sparkling woods, their happy parabolas contrasted with the shooting close by; the showing of concentration camp scenes to Kindler's fiancée, the scenes of misery on the wall and the girl shrinking back, startled by the rattle of the spool as it loosens for the run off.

Virtually on its own as a study in fear was André de Toth's *Dark Waters* (1944), in which Merle Oberon, victim of a shipwreck, is subjected to a bizarre series of aural and visual tortures in the Louisiana bayou so that her supposed friends can obtain her substantial fortune by declaring her insane. John Qualen, Fay Bainter and Thomas Mitchell as her "guardians" and Elisha Cook Jnr. as, characteristically, a beady-eyed plantation overseer, rig up, like Turhan Bey in *The Amazing Mr. X*, machinery to echo eerily Merle Oberon's name in the film ("Leslie, Leslie") through a barrage of cicadas. The mossy, crumbling mansion in the bayou, the tense conversations in which the criminals' real motives are disclosed, the eerie night with its moonlight, strange bird cries and splashes through the watery undergrowth are most enjoyably managed, and Elisha Cook being swallowed up with hysterical cries in slime provides a splendidly Gothic finale.

In the same mode was *Ladies in Retirement* (1940), directed with subdued intensity by Charles Vidor. The credits show a series of broken signs emerging from the Romney Marshes in the mist, a crow flapping on one of them: based on a celebrated French murder case this is the story of an impoverished girl, Ellen (Ida Lupino in her best screen performance), who becomes the companion of an old and spoilt former actress (Isobel Elsom) in a Romney Marshes cottage. Ellen brings into the house her pathetic sisters (Edith Barrett and Elsa Lanchester), both more than slightly dotty, who drive the old woman into a fury by plonking down spindrift on her very best tables or dropping a dead bird on the living-room carpet. Forced to make a choice between dismissal (and her sisters' expulsion to the madhouse) and murdering her benefactress, Ellen settles on the latter alternative. The murder scene is excellently staged — a song at the piano interrupted in mid-bar as the old lady is strangled off-screen, her pearls bouncing one by one on to the carpet. She is bricked up in the oven; the maid and her boy friend (very well played by Louis Hayward) finally bring the murderess to book. Not only the ensemble playing of the cast, but the director's iron control work up a high degree of suspense, and the art direction of the cottage and the studio marshes in their veil of mist is outstanding.

Hitchcock directed a number of lightweight films during the period, set in a melodramatic framework: *Rebecca* (1940), from Daphne du Maurier's Charlotte Brontë-ish story about a girl haunted by the presence of her husband's dead former wife; *Suspicion* (1941); *Spellbound* (1945), a novelettish concoction about the love affair of a psychiatrist (Ingrid Bergman) and a psychotic (Gregory Peck); and *Notorious* (1946), a story of spies in Buenos Aires. The first and last of these had points of interest: in *Rebecca*, the subtle suggestion of an evil and ghostly presence in a mansion, and Judith Anderson's dark portrait of the housekeeper, Mrs. Danvers; in *Notorious*, the complex photography of Ted Tetzlaff and the performances of Claude Rains and Madame Konstantin as a Fascist leader and his merciless mother. But the women's magazine conventions of these stories found the director notably ill-at-ease.

By contrast, Josef von Sternberg, master of *chinoiserie*, was entirely at home with his one major Forties melodramatic subject, *The Shanghai Gesture* (1941), adapted by a battery of writers from the 1920s Broadway shocker by John Colton, about a brothel madam in China. Here the house of ill-fame is turned into a gambling hell, presided over by Mother Gin Sling (Ona Munson), whose daughter Poppy (Gene Tierney) is the illegitimate result of a night of passion spent with Sir Guy Charteris (Walter Huston), Taipan of the China Trading Co. The truth of this is disclosed at a gigantic Chinese New Year's dinner party; Poppy finds the news of her birth too much: reviling Mother Gin Sling ("You're no more my mother than a toad!") she goads the Oriental tigress into such a passion that Mother Gin Sling slays her with a revolver. Sir Guy staggers out into the orgiastic New Year revels a broken man.

Sternberg's direction subtly suggests an atmosphere of decadence, greatly aided by a rich supporting cast of expatriates: Eric Blore's limping, shrill croupier, Leonid Kinsky's barman (repeated in *Casa-*

44

blanca), Marcel Dalio's gambling den functionary, Albert Basser-mann's senile ruin, Maria Ouspenskaya's dumb amah. The gambling den set is deservedly famous: a vast sunken hell-hole of greed and lust, it has a deliberately Dantesque quality, emphasised as Paul Ivano's craning camera surveys its monocled, turbaned and bejewelled deni-zens, precursors of the night creatures of *Gilda*, and of Siodmak's *The Great Sinner*. The images have an over-ripe opulence and squalor, and the chief performers are marvellous: Ona Munson as the Medusa-like Mother Gin Sling, with pretzel wig, claw fingernails and chunky rings; Gene Tierney's fabulously beautiful Poppy, wilful, spoilt and pouting, perched drunkenly on a bar, awaiting her lustful admirers as a flame awaits a moth. Sternberg's curiously humourless sensuality suffuses the whole film, especially in a scene in the apartment of Dr. Omar (Victor Mature), when he heartlessly accepts Poppy's enslavement to him: here the action carries a stinging erotic charge.

One whole group of Forties melodramas dealt with struggles for power in huge organisations, reflections in a way of competitive Holly-wood itself. And of these, two works stood out: *The Big Clock*, directed by John Farrow, written by Jonathan Latimer, and *Gilda*, Charles Vidor's film, written by Marion Parsonnet from a story by E. A. Ellington, photographed by Rudolph Maté.

The Big Clock (1948) remains one of the sound cinema's most seductive entertainments, photographed with unobtrusive but ingenious dexterity by John F. Seitz. From a scrappy and indifferent novel by Kenneth Fearing, Latimer has constructed a rich range of characters and situations. Most of the action takes place in the Janoth building, a New York mammoth publishing company headed by a wobbling lech-erous boss (played as a psychotic old baby by Charles Laughton), and his silken henchman (George Macready). A silent masseur, played by Henry Morgan, acts also as a lethal bodyguard. When Janoth murders his mistress with a sun-dial clock wrapped in green ribbon, he is forced to engage the resources of his organisation to track down the one witness to his guilt: a man glimpsed in a corridor at the top of a flight of stairs. Ironically, the magazine editor (Ray Milland) sent to head the investigation is himself the witness.

From the first tense editorial conference, flabby faces round a massive table, sycophants jumping to their feet at a snap of Janoth's fingers, to the tycoon's sudden, brilliantly shot, *Ivy*-like fall down a lift-shaft, the film never flags. Every part is ideally cast, from Rita Johnson's wry mistress to Elsa Lanchester's gurgling Greenwich Village artist, with her flocks of children and hideous *chef-d'oeuvre* of a pair of pray-ing hands. Above all, the giant clock which dominates the proceedings — nerve centre of the Janoth organisation — is magnificently created by the art department: with its endlessly ticking dials, pulsing dynamo, and gliding levers, it reminds one of the heart of *Metropolis*, and its impersonal energy is meaningfully shown pulsing through the mutual hatreds, the tensions of office life. As we glide along the endless shadowy corridors, penetrate the publisher's office where tycoon and familiar squabble, invade a conference room at the height of a tense exchange, we are brought very close to the feeling of commercial power.

Gilda (1946) is an even more extravagant evocation of tycoonery. Ballan Mundsen (George Macready) is a tungsten baron running a gambling casino in Buenos Aires: scarred and warped, his is an Hitler-ian presence, with ambitions for controlling the world. His massive South American house of sin is again a marvel of art direction, its central room filled with control panels that cut in or out the lights and noise of the saloons, its giant chambers filled with whirling wheels, crowds and a dazzle of chandeliers.

The film gains its tension from the relationship between Mundsen, his *protégé*, Johnny Farrell (Glenn Ford), and his wife, once Johnny's mistress, played by Rita Hayworth. The erotic strain is well conveyed through dialogue by Marion Parsonnet of a sharp-honed edge, the excitement and tension of carnival night interrupted by a murder at a cocktail bar, Gilda Mundsen's barbaric dance in a night-club, peeling off long black gloves, shaking back her shining mane of hair while the hands of patrons reach out to her through the darkness.

This is a film with the intense surrealist quality of a dream. Its

Buenos Aires is a creation totally of the imagination, with its winding dark streets, its gambling hell, Mundsen's white glittering house. The ambience is one of heat, decadence, sexual ferocity barely concealed behind civilised gestures and phrases. Maté's photography has a lacquered finish: the husband smoking a cigarette in silhouette, the first glimpse of Gilda, like every G.I.'s dream, sitting on a bed and throwing back her head in ecstasy, the wedding scene glimpsed through windows streaming with rain. George Macready gives a marvellous performance as Mundsen: the skull-like head, slashed from ear to mouth with a sword-scar, the level cold voice, the white skin create an impression of deathly and reptilian determination. Against this basilisk, Rita Hayworth plays with an extraordinary animal abandon: a healthy exuberant beauty haunted by suspicion and terror.

At Warners, the major film dealing with struggles among the executive set had, of course, to have cultural overtones. Just as Bette Davis or Joan Crawford pictures were given a touch of "class" by references to music ("Martinis . . . an acquired taste, like Ravel") or painting ("Excellent . . . a touch of Rousseau?") so the Brothers' first vehicle for Patricia Neal, whom they intended — for a time — to turn into a new major star, dealt with architecture. *The Fountainhead* (1949), from a crazy surrealist novel by Ayn Rand — she wrote the screenplay herself — told the story of a supposedly *avant-garde*, Frank Lloyd Wrightish figure, Howard Roark (Gary Cooper, too old and quiet for the part), who defies the conventional standards which turn functional city buildings into Greek temples with fluted pillars and pediments. He even goes to the extent of getting his mistress, architecture critic for *The New York Banner*, to blow up a housing estate because the builders betrayed his original concept. Finally, he waits for her, straddled on the roof of the tallest phallic symbol in the world, the Winand Building, while she goes up to him by external workman's elevator.

King Vidor's direction expertly matches the overblown, hectic quality of Ayn Rand's prose. The opening is impressionistically vivid: Roark's dismissal from college for his "advanced" notions, his one friend, an ageing architect (Henry Hull), collapsing with a heart attack, the stricken man driven to hospital in an ambulance in an extraordinary virtuoso sequence as the camera shows the Cross of Mercy super-imposed over the towers of Manhattan flashing in the sun. Later, everything grows more and more over-life sized, although Edward Carrere's sets, and Roark's buildings (Jack Warner cancelled Vidor's plans to engage Frank Lloyd Wright) are disappointingly rearguard and conventional. Vidor is at his best in the scene when the architecture critic Dominique Franchon (Patricia Neal) walks along the top of a quarry watching Howard Roark drive a phallic drill into the side of a cliff. Her white-skirted figure isolated against the skyline, his face tormented with desire, all in a white blaze of sunlight and chalk and a haze of dust, have much of the sensual impact of the director's handling of *Duel in the Sun*. Impressive, too, are the scenes in the newspaper office when its campaign for Roark brings it almost to closure, a sea of desks stretching away under harsh lights, a lonely figure picking its way to an office bringing a package of sandwiches.

Like big business, sport exercised an especial fascination for Forties producers of melodrama, and in *The Set-Up* (1949) and to a lesser extent in *Champion* (1949) and *Body and Soul* (1947) boxing was cleverly exploited as a theme. Robert Wise's *The Set-Up* was the most impressive film of the three: the story of a battered and ageing boxer (Robert Ryan) who becomes the victim of a "fixing" syndicate, the film was staged entirely at night and haunted by a vivid range of nocturnal characters: most notably, the icy gangster of Alan Baxter. The boxing scenes have a harshness, a sure feeling for cruelty and mob hysteria, that have seldom been surpassed. Within the brilliantly lit square, bodies writhe in pain and sweat; the bell clangs as they separate; the crowd — caricatured with all the savagery of a Daumier or a Gillray — swarms with sadistic women chewing bags of peanuts and shrieking abuse at the loser. The carefully orchestrated use of natural sound and of speech is a notable feature, and Milton Krasner's photography, flashy and sombre, creates a massive canvas of this inferno, moving out only to take in the scarcely less claustrophobic atmosphere of cafés, streets filled with searching people and neons late at night.

Less concentrated — the action of *The Set-Up* carefully preserves the unities — *Champion*, directed by Mark Robson, suffers from a rather

Mary Astor as Brigid and Humphrey Bogart as Sam Spade in John Huston's THE MALTESE FALCON, a melodrama of consistently cynical humour.

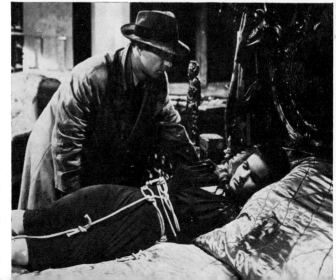

The mackintoshed loner, Alan Ladd, discovers a bound Veronica Lake in Frank Tuttle's film THIS GUN FOR HIRE.

Architect and critic —Gary Cooper and Patricia Neal—in a room that looks out on the towers of Manhattan: a scene from THE FOUNTAINHEAD, King Vidor's film of Ayn Rand's overblown novel.

An inside story of the fight world, Mark Robson's overly involved CHAMPION. Kirk Douglas played the title role and Arthur Kennedy (left) was his crippled brother.

too involved and flash-back ridden script. Moreover, for the agony and despair of Robert Ryan's great performance, Kirk Douglas substitutes a cold implacability. Only in the sensual tension of a beach scene with boxer and white swim-suited girl (Ruth Roman), in the occasional telling detail of life behind the arena, does this rather cheaply realised film achieve its ambitions. And *Body and Soul*, despite John Garfield's intensity as another boxer, is crippled by Robert Rossen's stiff and artificially posy handling, the kitschy quality of the central love affair between Garfield and Lilli Palmer; the film's technical accomplishment and the mannered, quasi-idiomatic script of Abraham Polonsky have a fatal softness at the centre.

In a related group can be placed the much superior *Force of Evil* (1949), this time directed as well as written by Abraham Polonsky, who was a victim of the blacklist. Based on a thick and complicated novel ("Tucker's People") dealing with the numbers racket, the film remains a masterpiece — poetic, terse, beautifully exact, a recreation in highly personal terms of the American underworld. The dialogue, with its Joycean repetitions and elaborate unpunctuated paragraphing, is unique in the American cinema, and at times achieves a quality of Greek drama, a poetry of the modern city. Played with great feeling by John Garfield and Beatrice Pearson (an odd, diminutive girl who appeared in only one other film), *Force of Evil* is dominated by the acting of Thomas Gomez, tyrannically forceful and hysterical as a fat man caught up in the racket. And, among many fine scenes, two stand out: the murder of a book-keeper (Howland Chamberlin), in a cellar, his glasses smashed, his face splashed with blood, his voice whining with terror; and the last descent of the young central figure played by Garfield down flights of steps into what will be a foredoomed existence of misery and squalor.

Realism, too, marked Fred Zinnemann's *Act of Violence* (1948) and Jules Dassin's *The Naked City* (1948), a film linked in manner if not in matter with the sociological melodramas discussed in another chapter. Jules Dassin's direction conveyed a sense of the heat, explosive cruelty and savagery of New York, William Daniels's cameras tracking excitingly through markets and across bridges, dollying into tall windows, following with a hound's determination the police chief (edgily played by Barry Fitzgerald) as he sets out to trap a killer. Anthony Mann's *T Men* (1948) — less attractively made, rather clotted and over-grim — also conveyed a sense of the raw lives of detectives in a big city. It was a *genre* that broke free from the artificial studio gloss of films like *Laura* to admit the audience to the real world behind the world it saw every day, and television has owed everything to its breakaway techniques.

These impersonal records of crime, striking though they are, finally lack the magic of the black film, which depended on the recreation of a total imaginative world within the studio. Reality, disorganised and loose, broke up the perfect cohesion of a universe that once had — from U.F.A. via Paris — unleashed itself without restraint from sound stage to audience.

4. Fantasy and Horror

WHEREAS THE Thirties had seen the birth of some of the cinema's most potent fantasy figures—Dracula, Frankenstein, the Mummy — and the emergence of such players as Karloff, Lugosi and Lionel Atwill, Forties fantasies were by contrast gentler, reflecting perhaps a reaction from the stresses and violence of the all too real war. Certainly there were ghosts and "creatures" galore, but they were seldom terrify-ing and often downright benign. Claude Rains, for example, twice found himself playing emissaries from the Other Side (*Here Comes Mr. Jordan, Angel on My Shoulder*), or pitiable grotesques (*Phantom of the Opera*), but neither he nor the films were in any way frightening, or intended to frighten. Ghosts, in fact, were rather nice throughout the Forties (with, of course, some prominent exceptions). A major pre-occupation was with celestial and nether regions, both of which became quite familiar locations to Forties audiences. Heaven, for instance, was shown in *The Blue Bird* as a place of gorgeous cloudscapes alive with cherubim, and hell in *Heaven Can Wait* as an ultra-modern salon presided over by a genial bearded Devil (Laird Cregar). Geniality was the keynote, too, of the Devils of Rains (*Angel on My Shoulder*) and Walter Huston (*All That Money Can Buy*): even the Prince of Darkness, it seemed, was not so horrible after all.

Whimsy went hand in hand with geniality in films which gently but decisively pulled reality awry. In *It Happened Tomorrow*, Dick Powell could read tomorrow's news today; in *It's a Wonderful Life*, James Stewart was permitted to see what would have become of his home town had he never been born; in *Turnabout*, John Hubbard and Carole Landis had to cope with the consequences of a sudden exchange of sex. Spectres were not immune from the prevailing mood of twee pleasantness and charm: Rex Harrison's bearded sea captain spectre in *The Ghost and Mrs. Muir*, conducting a very spiritual love affair with Gene Tierney; Spencer Tracy in *A Guy Named Joe*, turning up at odd moments to help the war effort by his ghostly exhortations; Charles Laughton in *The Canterville Ghost*, roguishly carrying his head around under his arm; Joan Blondell in *Topper Returns* . . . the list is long.

Sometimes ghosts turned nasty, as in *The Beast with Five Fingers* or *The Woman Who Came Back*, but there was generally a "natural" explanation at the picture's end which unconvincingly sought to account for the odd goings-on which preceded it. Or else the spirit was just disagreeable, like the one in *The Uninvited*, making flowers wither or causing temperatures to drop disconcertingly or gliding like cigarette smoke at the top of a dark staircase.

Universal was undoubtedly the leading fantasy-horror studio. In addition to carrying on the Dracula-Frankenstein-Mummy series in ever-cheaper degradations, it invented new ones like the Wolf Man or the Inner Sanctum Mysteries, and also spawned a whole sub-culture of ghouls, mad scientists and creeps, often impersonated by Lon Chaney Jr., Lionel Atwill or George Zucco. This was the studio also of Susanna Foster screamers, Maria Montez exotica and such A-class fantasy films as *Flesh and Fantasy* and *A Night in Paradise*, more often than not in colour.

51

Quantitatively, Monogram came next, with its "quickie" exploitation pieces, frequently featuring John Carradine or Karloff; then Republic, which put von Stroheim through some quite fantastic paces; R.K.O., which boasted in Val Lewton perhaps the leading horror producer of the decade; Columbia, where Lugosi the Vampire and assorted spectres cavorted; Paramount, which made spasmodic but distinctive contributions to the fantasy-horror genre; and finally M-G-M and Fox, neither of which seems to have had much interest in it. Bringing up the rear were assorted independents whose productions — such as *The Woman Who Came Back* or *The Amazing Mr. X* — often achieved standards comparable to the best of the majors.

The decade began auspiciously with two of the most splendid of all fantasy films, both intended nominally for children: Walter Lang's *The Blue Bird* (1940), suggested by Maurice Maeterlinck's story, and Alexander Korda's *The Thief of Bagdad* (1940). The Korda film has since been imitated but never equalled in its creation of a fairytale world of marvel and wonder. Its script, written by Lajos Biro with assistance from Miles Malleson and Sir Robert Vansittart, drew its inspiration mainly from Powys Mathers's translation of The Thousand and One Nights. It tells in flashback the complex story of Ahmad (John Justin), grandson of Haroun-al-Raschid, and his conflict with his evil Grand Vizier, the necromancer Jaffar (Conrad Veidt). Both love the beautiful daughter of the Sultan of Basra (June Duprez), but Jaffar uses his magic skills to blind Ahmad and turn his erstwhile companion, the little thief Abu (Sabu) into a mongrel dog. When the princess submits to Jaffar's embrace, the pair revert to their normal state: Abu undergoes a series of bizarre adventures, while Ahmad, aided by a flying carpet, a magic bow and arrow and a monstrous genie (Rex Ingram) released from a bottle, kills Jaffar and marries the princess as his little friend rides off into the blue on the carpet.

Three directors (Michael Powell, Tim Whelan, Ludwig Berger) are credited, but the guiding hand throughout is clearly Korda's. Aided by his brother Vincent's sumptuous sets, the largest and most powerfully lit up to that time for a colour picture, by Georges Périnal's sophisticated and tastefully decorative photography, by the protean inventiveness of the special effects department, and by the barbaric quasi-oriental score of Miklos Rozsa, Korda created some of the most striking fantasy sequences in all cinema: the Temple of the Goddess of the All-Seeing Eye, a vast monochromatic hall in which the one-eyed idol broods, soon to be deprived by Abu of her precious ruby orb ("Not for ten thousand years will she grow another", the genie tells him); the Flying Horse and Magic Carpet, special-effects triumphs; the Silver Maid, a multi-armed mutant fashioned by Jaffar from Halima, his former assistant, as punishment for her disloyalty. The scene in which the Silver Maid, her six arms weaving in a quasi-Balinese dance, stabs the Sultan in her embrace at Jaffar's command, carries a wealth of Freudian overtones, and indeed the whole film may fairly be regarded as a culmination of the Teutonic tradition begun at U.F.A. and Dekla-Bioscop in the 1920s, an impression reinforced by the directorial presence of Ludwig Berger and by Conrad Veidt's performance as Jaffar. The highlights of his face sprinkled with gold dust, his grey-green eyes accentuated in high close-up, his sinisterly accented voice purring its spells and curses, Veidt plays the malign sorcerer with disturbing conviction and power. This is one of the great performances of the fantasy cinema, demonically overpowering at such moments as that in which he blinds Ahmad, turns Abu into a dog, or summons up a storm at sea to drown Abu and his princely friend. To it the film owes much of its special ambience, one of wonder and delight in the free reign of the imagination, in touching the wellspring of myth and fable. In 1945 Columbia made a feeble imitation, *A Thousand and One Nights*, shamelessly plagiarising many of its ideas and even using its genie, Rex Ingram, in a similar role; but this, like many other subsequent imitations, was merely a pale shadow of the original.

Beside *The Thief of Bagdad*, *The Blue Bird* may seem relatively minor, yet it, too, is a film of much beauty. Lavish and expensive, it relegated Maeterlinck to the background to provide a fitting vehicle for Shirley Temple, then at a difficult stage of her career. She played Mytyl, sister of Tyltyl (John Russell). Their father (Russell Hicks), a poor woodcutter in the play, became a Tyrolese patriot about to join Andreas Hofer against Napoleon. His children still sought the Blue Bird of Happiness, accompanied by "human" incarnations of their dog Tylo (Eddie Collins), their cat Tylette (Gale Sondergaard) and Light (Helen Ericson). Their quest took them into the Lands of Memory and Luxury (the latter presided over memorably by Nigel Bruce and Laura Hope Crews), and into the Kingdom of the Future, an exquisite sequence in which the souls of unborn infants are shown departing for their earthly destinies in a fleet of ships with billowing sails, afloat on a sea of clouds. Heavily influenced by both *Snow White* and *The Wizard of Oz* (the children's Wonderland-style companions, the Technicolor dream scenes framed by sepia "reality"), *The Blue Bird* was nevertheless often charming and visually sumptuous, but it was critically and commercially a failure.

Spectres and spirits have haunted the cinema from its earliest days, with the Devil himself making frequent appearances: one thinks of Jannings in Murnau's *Faust*, numerous apparitions from the German cinema. The Forties' spectres had much in common with Jannings' Mephistopheles, little with their more demonic Teutonic cousins: jovial and gay, or wistful and contemplative, they usually meant no harm to anyone, and quite often were rather fun to have around.

Even the Devil, as incarnated by (respectively) Walter Huston, Laird Cregar and Claude Rains, was an entertaining creature. Huston played him in William Dieterle's *All That Money Can Buy* (1941, also called *The Devil and Daniel Webster*) as Mr. Scratch, a lecherous winking hick with heavy stubble and battered hat, perching on a fence outside the New Hampshire farmhouse of Jabez Stone (James Craig) in 1840. A handsome film, with its fine-textured sepia images capturing the rural township and landscapes like a series of Grant Wood paintings, it suffered from stolid and prosaic direction, without the seeming spontaneity that fantasy ideally demands. And its didactic solution to a moral problem by an appeal to patriotism was echoed the following year in Stuart Heisler's *The Remarkable Andrew*, written by

Dalton Trumbo, which had the ghost of Andrew Jackson, played by Brian Donlevy, come to the assistance of William Holden, determinedly fighting corruption in a small town.

Unlike Huston's scraggy and unkempt Mephisto, Laird Cregar's in Lubitsch's *Heaven Can Wait* (1943) was effetely elegant and suave, occupying a de luxe reception room from which he was able to consign Florence Bates to hellfire via a trapdoor. Claude Rains's interpretation in Archie Mayo's last film, *Angel on my Shoulder* (1946), had the Devil as a cultured rogue, sly and humorous, but here the author Harry Segal seemed merely to be repeating himself, for the film was uncomfortably similar to *Here Comes Mr. Jordan* (1941), based on a Segal story, in which Rains also appeared, not as the Devil but as a heavenly functionary in charge of despatching souls of the deceased on their predestined journeys. He sends a boxer, Joe Pendleton (Robert Montgomery) back to earth as the inhabitant of the body of a crooked financier, just murdered by his wife (Rita Johnson) and her lover (John Emery). There are numerous complications, few of them amusing, before Montgomery wins a title match and also the hand of Bette Logan (Evelyn Keyes). A clumsy and confusing device was to have Montgomery appear as himself to the audience but supposedly as a different person to the film's characters. However, *Here Comes Mr. Jordan* was sufficiently successful for the same director (Alexander Hall) and two of its cast (Edward Everett Horton and James Gleason) to collaborate in 1947 on a Technicolor musical sequel, *Down to Earth*, discussed in the chapter on musicals.

Altogether superior was Frank Capra's *It's a Wonderful Life* (1947), which, from its opening montage of small-town winter streets and houses preceding an ascent to "Heaven," through its succession of superbly managed set-pieces — notably a high school dance, *circa* 1928, with the dance floor parting to reveal a swimming pool and the entire company, clothes and all, falling in — provided a constant display of high-powered virtuosity. Henry Travers was a heavenly messenger sent to show despondent and suicidal James Stewart a vision of the town as it would have developed had he never been born: a sin city of gin-mills, strip-joints and similar attractions replacing *The Bells of St. Marys* as town entertainment, and Gloria Grahame descending to prostitution and being dragged off, shrieking and protesting, to gaol. This was magnificent, passionate, full-throated film-making, aided immeasurably by the contributions of the photographers Joseph Walker and Joseph Biroc, and by the editing of William Hornbeck.

Henry Travers was not the only supernatural visitant sent to straighten out mere mortals' affairs. In Victor Fleming's *A Guy Named Joe* (1944), the ghost of departed bombardier Spencer Tracy returned periodically to instil courage into survivors Irene Dunne and Van Johnson. Rex Harrison as a dead sea captain in Joseph L. Mankiewicz' *The Ghost and Mrs. Muir* (1947) materialised at odd moments to point up the unworthiness of the man (George Sanders) with whom widow Gene Tierney contemplates remarriage. Jolly Charles Laughton was *The Canterville Ghost* (Jules Dassin, 1944), a travesty of the Wilde story which updated it to wartime England, and Jack Benny in Raoul Walsh's *The Horn Blows at Midnight* (1945) was the Angel Athanael, sent to earth to sound the trumpet of doom.

Joan Blondell was another comical spectre in Roy Del Ruth's *Topper Returns* (1941), a sequel to Hal Roach's *Topper* and *Topper Takes a Trip*, in which she lured Topper (Roland Young), his dimwit wife (Billie Burke), their coloured chauffeur (Eddie "Rochester" Anderson) and their maid (Patsy Kelly) into a series of fast-moving, well-paced and funny adventures with trapdoors, secret passages and the comic possibilities of invisibility in search of a masked and hooded murderer.

Thorne Smith, author of *Topper*, also provided the original material for René Clair's deft fantasy-comedy *I Married a Witch* (1942). This featured Cecil Kellaway and Veronica Lake as the ghosts of two seventeenth-century sorcerers (father and daughter) burnt in Puritan days who return to plague the descendant (Fredric March) of their persecutors. The film is one of Clair's happiest productions, gently satirical, playfully bizarre and full of a mocking though never malicious wit. Its special delight is Kellaway's pixyish sorcerer, revelling in his white magic and bringing the picture to a chuckling close with his tipsy ditty coming from a rocking liquor bottle in a cleverly constructed cage.

Kellaway turned up again in David O. Selznick's and William Dieterle's *Portrait of Jennie* (1949), not as a ghost this time but as a sympathetic art dealer. In this lushly beautiful and unashamedly romantic work — arguably the director's best film — Robert Nathan's novel was turned into a haunting series of exquisite images, some in colour, some in sepia, some in black-and-white. (On its original release, the final sequence involving a sea-coast storm was tinted green and shown on an enlarged "cycloramic" screen.) Jennifer Jones was the spirit of a departed girl with whom artist Eben Adams (Joseph Cotten) falls in love. Her song indicates her physical remoteness from him in a real world:

> Where I come from
> Nobody knows;
> And where I'm going
> Everything goes.
> The wind blows,
> The sea flows —
> And nobody knows.

Each of the two principal characters' five encounters — particularly a dazzling ice-skating scene in Central Park, and their final meeting at the height of a furious storm which recalls the mystical flavour of a Thomas Hardy novel — was gloriously photographed by Joseph August, while the playing of the stars and a fine supporting cast was beyond praise. *Portrait of Jennie* remains one of Hollywood's most touching excursions into fantasy.

Alas, not all spectres proved agreeable. A rather nasty one materialised in Lewis Allen's *The Uninvited* (1944), based on Dorothy Macardle's novel *Uneasy Freehold*. Set in a Hollywood-England of continual sunshine, chintz curtains and cute village streets, this was nevertheless a film of subtle and eerie power, photographed in deceptively high key. In a scene which invariably terrified audiences, a pair of large doors suddenly and noisily blew open for no apparent reason. Cornelia Otis Skinner provided some splendidly Gothic overacting as the custodian of the local asylum who goes insane herself during a thunderstorm, though the evil ghost itself, when challenged by Ray Milland, looked disappointingly like a wisp of cigarette smoke.

The Beast With Five Fingers (Robert Florey, 1947) involved a dead pianist's hand seemingly returned from the grave to commit murder. One of the Warners' rare Forties' excursions into straight horror, its scenes of the disembodied hand playing the piano (Bach), scuttling across the floor, disarranging the contents of a bookshelf or, its fingers wriggling like antennae, discovered behind a set of encyclopedias, carried a powerfully macabre charge. Peter Lorre, bald, his haunted bulbous eyes staring in terror, played Hilary, the pianist's secretary, as a deranged bookworm, constantly fearing the hand's reappearance. When it does finally appear, slowly emerging from a cigar box, he vainly attempts to nail it to a table, then to throw it into the fire, but with supernatural tenacity it survives both these ordeals to crawl up to his throat and strangle him.

In its final form the film could only suggest Florey's original intention, which was to shoot the whole story *Caligari*-like as seen through Hilary's distorted brain. Gradually, the audience would discover that what they were seeing was the tormented man's vision, not a depiction of objective reality. By the time Jack Warner had cut the picture, most of this was gone except for the idea of Hilary's hallucination, conveyed by the hand's fading out of sight after it has apparently throttled him. Florey practically disowns the release version.

Throughout the early Forties, Hollywood's most imaginative, literate and intelligent fantasy-horror films came from R.K.O., the work of the producer Val Lewton, and they set a standard that has since proved a model for the genre. Born in 1904, Lewton was a freelance writer, story editor for Selznick and novelist before being assigned to low-budget horror movies. His film formula was basically simple, but until then all too seldom applied in practice: it relied on suggestion, the power of the unknown, the oblique. It used the resources of cinema — sound, silence, shadow — to hint at what it dared not show. This was a cinema of calculated understatement: conversations polite, low-pitched, the social proprieties scrupulously observed. At its best the formula resulted in some of the most frightening excursions into the macabre the screen has yet given us. Unfortunately it was often allied to a rather self-conscious literariness which vitiated some otherwise splendid films.

Lewton's first production, *Cat People* (1942), set the tone for the remainder of his output and used many of the personnel — director Jacques Tourneur, writer DeWitt Bodeen, cameraman Nicholas Musuraca, set designer Albert d'Agostino, editor Mark Robson, performers Kent Smith, Simone Simon, Tom Conway — who collaborated with him later. It was the story of Irene Dubrovnik (Simon), a Balkan-born girl working as a dress designer in New York who under stress becomes an outsize homicidal cat. Careful — perhaps over-careful — the film today seems so understated that much of its intended effect is dissipated. But it remains full of atmosphere and benefits enormously from Musuraca's exquisite low-key photography and d'Agostino's cosy, intimate art direction. Its high-spots — Jane Randolph pursued by some nameless, snarling Thing through a nocturnal Central Park, and threatened by a similarly insubstantial horror in an otherwise deserted basement swimming-pool — still carry a potent charge, but its total impression is distinctly tepid.

Lewton's next film, *I Walked With a Zombie* (1943), again directed by Tourneur, is by contrast an almost unqualified triumph. Here the hints, the understatement, the avoidance of crude shocks, result in some passages of superb eeriness, achieved on a minuscule budget and a rush shooting schedule. A kind of West Indies *Jane Eyre*, it runs less than 70 minutes and holds the attention throughout. With a calypso singer (Sir Lancelot) commenting in rhymed couplets on the action like a Haitian Greek chorus, it builds up to an impressive climax in its voodoo ceremony and what precedes it: the walk through the sugar plantations, the throbbing drums, the grotesque voodoo symbols, the white-clad zombie herself, the erotic gyrations of a voodoo celebrant.

The Leopard Man (Tourneur, 1943) was almost as good. Here Dennis O'Keefe was a reporter engaged to determine the nature of a killer who leaves leopard-like claw marks on his victims in a New

Mexico city. Strongly reminiscent of *Cat People* — with a girl in one scene being followed through deserted nocturnal streets, dustbin lids clattering noisily to the ground — it recalled also the Jack the Ripper theme in that those murdered were usually women of the night. At the end it offered a rational explanation, the murderer being apprehended at the height of a picturesque religious procession, but not before a girl had been brutally clawed to death, her blood flowing under a jammed door which her mother is vainly trying to open.

With *The Seventh Victim* (1943), Lewton gave former editor Mark Robson his first chance to direct and actress Kim Hunter her first screen role. Set mainly in a highly stylised studio New York, it opened with a quotation from John Donne (Holy Sonnet VII) as it traced the efforts of Hunter — a holy innocent loose in an unholy city — to locate her missing elder sister. The search leads her to murder and into a strange half-world of sleek diabolists, private sleuths, smooth psychiatrists and failed poets. Extraordinarily suggestive, the film cleverly conveyed a sense of something evil happening or having happened just off-screen, especially in such scenes as the subway ride in which the body of a murdered man is dragged on to a train by two men pretending he's a drunk they're propping up, the gathering of wealthy diabolists at which Hunter's sister Jacqueline (Jean Brooks) is offered a poisoned drink, the *Psycho*-like sequence in which Hunter is admonished by the lesbian devil-worshipper Mrs. Redi, glimpsed as a menacing black presence through a plastic shower curtain, and Jacqueline's suicide, conveyed by the sound of a chair kicked away as she hangs herself off-screen and a voice repeats the introductory Donne quotation. Often considered Lewton's best film, *The Seventh Victim* suffered from a general air of bookishness and a ludicrous finale in which the (predominantly foreign) satanists bow their heads in shame as Tom Conway recites the Lord's Prayer.

Neither *The Ghost Ship* (Robson, 1943) nor *The Curse of the Cat People* (Robert Wise, 1944) was in any way remarkable, but *The Body Snatcher* (1945), based on Robert Louis Stevenson's treatment of the Burke and Hare story, which united Lewton for the first time with Boris Karloff, had many fine moments. Under Robert Wise's direction,

Karloff and Henry Daniell made a wonderfully malevolent pair of ghouls, while Bela Lugosi as their hireling was admirable also. Its scenes of young girls being snatched off the dark Edinburgh streets to provide anatomists' corpses carried a sense of unmitigated evil, and its final moments — Daniell driving a hearse with Karloff's corpse beside him falling out of its shroud and almost encircling him in its waxen arms as the dead man's voice repeats "Never get rid of me, never get rid of me" to the galloping horses' rhythm — were bravura horror.

Karloff appeared also in Lewton's two final ventures into the macabre, both directed by Mark Robson. *Isle of the Dead* (1945), suggested by Boecklin's famous painting which appears behind the credits, is Lewton's masterpiece and one of the screen's most brilliant exploitations of the fear of the unknown. Strictly speaking, nothing happens in it that cannot be naturally explained, yet it can produce a *frisson* of transcendental terror achieved by few other films. Its final scenes rise to a crescendo of *Angst* by the use of ingeniously simple means: the camera slowly approaches a coffin in which we know a woman lies buried alive, about to awaken at any moment, as water drips — the only sound we hear — on to its wooden lid. Suddenly there is a cry from the coffin interior as the lid is forced open with a screech of hinges, the screen at one moment going dark as we peer into the gloom waiting for the coffin's white-shrouded occupant — sent insane by her experience — to emerge. If Lewton had made nothing else, he would surely be remembered for this.

Bedlam (1946), also directed by Robson, represented a come-down. Set in London's famous eighteenth-century lunatic asylum, and suggested by Hogarth's engravings, it was too over-literary by far. But Karloff's performance as the sadistic superintendent was quite interesting, and there was a scene long before *Goldfinger* of someone — a youth this time — suffocating to death under a coat of gold paint. Karloff received his come-uppance at the hands of a kangaroo court of inmates presided over by Ian Wolfe, his face last glimpsed as it gradually disappears behind a brick wall which his persecutors — all former victims — are building to inter him alive.

Lewton clearly influenced many subsequent horror films, notably

61

The Woman Who Came Back, directed by Walter Colmes in 1945. Here, despite tentative and inexperienced handling, Colmes, a former radio writer, achieved the difficult feat of creating tension and menace in broad daylight. Nancy Kelly played a bus crash victim who imagines she is the reincarnation of a 300-year-old witch, Elizabeth Tryster, burned to death in 1645. Her delusion stems from a weird old woman passenger on the fatal bus — of which Kelly is the sole survivor — and is most strikingly shown when her mirror reflection dissolves momentarily into the crone's hideous features. Several other alarmingly eerie sequences, subtle and oblique, revealed Colmes as a Lewton disciple who had learned his lesson well.

They included a very *Cat People*-like scene of a woman who suspects Kelly of being a witch being followed by the jingling sound of a sinister dog's name tag; Kelly returning from church, the buzz of a lawnmower the only sound we hear as the sullenly suspicious townsfolk affect not to notice her; the Rev. Otto Kruger in the church pulpit, the camera dollying around him as he delivers a pacifying sermon to the tense, restless congregation; Kelly reading about superstitions as a storm rages and a shutter bangs to and fro; her venture into the church crypt to read the witch lore, and discovering the dog (companion of the deceased old woman and by implication her familiar) blocking the trapdoor entrance.

At R.K.O., only John Cromwell's *The Enchanted Cottage* (1945), on the screenplay of which his former colleague DeWitt Bodeen collaborated, offered Lewton serious competition in the fantasy field. In it, Robert Young as an embittered, facially disfigured flier and Dorothy McGuire as his gawkily ugly wife were magically transformed into Beautiful People (well, almost) by a kind of astral emanation distilled from the collective happiness of past honeymooners who had occupied their cottage. Basically sentimental and bathetic, the film was redeemed by Cromwell's characteristically fine craftsmanship and by the expert supporting performances of (among others) Mildred Natwick, Hillary Brooke and Herbert Marshall.

★   ★   ★

At Universal, too, a plain Jane was inexplicably metamorphosed into a raving near-beauty: Betty Field in the first segment of Julien Duvivier's tripartite *Flesh and Fantasy* (1943) donned a carnival mask bought off a strange old man in a strange toy shop and when Robert Cummings removed it her features, hitherto unattractive, had somehow taken on the mask's symmetrical contours. Easily the film's best episode was its second, a superb adaptation of Oscar Wilde's *Lord Arthur Savile's Crime*. From its beautiful opening shot of two hands — the palmist's (Thomas Mitchell) and his subject's (Edward G. Robinson) — it provided a succession of stylised pseudo-London images, strongly recalling Pabst's *Dreigroschenoper*, and a gallery of memorable performances from British players like Sir C. Aubrey Smith, Dame May Whitty and Doris Lloyd. The scene in which Robinson leaves the house of the clergyman (Smith) whom he has tried to murder to make the soothsayer's prediction come true, and emerges into a sinister, foggy cobbled alley, was like something out of *The Student of Prague* or *The Street*. And the palmist's slaying on a decoratively artificial Thames bridge allowed photographers Stanley Cortez and Paul Ivano a field-day, as did the circus grounds and the final (rather weak) story — involving Charles Boyer as a tightrope walker — into which the bridge scene ingeniously led.

Linking *Flesh and Fantasy*'s three segments was a feeble device in which the tales are related by a weird little man (David Hoffman) who deserves mention also as the owner of the face in the crystal ball atop a table in a well-stocked library which introduced each of Universal's Inner Sanctum Mysteries with some appropriate remarks. Typical of the series was Harry Young's *The Frozen Ghost* (1944), which featured Martin Kosleck giving his frenzied all to the part of a deranged plastic surgeon demoted to custodian of Tala Birell's wax museum.

Simultaneously, the same studio produced pedestrian sequels to *Frankenstein*, *Dracula* and *The Mummy*, adding only the Mad Doctor and the Wolf Man to its bestiary, and also such shilling shockers as *The Mad Ghoul* (with George Zucco, 1943), and *Night Monster* (with Lionel Atwill, 1942). Nor must we forget Roy William Neill's Sherlock Holmes films, which in such prodigally inventive efforts as *Sherlock*

Holmes and the Spider Woman (1943) gave many an A-class fantasy quite a run for its money, or the series of films exploiting the invisibility gimmick, some for thrills, some for laughs, a few for both: the hilarious *Invisible Woman* (A. Edward Sutherland, 1940), *The Invisible Man Returns* (Joe May, 1940, with Vincent Price), *Invisible Agent* (Edward L. Marin, 1942) and *The Invisible Man's Revenge* (Ford Beebe, 1944).

On a higher budget level, Universal put Susanna Foster and Maria Montez into several elaborate Technicolor fantasy extravaganzas. Miss Foster screamed and trilled her way through Arthur Lubin's lavish remake of *Phantom of the Opera* (1943), in which Claude Rains played Erique Claudin, an acid-scarred maniac, and through George Waggner's *The Climax* (1944), in which Boris Karloff perished in a blaze of glory with the corpse of his murdered mistress which he had kept in a luxurious and — to judge from its splendid state of preservation — presumably airtight apartment for nigh on twenty years. Not even Hal Mohr's handsome colour photography could redeem these films' galloping silliness, nor that of Arthur Lubin's *A Night in Paradise* (1946), the studio's most lavish flop, a pseudo-mythological and legendary farrago with Thomas Gomez as Croesus and Turhan Bey as Aesop.

Gorgeously mounted, these monstrously vulgar entertainments had a dotty splendour all their own, a magnificent lunacy made possible by Hollywood's palmiest and most profitable decade. As for Miss Montez, after queening it at Universal throughout the war, she still continued her expensive masquerading on leaving the studio, notably in the 1948 *Siren of Atlantis*, another version of the much-filmed *L'Atlantide*, directed by several hands, including Arthur Ripley and Gregg Tallas.

Vampires and werewolves proliferated so profitably at Universal that they also turned up at Columbia, where Lugosi in *Return of the Vampire* (Lew Landers, 1943) disintegrated in fatal sunshine before the audience's very eyes, Karloff played a series of demented scientists, Lorre was the unhappy owner of *The Face Behind the Mask* (Robert Florey, 1941) and Nina Foch gave Simone (*Cat People*) Simon stiff lycanthropic competition in Henry Levin's *Cry of the Werewolf* (1944).

Monogram and Republic furnished many a lower half of a horror

Walter Huston's entertaining devil, Mr. Scratch, tempts the simple New Hampshire farmer (James Craig, at left) in William Dieterle's handsome but stolid production of ALL THAT MONEY CAN BUY.

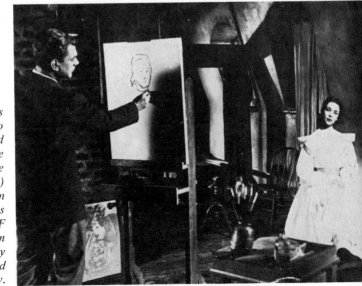

Joseph Cotten as the artist who becomes infatuated with the mysterious Jennie (Jennifer Jones) in William Dieterle's PORTRAIT OF JENNIE, an unashamedly romantic and touching fantasy.

Jean Brooks (in armchair) under pressure at a meeting of the secret society of devil worshippers during Val Lewton's production of THE SEVENTH VICTIM, directed by Mark Robson.

Hurd Hatfield as Dorian in Blue Gate Fields, from Albert Lewin's pictorially masterful adaptation of Oscar Wilde, THE PICTURE OF DORIAN GRAY.

double bill with their cheapie exploitation pieces, among them Erich von Stroheim in *The Lady and the Monster* (George Sherman, 1944, based on Curt Siodmak's *Donovan's Brain*), unforgettable for von Stroheim's rasped command to Vera Hruba Ralston to "get the giggly saw"; Karloff in *The Ape* (1940), in which he committed murder while encased in a gorilla skin; Carradine in *Revenge of the Zombies* (1943) and *Face of Marble* (1946), in both of which he was a crazed doctor; and others like *King of the Zombies*, *Human Monster* and *Valley of the Zombies*, all as dismal as their titles suggest.

The major studios seldom essayed horror/fantasy, but when they did it was usually in a big way. M-G-M's sole A-grade contributions to the genre were Victor Fleming's *Dr. Jekyll and Mr. Hyde* (1941), notable mainly for some kinkily suggestive dream sequences in which Spencer Tracy enthusiastically flogs Ingrid Bergman and Lana Turner as they draw him along in a chariot, and Albert Lewin's famous version of Oscar Wilde's *The Picture of Dorian Gray* (1945).

This was a film of immaculate design (Hans Peters) and visuals of a lacquered, *fin de siècle* elegance (Harry Stradling's photography deservedly won an Academy Award), providing the novel with an almost perfect cinematic equivalent, despite the fact that its screenplay inevitably vulgarised the original: Sibyl Vane, for instance, was no longer a Shakespearian actress but a music-hall singer, and George Sanders's Lord Henry Wotton, spouting Wilde-and-water epigrams, was a paltry Mephistopheles indeed. Pictorially, though, the film was masterly: the butterfly trapped in formaldehyde, a brilliant symbol of Dorian's exquisite imprisonment in his transcendental curse; his Eastern *soirée* at which a Balinese dancer performs gyrations similar to those of *The Thief of Bagdad's* Silver Maid; his visit to a lurid brothel in Blue Gate Fields as a gaunt pianist thrums the Chopin *étude* which Dorian had used to seduce the luckless Sibyl; the country shooting-party at which Sibyl's brother is accidentally killed, beautifully captured in images as sharply defined as those of a steel engraving; and of course the decaying portrait, the work of Ivan Le Lorraine Albright, which — startlingly inter-cut in colour into the movie's predominant monochrome — was as voluptuously hideous as Wilde himself could have wished. Hurd Hatfield's Dorian, waxen, pallid and enigmatic, his thin soft voice hinting at all manner of over-refined debauchery, Angela Lansbury's Sibyl, a touching virginal creature never for a moment ridiculous, or Douglas Walton's Alan Campbell, fidgety and crushed beneath the weight of Dorian's power over him, were excellent, while Cedric Hardwicke's uncredited and authoritatively delivered narration persuasively filled in the chief character's motivational gaps.

Paramount began the decade with Ernest B. Schoedsack's *Dr. Cyclops* (1940). Albert Dekker, bald and bespectacled, played Dr. Alexander Thorkel, a maniacal experimenter on the Karana River, at the headwaters of the Amazon, who reduces a party of visiting scientists to doll-like proportions and, in a peculiarly repellent scene, snuffs out the life of one of them with a wad of cotton-wool soaked in ether. His victims' struggles with seemingly gigantic insects, cats, etc. provided a special-effects department's field-day, and Thorkel met his doom when, deprived of his essential spectacles (hence the title), he fell to his death down a well.

In 1944, Nils Asther appeared in *The Man in Half Moon Street*, based on Barré Lyndon's play about a discoverer of a youth-prolonging elixir; his rapid ageing on-camera in a railway carriage was the neatest case of instant decrepitude seen on the screen since Margo's metamorphosis in *Lost Horizon*. Paramount's final fling at fantasy occurred in John Farrow's *The Night Has a Thousand Eyes* (1948), also written by Lyndon. Here Edward G. Robinson as a vaudeville clairvoyant (a switch from his part in *Flesh and Fantasy*) cannot avert himself or others from the predestined fate which he foresees for them.

More spiritualistic jiggery-pokery figured in Bernard Vorhaus's *The Amazing Mr. X* (also known as *The Spiritualist*, 1948). Those two *echt*-Forties people, Turhan Bey and Lynn Bari, played respectively a phony medium and the supposed widow with whose "departed" husband he claims he can communicate. Long before the days of transistor tape recorders and stereo, Bey was able to construct sonic miracles in his house and on a beach to give Miss Bari some unsettling aural illusions. Her husband (Richard Carlson), whose "dead" voice had repeatedly called her name, turned out to be alive all along, the whole thing being an elaborate plot to drive her insane. Scarcely any of its 78 minutes were dull, and John Alton's decorative low-key black-and-white images were constantly watchable.

Unconsciously funny, *The Amazing Mr. X* drew unintended laughs while playful fantasies like Hal Roach's *Turnabout* and René Clair's *It Happened Tomorrow* (1944) set out deliberately to amuse. In *Turnabout* — based on a Thorne (*Topper*) Smith story — John Hubbard and Carole Landis played a married couple so dissatisfied with their respective lots that a sacred Indian idol switches each into the other's body. What could have been a tasteless transvestite giggle was made genuinely funny by refreshingly "natural" playing and direction.

It Happened Tomorrow also had fun with its central premise: a ghostly old man presents a cub reporter of the 1890s (Dick Powell) for three days in succession with a copy of tomorrow's newspaper a day before it could have gone to press. Rushing to put his byline on scoops before they happen, he is stopped short on the third day by an announcement of his own death. All ends happily (this, after all, is Clair), and assisting in the frolics are Linda Darnell, Jack Oakie and Sig Rumann. This is one of the director's most beguiling divertissements.

Forties fantasy was one of the many cinematic casualties of the succeeding decade: like everything else, the *genre* became cruder, coarser, more mechanical, appealing increasingly to moronic or perverse tastes (or both). Nearly all its products acquired a sci-fi gloss and — with very rare exceptions — the sense of wonder so often communicated in the best examples of the mode became a thing of the past. Only in television series like William Frye's *Thriller* or Joseph Stefano's *Outer Limits* has there since been achieved in this field anything comparable to what Val Lewton and his contemporaries were making twenty or more years ago.

5. Problem and Sociological Films

THE THIRTIES was a decade of militant social consciousness in films and in the arts generally: the after-effects of the Depression and a preoccupation with what used to be called the "underprivileged" resulted in a series of films reflecting the predominantly Left-oriented flavour of the time. By the Forties, much of the impetus for these pictures had played itself out. Although belonging technically to the succeeding decade, films like *The Grapes of Wrath*, *Of Mice and Men* and *Tobacco Road* were really Thirties products, deriving their intellectual and emotional sustenance from the era of the New Deal and the Group Theatre. With one or two notable exceptions such as *The Ox-bow Incident* and *The Lost Weekend*, sociology lay dormant in Hollywood until after World War Two, which not unnaturally tended to displace everything else from the non-escapist screen.

Then, between 1946 and 1949, the floodgates opened: problem pictures were suddenly fashionable. Racial prejudice involving Negroes and Jews, insanity, alcoholism, rehabilitation of ex-servicemen, juvenile delinquency, euthanasia and political corruption provided material for some of the decade's most outstanding productions. Simultaneously, a new trend towards "realism", towards non-studio shooting in actual locations, a trend largely started by the "March of Time" producer Louis de Rochemont, resulted in a marriage between Hollywood craftsmanship at its best and the demands of verisimilitude that spawned a notable series of semi-documentary crime melodramas, many based on real-life cases: *Boomerang!*, *The House on 92nd Street*, *Call Northside 777* typified the style.

Here — as indeed throughout the decade — the leading studio was Fox, even if, as Richard Winnington accurately pointed out, Darryl F. Zanuck often took up themes that others had initiated. Fox's leadership in this field began in 1940 with *The Grapes of Wrath*, continued with *The Ox-bow Incident*, and after the war resumed with *Pinky*, *Gentleman's Agreement* and *The Snake Pit*.

This was the time also when Stanley Kramer came to prominence with *Home of the Brave* and Adrian Scott at R.K.O. made the best of all anti-anti-Semitism pictures, *Crossfire*. Mark Hellinger at Universal, with Jules Dassin, raised the realistic crime thriller to new levels of craftsmanship with *The Naked City*, having preceded it with a powerful if melodramatic study of prison injustice, *Brute Force*. At Columbia, John Derek was the Forties' answer to the Thirties' Dead End Kids, another criminal moulded not by an evil character but by an evil environment. Here, too, Broderick Crawford impersonated Huey Long in *All the King's Men*. At Paramount, Ray Milland staggered alcoholically through Wilder's *The Lost Weekend*, while M-G-M's only contributions to movie sociology were Mervyn LeRoy's *Blossoms in the Dust* and Clarence Brown's version of William Faulkner's *Intruder in the Dust*.

These films were more or less sincere, unsensational, often too high-minded and sentimental. But with all their simplistic faults they are preferable to the artificial frenzies of *The Blackboard Jungle* or the slick, machine-tooled forgettability of the typical television "think" piece.

Ford's *The Grapes of Wrath* (1940) remains as magnificent today as when it first appeared, undated, its compassion and truthfulness transcending the ideological limitations which some have sought to impose on it, and which the director has contemptuously repudiated From John Steinbeck's Zolaesque novel of the displaced "Okies" of the 1930s, Ford made a film of passionate sobriety, controlled eloquence, and unsentimental power. Nunnally Johnson's excellent script followed the Joads — Ma (Jane Darwell), Pa (Russell Simpson), Grampa (Charlie Grapewin) and Tom (Henry Fonda) — as they make their way, like the biblical Israelites, from drought·ravaged Oklahoma to the Promised Land of California, there to encounter, not milk and honey, but the harsh ugliness and corruption of a transit camp. In almost flawless performances, only occasionally suggesting city slickers slumming, the Joads came wonderfully alive, carrying their symbolic burdens lightly, and if they seemed at times unnecessarily idealised, and their speeches implausibly literary, that scarcely diminishes the film's stature. Jane Darwell as Ma was especially fine, and moments like those in which she burns her belongings before quitting her lifelong home for good, or proclaims the indestructibility of "the people that live", are among the most moving in the film. Henry Fonda's Tom — fundamentally decent, a felon through force of circumstance — remains the best thing he has done on the screen, while John Carradine's Casy, a preacher-cum-labour organiser, is hardly less good. Despite an occasional tendency to artiness, Gregg Toland's images, deglamorised, unpretty, stark, a world away from the flashy pyrotechnics of *Citizen Kane* or the photographic muscle-flexing of *The Westerner*, helped give the film its air of "inevitability", a masterly illusion of reality. Contrary to what has often been stated, the musical score does consist of more than solo accordion — sometimes almost a full orchestra — but Ford here generally dispenses with music altogether. Stylistically years ahead of its time, *The Grapes of Wrath* is one of the few films thoroughly to deserve its reputation as a masterpiece. The decade produced nothing nobler.

The same year saw coincidentally another distinguished Steinbeck adaptation when Lewis Milestone made *Of Mice and Men* for the producer Hal Roach. Before the credits, two men, George (Burgess Meredith) and Lennie (Lon Chaney Jr) are seen fleeing from a posse. They hide in a ditch, hop a train at night, and the titles appear on the box-car. Thus dynamically, swiftly, the mood is set, and the events that follow — the farm scenes, the simple-minded Lennie's accidental killing of the boss farmer's flibbertigibbet wife, George's mercy-killing of Lennie — take place against a background of economic misery coupled with rural lyricism, a combination that brings out some of Milestone's finest qualities: a beautiful feeling for the farm, the land and its workers, caught notably when the boss's wife (Betty Field) goes for a provocative walk among the hay-harvesters; and an instinctive sympathy for the pathos, loneliness and tawdry pleasures of the itinerant farm hands. Although the film's acting is more stylised than naturalistic, and Charles Bickford's white-shirted, all-understanding overseer Slim bears more than his share of symbolism, this is perfectly in keeping with its essential character of a morality play, a bit contrived, perhaps, but none the less sincere and affecting. As in *The Red Pony*, Aaron Copland's score, fresh and simple, beautifully complements the visuals, and Lon Chaney's Lennie, Burgess Meredith's George and Betty Field's foolish, bored victim could hardly be bettered.

Further exploration of the plight of the downtrodden occurred in John Ford's *Tobacco Road* (1941), adapted by Nunnally Johnson from Jack Kirkland's long-running play and Erskine Caldwell's novel. The film is considerably below the level of *The Grapes of Wrath*: the film-makers turned the original drama of dirt, malnutrition and moral decay among Georgia backwoods farmers, with its countrified sexuality and Rabelaisian humours, into a bucolic, folksy farce, complete with changed ending and cleaned-up situations. Charlie Grapewin was admirable in the part of Jeeter Lester, created on the stage by Henry Hull in 1933, but Gene Tierney as Ellie May, caked with studio dirt, was altogether wrong, and not even Ford's most careful craftsmanship could redeem the film's betrayal of its source.

Though its intentions were commendable, William Wellman's *The Ox-bow Incident* (1942), based by the screenwriter-producer Lamar Trotti on Walter van Tilburg Clark's novel, and in turn on an actual incident in 1885, emerged distinctly flawed. A condemnation of lynch law, it continued the tradition of Fritz Lang's *Fury* (1936) and Mervyn LeRoy's *They Won't Forget* (1937), while achieving the force of neither. In a Western setting, it depicted the mob killing of three men accused of murder who later prove to have been innocent: the anti-lynching argument would surely have been reinforced had one of them been guilty. This contrivance extends also to the lynchers, represented chiefly by a bloodthirsty ex-soldier and a lewd sadistic virago (well played by Jane Darwell). Patently studio "outdoor" sets and slack, uncommitted direction compromised the film still further. That it yet achieved a certain power was due mainly to its intelligently written dialogue and the theatrically accomplished playing of its cast, which gave it ahead of its time the air of a competent television problem play.

71

While the international scene was largely covered by films dealing directly or indirectly with the war, there were also a few which dealt memorably, often brilliantly, with domestic politics. Here the leading director was Frank Capra, who in the Thirties with *Mr. Deeds Goes to Town* and *Mr. Smith Goes to Washington* had brought something new to the American cinema: the sociological morality play, the struggle of the good, the true and the beautiful against the forces of corruption and evil, played with the entire U.S. as its background. With his script-writing collaborator, Robert Riskin, Capra in 1941 made perhaps his greatest film in this mode, *Meet John Doe*. An impassioned plea for "little people" and Democracy, it delivered its naive utopian message with such fervour, such full-throated enthusiasm, and above all with such dazzling cinematic *panache* that, watching it, even the most cynical realist must succumb to its enchantment.

Taking seven months to make, and costing a million dollars (a large budget at that time), *Meet John Doe* is a sermon delivered by a master technician. Capra's virtuosity astonishes in the scenes of a mass rally in the rain, the director in his manipulation of crowds and his organising of the images displaying an almost peerless cinematic command. The final clock-tower scene, the snow falling gently, the three main protagonists confronting each other in a life-or-death showdown, carries an emotional punch undiminished by time.

It is probably safe to guess that Victor Saville and George Cukor had Capra's film in mind when in the following year they made *Keeper of the Flame*, based by the screenwriter Donald Ogden Stewart on a novel by I. A. R. Wylie. For here too was a quasi-Fascist would-be dictator — albeit dead — who very nearly assumes power in America. Opening with the death of this man, Robert Forrest, in a car crash in a storm at night, it followed the efforts of a reporter (Spencer Tracy) to discover the truth about the seemingly upright political hero from his widow (Katharine Hepburn), his mad mother (Margaret Wycherly) and his sinister, thickly bespectacled secretary (Richard Whorf). The truth is that Forrest was a traitor, his democratic posturings — he even had his own Boy Scout troop — a sham. For learning this, the secretary tries to kill the reporter and Forrest's widow (who are by now in love) and when this fails he commits suicide by walking into the path of a speeding car.

The deadening hand of Charles Foster Kane lies heavily on this film, thematically and stylistically: thematically in its probing into the life of a man who dies at its beginning and its revelations about his past; stylistically in its Xanadu-like Forrest estate surrounded by huge pieces of ironwork, often photographed menacingly from below eye level and hung with "no trespassing" and "keep out" notices; in Richard Whorf's appearance, recalling Thompson's, the reporter's, in *Kane*; and in the press conference scene, a virtual duplicate of the one in Welles's film following immediately on the "newsreel". Its emotional temperature, however, is altogether too low, too tepid, muffling its impact. It lacks urgency, a sense of high drama, so that its good ideas — Forrest's funeral, duped mourners weeping under umbrellas, some acerbic character "bits" by Percy Kilbride and Audrey Christie — go for little.

Hollywood left U.S. politics alone after that until 1947, when Capra returned to this theme with *State of the Union*, based on a hit stage play by Howard Lindsay and Russell Crouse. This, too, starred Tracy and Hepburn, the former as an idealistic presidential candidate who has his ideals whittled down through contact with the evil represented by Angela Lansbury's predatory newspaper proprietress and Adolphe Menjou's cunning political manoeuvrer. Less allegorical, more down-to-earth than *Meet John Doe*, *State of the Union* was still vintage Capra, its rogues' gallery of corrupt industrialists, labour leaders and backstairs political string-pullers making a distinctly more striking impression than Tracy's honourable industrialist-cum-candidate, despite the actor's excellent performance. Lansbury's Kay Thorndike — a trench-coated believer in power, she inherits her belief from her publisher father (Lewis Stone) and cynically uses sex to further it — was one of her most acrid portrayals, while Van Johnson as Tracy's disillusioned but loyal aide and a gathering of Capra "regulars" helped give the film its characteristic Capra tang, with rat-a-tat dialogue delivered expertly and a slam-bang climax as Tracy, amid the hoop-la and ballyhoo of a coast-to-coast radio election *spiel*, exposes the corruption of it all to the consternation of his crooked supporters and the delight of his staunch wife.

Even more disenchanted, and leavened by no last-minute rush to join the side of the angels, was Robert Rossen's *All the King's Men* (1949), adapted by the director from Robert Penn Warren's novel which was in turn suggested by the career of Louisiana's governor Huey Long. Perhaps because it lost an hour's running-time before release to bring it down to 109 minutes, *All the King's Men* suffered from choppy continuity and unsatisfactory character motivation. Willie Stark (Broderick Crawford) is shown first as a hick lawyer moved by a seemingly sincere concern for the downtrodden. Then, as he tastes power and realises the charismatic nature of his appeal, he changes into a drunken, juggernauting egomaniac, a potential national dictator stopped only by an assassin's bullet. The trouble was that the change, instead of being gradual, became too abrupt, and Stark's psychology consequently made little sense. But the film did have a restless, nervous intensity, full of gusto and drive and colour: behind the credits we see torchlight processions, campaign barbecues, banners borne aloft proclaiming support for Stark. He is revealed in short, staccato sequences, at a football stadium, haranguing a fairground crowd, bulldozing legislators, posing for cameramen with his estranged family. All these passages, and those connected with the hustings and political campaigning, have an electric fire and vitality, utterly American.

So much for domestic politics. Until the Cold War, films dealing with the international scene were mostly confined to those about World War Two. An exception was *The Searching Wind* (1946), Hal Wallis's intelligent and civilised version of Lillian Hellman's stage success, adapted for the screen by the playwright and directed by William Dieterle. This was a rarity, a film of ideas that presented a valid point of view in terms of believable action and conflict and character. Set mostly in Europe, it surveyed the diplomatic career of a fictional American ambassador, Alexander Hazen (Robert Young) as he encounters Fascism first in Rome in 1922 as Mussolini marches on the city, in Berlin in the early 1930s when Nazism emerges as Germany's dominant force, in Madrid at the height of the Spanish Civil War, and finally in Paris at the time of the Munich Pact. Its message — that isolationism is outdated and that America must concern itself with happenings in Europe and elsewhere — was intertwined with Hazen's personal involvement with a newspaperwoman, Cassie Bowman (Sylvia Sidney) and his gradually deteriorating marriage to Emily (the admirable, underrated Ann Richards). To the probing acerbity of Miss Hellman's lines, Dieterle's *mise en scène* and Hans Dreier's and Franz Bachelin's art direction provided ideal foils, reproducing a semblance of diplomatic high life in Rome, Paris and Washington that clothed the film's arguments in a stylised approximation of reality. From a strong cast two stood out: Dudley Digges as Moses Hazen, a splendid portrayal of an aristocratic American in a now defunct tradition of great acting (he played this part 500 times on the stage); and Albert Bassermann as Count von Strammer, a brief but unforgettable appearance in which the aged *doyen* of the German theatre impersonated a time-serving diplomat of the von Papen type with knowing mastery.

When the U.S.S.R. emerged as the principal international villain in the latter half of the Forties, Hollywood reflected the trend in a cycle of none too distinguished films that began with William Wellman's *The Iron Curtain* (1948). Allegedly based on the memoirs of Igor Gouzenko, this featured Dana Andrews and Gene Tierney as the most unlikely Russians since the Barrymore trio played the Romanoffs, while Berry Kroeger, June Havoc and others contributed little more than unintentionally comic turns. Only Stefan Schnabel's spy-ring boss — cynical, ruthless, a cigarette drooping moodily from the corner of his mouth in the best Fritz Lang tradition — and Charles G. Clarke's excellent Ottawa location photography saved the film from being a total write-off. It was swiftly followed by R. G. Springsteen's *The Red Menace* (1949), a ludicrous but often artily shot purported "exposé" of U.S. Communists' methods that even *Time* magazine found indefensible, and George Sidney's *The Red Danube* (also 1949), which showed the Russians' efforts to forcibly extradite ballerina Janet Leigh from Vienna foiled by Major Walter Pidgeon and Mother Superior Ethel Barrymore. These crude and foolish pantomimes did the cause of anti-Communism probably more harm than good.

Although set in the 1930s, John Huston's *We Were Strangers* (1949) had an almost timeless political relevance. In Havana in 1933, during the Machado dictatorship, a group of revolutionaries and patriots plan to assassinate a member of the prominent and corrupt Contreras family, dig a tunnel to the clan's vault in the Colon Cemetery and — when Machado and his henchmen are gathered together for the obsequies — blow the lot to smithereens. At the last moment the funeral venue is changed, the elaborate preparations go for nothing, and most of the chief conspirators are killed. An uneven but often striking film, *We Were Strangers*' best passages were those in the tunnel, as the diggers' nerves become progressively more strained and the claustrophobic danger of their situation exacerbates the tension. Jennifer Jones as China Valdes, a Cuban patriot, performed a difficult role with her customary intelligence: the sequence in which she sees her brother shot by Machado thugs had a newsreel-like immediacy in the finest tradition of neo-realism.

New themes began to emerge in the decade's latter half. In 1947, for instance, racial intolerance became for the first time an acceptable Hollywood screen subject. That year, two films revolved around anti-Semitism. The first, Edward Dmytryk's *Crossfire*, was quite the better; it is, indeed, one of the Forties' finest films, a position it would still hold even if it had been — to stretch a point to its limit — actually in favour of anti-Semitism. Its merit lies not so much in its espousal of liberal sentiments or even in its recognition — daring at the time for an American commercial film — of the existence of anti-Semitism in U.S. society as in its marvellous rendition of the seamy underside of a big city at night, its superb writing (by John Paxton), and its almost perfect ensemble playing.

It opens with an interior shot, plunging us without preliminaries straight into the action: on an apartment-room wall we see in shadow a man being beaten up and left for dead. The remainder of the film is spent attempting to discover not only who killed the victim but also *why* he was killed. The search takes in a group of army men on leave, an

Irish police inspector, and a bar-room floozy and her ambiguous "admirer". The killer is soon made clear: he is a psychopathic bully and sadist (played by Robert Ryan). What takes longer to ascertain is his motive. This, it finally emerges, is inflamed prejudice, for the dead man (Sam Levene) was Jewish, and the murderer killed him in an alcohol-induced rage.

Dmytryk and Paxton delineate their milieu hauntingly: an all-night movie theatre, a seedy bar, a military hotel, a cheap apartment, all bathed in that peculiar midnight-to-dawn atmosphere that ordinary surroundings acquire at those muted subdued hours. Gloria Grahame's Ginny, bedraggled and sardonic, is a typical inhabitant of this night world, and so is her "boyfriend" (Paul Kelly), a pathological liar. Their scenes together have a bitter, witty edge and contain some of the film's best writing.

But it is Robert Ryan's psychopath, Montgomery, that stays most in the mind: deceptively soft-spoken, seething with suppressed tensions and feelings of inferiority, it is a frightening portrait, particularly in such scenes as that in which he strangles his accomplice-victim Floyd (Steve Brodie) with a necktie or scrapes away raspingly with a safety razor as a simpleminded fellow soldier delivers a phony police "message" to him in the hotel washroom, laying the trap that will be his undoing. Predictably, the film's didactic sections are its weakest: Robert Young's sermon on tolerance, the loaded contrivance whereby Levene's murdered Jew is revealed to have been an honourably discharged veteran (surely it would still have been wrong to kill him if he had been a draft-dodger, a profiteer, a degenerate?). But as a beautifully organised and proportioned melodrama, written, directed and acted with unostentatious excellence, and creating its own poetically heightened "reality", *Crossfire* has few rivals.

Gentleman's Agreement, the other 1947 film with anti-Semitism as its theme, has few rivals either — for superficiality, banality, or ineptitude. Despite fine craftsmanship — Arthur Miller's photography, some exquisite sound-recording — this emerged as a distressingly phony affair. Gregory Peck played a magazine writer masquerading as a Jew for six months for a series of articles on anti-Semitism. Moss Hart's screenplay, slick and self-conscious, examined the effects this impersonation had on the writer's private life: on his fiancée (Dorothy McGuire), his co-worker (Celeste Holm), his mother (irritatingly played in her most sub-Brechtian manner by Anne Revere). It was left to John Garfield as a Jewish serviceman to try to bring a semblance of sincerity and authenticity to the punch-pulling proceedings, but he could not save the film. A TV-style problem piece *ante diem*, *Gentleman's Agreement*'s compromises and evasions derived largely from Laura Z. Hobson's original novel, while Elia Kazan's uninvolved, routine direction did little to help.

Kazan brought more — though not much more — passion to *Pinky*, one of a number of films on the Negro question released in 1949. Here Jeanne Crain played a light-skinned Negress who returns to the South after having "passed" as a white in Boston. Screenwriters Philip Dunne and Dudley Nichols provided two sharp and ugly scenes that stood out markedly from the film's general sentimentality and dishonesty: one in which Pinky is bullied on a roadway by two callous whites, another in which she is cruelly patronised and insulted by a bigoted customer (brilliantly played by Evelyn Varden) in a store in which she works as a helper. For the rest, it was no less compromised than *Gentleman's Agreement*. Joe MacDonald photographed it immaculately, especially in the climactic trial sequence presided over by the excellent Basil Ruysdael, but it remained a patently false film.

Stanley Kramer's *Home of the Brave*, directed by Mark Robson — the film that started the Negro cycle of 1949 — was little better. Cheaply made, it was adapted by Carl Foreman from Arthur Laurents's 1945/6 play in which the protagonist had been a Jew. Here he became a coloured serviceman (James Edwards), crippled and amnesiac through battle shock after a reconnaissance expedition to a Jap-held island on which his best friend had been killed. A psychiatrist (Jeff Corey) uses narcosynthesis to extract from the soldier the confession that under stress during the manoeuvre his deceased buddy had called him a "nigger", thus precipitating his mental and physical crisis. This was not one of Kramer's better films, its generally feeble air emphasised by some distractingly unreal jungle sets.

Unreality was eschewed altogether in Clarence Brown's film of William Faulkner's *Intruder in the Dust*, which appeared towards the end of 1949. Shot almost entirely in the author's home town of Oxford, Mississippi, it focused on the events of two days during which a stubborn, proud Negro, Lucas Beauchamp (Juano Fernandez) is held in the town gaol on suspicion of having murdered a white man by shooting him in the back. This is one of Clarence Brown's last and best films, recalling his masterpieces of the 1930s, *Ah, Wilderness!* and *Of Human Hearts* in its depiction of small-town life. But while those films were affectionate, *Intruder* is harsh and bitter (though not as misanthropic as *Fury*). It is also restrained — perhaps too restrained, resulting in a rather muted and bland effect. Juano Fernandez makes of Lucas a dignified, imposing figure, too scornful of whites to reveal the truth of his innocence, and the 14 professional actors among a cast of 500 enthusiastic amateurs recruited from Oxford's residents do much to lend the film its air of manifest sincerity.

Shooting in actual locations using local residents, as in *Intruder in the Dust* and *All the King's Men*, were stratagems relatively new to Hollywood, and for their widespread adoption in the late Forties one man is largely responsible: Louis de Rochemont. To the 1949 Negro cycle de Rochemont contributed *Lost Boundaries*, based, like all his features, on a real-life case, that of a New Hampshire University student, Albert Johnson, son of a light-skinned doctor who for 20-odd years had practised in New Hampshire while "passing" as a white man. The boy's discovery of his racial background came only after his father had unsuccessfully tried to obtain a wartime commission in the U.S. Navy. Meeting Johnson, de Rochemont resolved, with the help of roving *Reader's Digest* reporter William L. White, to turn his story first into a book, then into a film. To shoot it, he and the director, Alfred Werker, went to Maine and to Portsmouth, New Hampshire, using no artificial sets and as extras the locations' actual inhabitants.

The film's chief burden was carried by Mel Ferrer as the elder Johnson, renamed Dr. Carter. As the Negro doctor forced to renounce his race to follow his career he contributed an earnest, thoughtful performance, ably supported by Beatrice Pearson as his wife. If the depiction of their plight tended to soften the probable actual consequences of a similar real-life situation, it was nevertheless a worthy addition to the growing number of Negro problem pictures which — with such titles as *No Way Out* and *The Defiant Ones* — continued into the Fifties.

De Rochemont had preceded *Lost Boundaries* with an impressive list of semi-documentary features, made mostly at Fox. Born in 1899, he put together his first movie camera at 12, his first two-reelers (publicising the U.S. Navy, in which he was a World War I line officer) in the early Thirties, and at that time also produced an experimental newsreel-style dramatisation of some historical highlights called "March of the Years". Thus began a series which in 1935, in collaboration with *Time* magazine's circulation manager Roy E. Larsen, developed into the famous award-winning "March of Time" short subjects. When in the Forties de Rochemont turned to features he incorporated many devices made familiar through "The March of Time", notably the stentorian narrator's voice — since become virtually a cliché — which introduces and closes a film to lend it an appearance of verisimilitude.

A domestic spy drama, *The House on 92nd Street* (1945), directed by Henry Hathaway — with whom de Rochemont was again to collaborate — inaugurated the postwar semi-realist trend. It continued with *Boomerang!* (1947), Elia Kazan's classic deglamorisation of the glossy studio *roman policier* typified by *Laura* and *Johnny Eager*. This was based on a true case as reported by Fulton Oursler writing under the name of Anthony Abbot. It took place in a small Connecticut town in which an Episcopalian minister is shot dead, and the guilt or innocence of the accused man (Arthur Kennedy) is investigated by District Attorney Dana Andrews. Impressionistically portraying an entire community, *Boomerang!* showed the police as overworked, irritable, grey little men without much sleep, reporters as panicky and tired, and the average American as harassed and tense through ceaseless everyday pressures.

The film suffers, however, from a self-defeating caution and sobriety: too quiet and unsensational, it emerges as rather drab and colourless. But its picture of an America that demands a total commitment to one's job, impersonal and pitiless, is unsparingly real.

Katharine Hepburn and Richard Whorf, widow and secretary of a seemingly upright political hero, in KEEPER OF THE FLAME, directed by George Cukor.

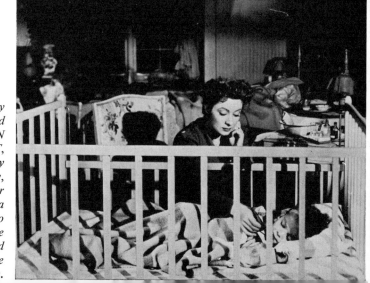

The exquisitely designed BLOSSOMS IN THE DUST, directed by Mervyn LeRoy, featured Greer Garson as a Texas woman who helped relieve the stigma attached to illegitimate children.

The alcoholic (Ray Milland, at left) is reduced to purse-stealing in Billy Wilder's powerful THE LOST WEEKEND.

John Farrow's THE HITLER GANG, a bitingly intelligent and impressively mounted depiction of the Nazi rise to power, showed (left to right) Luis van Rooten as Himmler, Martin Kosleck as Goebbels, Robert Watson as Hitler, and Victor Varconi as Hess.

Thereafter, films based on true incidents, filmed "where it happened", proliferated. One of the best was Hathaway's *Call Northside 777* (1948), about a Chicago reporter's attempts to locate a witness who can prove the innocence of a Polish-American (Richard Conte) serving a long-term prison sentence for complicity in murder. Directed in a deceptively "throwaway", understated, seemingly casual style, superlatively shot in and around Chicago by Joe MacDonald, its highlights were James Stewart as the reporter making the round of the Polish doss-houses in an attempt to find the missing witness's address, finally wheedling it from a gross, ageing barfly, and his arrival at the designated apartment-house, electrifyingly atmospheric, with the elevated chugging nearby, the eerily deserted landing and stairway and then the taut, excitingly played confrontation between the reporter and the witness (Betty Garde), a scene of masterly tension and cathartic release.

The writer-director Crane Wilbur, that specialist in prison pictures, lost little time in dramatising a gaol break that occurred in Canon City, Colorado, on December 30, 1947. The resulting film, *Canon City* (1948), for all its clichés, rang somewhat truer than Mark Hellinger's effort of the previous year, *Brute Force*, directed by Jules Dassin, which, while purporting to be a serious study of gaol conditions, more closely resembled a Grand Guignol melodrama in a penitentiary setting.

The Naked City, Hellinger and Dassin's subsequent collaboration (1948), followed the de Rochemont-inspired trend by being shot almost entirely in New York, as did Henry Hathaway's *Kiss of Death* (1947). William Keighley's *The Street With No Name* (1948) was similar, filmed largely on location and showing how an F.B.I. agent infiltrated and then broke up a gang of criminals.

While crime melodrama took on a new, documentary-style look, the straightforward "problem picture" remained for the most part closely confined to the studio. Mervyn LeRoy's *Blossoms in the Dust* (1941) was an exquisitely designed production (photographed jointly in Technicolor by Karl Freund and W. Howard Greene) in which Greer Garson played Mrs. Edna Gladney, a Texas woman who did much to remove the nineteenth-century social stigma from illegitimate children. Anita Loos's script played free with fact and was shamelessly sentimental, but the film nevertheless had a real feeling for its subject. As a soap opera-cum-message picture, discreetly directed and bathed in lovely pastel colours, it yielded much enjoyment.

The Lost Weekend (Billy Wilder, 1945) is probably the Forties' most famous problem picture, and today loses little of its original power. Inevitably, it compromises: the serious treatment of alcoholism was such a radical departure from normal Hollywood fare that its box-office concessions — the elimination of the novel hero's homosexuality, his improbable redemption through the love of a good woman (Jane Wyman) — can be forgiven. What it retained mattered more: a detached compassion, a clinical sympathy for its neurotic protagonist, quite different from the indulgence accorded such *monstres sacrés* as Norma Desmond or Chuck Tatum.

Ray Milland's Don Birnam ("I'm not just a drunkard — I'm a drunk!") is a failed writer, an anxiety-prone weakling who uses alcohol as an escape. As the film opens he is shown living on the charity of his brother (unpleasantly played by Philip Terry). A number of short, episodic scenes mount gradually in intensity until the two climactic passages, which occur respectively in an alcoholic ward and at Birnam's apartment during a fit of *delirium tremens*. These are both "big" scenes, helped considerably by Miklos Rozsa's theremin-dominated score.

Yet other sequences convey Birnam's agony even better: his attendance at a performance of *La Traviata* as, during the Drinking Song, shots of his increasing discomfiture are intercut with shots of the on-stage singers' mock-joyous abandonment to drink, in an editing juxtaposition of which Pudovkin would surely have approved; his attempt to pawn his typewriter on Third Avenue on Yom Kippur, with both Jewish and Catholic pawnshops simultaneously shut; and, in particular, the scene in Harry and Joe's Bar, played and directed with exemplary delicacy and finesse, in which Birnam robs a girl's handbag, and is thrown out protesting "I'm not a thief!" as a mousy little balding pianist leads the customers in singing "Somebody Stole My Purse!" to the tune of "Somebody Stole My Gal."

Wilder has seldom used his camera more daringly, almost immersing it in a glass of whisky, having it contemplate a gigantic closeup of Milland's opening eye, or stare glumly at the ugly ceiling of the alcoholic ward. Telephones, overturned lampshades and, of course, bottles loom menacingly in the foreground of the compositions, while John F. Seitz's New York exteriors capture in drab greys and blacks a city stripped of glamour and allure. Holding it all together is Milland's admirable performance, conveying the character's softness, his voluptuous surrender to indulgence, to perfection.

Certainly *Smash-up* (Stuart Heisler, 1947, also called *A Woman Destroyed*), which attempted to do for lady dipsomaniacs what Wilder's film had done for men, offered its prototype little serious competition. Susan Hayward played a nightclub entertainer who hits the bottle and the skids, with severe romantic rivalry from a jealous and nasty Marsha Hunt on the way (an excellent sequence shows the two women fighting hysterically in evening dress in a nightclub powder room, shot partly from floor level). Stanley Cortez's shadowy and supple camerawork is consistently worth watching, at one time using a shot through a glass (à la *Humoresque*) of Hayward starting a number. The film has a soft sheen, a feeling of luxury and almost claustrophobic sumptuousness, in marked contrast to Wilder's relatively faithful realism.

Insanity also proved a tempting — and permissible — subject, and Mary Jane Ward's novel *The Snake Pit* became a film (1948) in which Olivia de Havilland's bravura performance and Anatole Litvak's gimmicky direction could not wholly disguise its fundamentally opportunist and sensational approach. Here, a New York asylum was shown as a place of heartless incompetence, even of brutality, its inmates at the mercy of callous warders and unsympathetic doctors, and its "cures" a combination of seemingly arbitrary electric shock treatments and cosy chats with an all-knowing, all-understanding psychiatrist (unctuously played by Leo Genn), a portrait of Freud handily hanging behind him as he delivered his simplistic diagnoses.

De Havilland's fellow inmates were actressy grotesques: Ruth Donnelly's squinting comic turn, Betsy Blair's wordless ninny, Celeste Holm's dewy-eyed asylum veteran. Litvak's handling was alternately sentimental — the lunatics sing *Goin' Home* at a dance, tears coursing down their cheeks — and sensational: they are seen as in an hallucinatory pit, writhing and twisting all too picturesquely in a sub-Dantesque *Totentanz*. As a serious examination of mental illness the film, with its pop psychiatry and glib superficiality, was worthless. But as an actress's and technicians' field-day it offered de Havilland, Litvak and the photographer Leo Tover an ideal opportunity for display. De Havilland's performance — disciplined, electric, the product of a rare union of intuitive and cerebral histrionic talent — was worthy of a better film, while Litvak made of such sequences as her interrogation by a foolish finger-wagging doctor (Howard Freeman) — a window rattling distractingly, the medical board scrutinising her intently — exercises in *ersatz* satire-cum-melodrama.

Juvenile delinquency had been a Hollywood staple since *Dead End* and the Kids to which it gave birth. The Forties' most ambitious contribution to this overworked genre was Nicholas Ray's *Knock on Any Door* (1949), based on Willard Motley's novel. John Derek was the misunderstood product of a shabby environment whose progress from slum to deathchamber via reform school was synthetically charted. Humphrey Bogart delivered the film's message in a jury speech at the boy's trial — in essence, that criminals are made, not born — with understandable weariness.

No sooner was the war over than the problem of ex-servicemen's readjustment manifested itself on the screen in Samuel Goldwyn's and William Wyler's *The Best Years of Our Lives* (1946). A banal, occasionally cynical tribute to the American way of life, it somehow later acquired a reputation as a film with radical values, although it is actually about as radical as a manifesto of the John Birch Society. Set in the fictitious mid-Western town of Boone City, it examined three returning soldiers — ex-banker Fredric March, ex-soda-jerk Dana Andrews, and Harold Russell, an actual handless veteran — as they try to pick up the threads of their pre-war existence. Presumably its "radicalism" consisted of March's advancing an unsecured loan from his Cornbelt Trust Co. to an honest young farmer, likewise a war veteran; but any doubts on this score are immediately resolved by a scene in which March endorses the values of big business — albeit drunk — to a formal gathering of company officers, as his wife (Myrna Loy) smiles approvingly in close-up. The script celebrates — somewhat dishonestly — the traditional America of free enterprise and staunch family life, but it emerges as nearly all novelette, alarmingly foreshadowing television's *Peyton Place*, as March's daughter (Teresa Wright) has her affair with the unhappily married Andrews, sheds tears over shelling peas in the kitchen with her understanding Mom, and behaves throughout with merciless "niceness". It's true that Harold Russell does give a remarkable performance — considering he had no previous acting experience — and that March is, as always, excellent, making of the character of Al rather more than is in the script. But Wyler's handling for Goldwyn is mostly so anonymous and pedestrian, so tepid and attenuated, that it reduces the film's visual interest to practically nil. Perhaps the best sequence directorially is that in which the three veterans, together behind the plexiglass nose of their plane, return to their home town for the first time in years: the sense of comradely intimacy, of shared reminiscence and anticipation, is nicely conveyed, as is their arrival ("Good old Jackson High", etc.), and taxi ride to their respective homes.

For its euthanasia drama — variously known as *An Act of Murder, Live Today For Tomorrow* and *I Stand Accused* — Universal transposed Ernst Lothar's novel *The Mills of God* from a European to an American setting and cast Fredric March as the stern, upright, rather merciless judge who poisons his wife (Florence Eldridge) when he learns she is suffering from an incurable disease. Crude and strident when set beside today's TV medico soap operas, the film (directed by Michael Gordon, 1948) was almost fatally flawed by Daniel Amphitheatrof's noisy, inescapable score, underlining every crisis and climax with hideous cacophony. Between its crashing chords, March, Eldridge, Stanley Ridges and Geraldine Brooks could occasionally be heard giving creditable performances, while the portentous pre-credits opening and a scene in which Eldridge has a delirious turn in a mirror-maze, the irony over stressed as distorted faces laugh indifferently at her plight, were unfortunate attempts by the director to impose "style" on his subject. This was an "interesting" film, sadly dated now, and superseded in most respects by *Ben Casey*, *The Defenders*, and *The Eleventh Hour*. Perhaps sociology, after all, is best left to the tube: certainly the Forties, which excelled in other modes — the musical and melodrama, for example — scored too few outright successes with this one.

6. War Propaganda

ALTHOUGH THE U.S. did not officially enter World War Two until 1941, its movie industry had naturally been well aware of what was happening in Europe and reflected it in several notable pictures. With American involvement, the number of feature films directly dealing with the war increased, and their purpose changed. Whereas they had until then been passionately anti-Nazi, they now combined anti-Nazism with exhortations to the American public. As the war progressed and widened to include the Pacific, Japanese were added to Germans as enemy figures, and Californian backlots did duty for all climes and terrains from the plains of Russia to the sands of Iwo Jima.

In retrospect, most Hollywood movies depicting Occupied Europe and the conduct of the war seem grotesquely unreal. One only has to compare them with documentaries made by professional feature directors — the *Why We Fight* series, for example, or *The Memphis Belle*, or *The Battle of San Pietro* — to be struck by the difference between studio and actuality. Yet despite themselves they captured something of the mood of the time, something of the fervour and exhilaration of an experience central to the lives of all who lived through it. When, in *Casablanca*, the Horst Wessel Song is drowned out by the Marseillaise in Rick's Café, it is a scene no one but a team of Hollywood scriptwriters could have conceived, but its passion and intensity — perfect reflections of the *Zeitgeist* — can still strike sparks today.

Perhaps because they *did* reflect their time so faithfully, the war propaganda movies of the Forties date more noticeably than those of any other *genre*. What, after all, is more dated than yesterday's war? Those smooth Nazi villains, the Veidts, the Premingers, the Koslecks, those downtrodden peasants impersonated by Nazimova or Una O'Connor, those multi-racial Allied platoons seemingly all composed in equal proportions of Negroes, Jews, Irish and Italians — how quaint, how *vieux jeu* they look now! Not to mention those snarling Japanese rapists and torturers, Yellow Perils incarnate, with identical horn-rims framing their slit Oriental eyes, who grunted and jabbered their way through countless Pacific jungles in the latter part of the war! They are about as far removed from Sessue Hayakawa's complex colonel-commandant in *Bridge on the River Kwai* (1956) as James Mason's Rommel in *The Desert Fox* (1953) is removed from von Stroheim's impersonation of the same figure in *Five Graves to Cairo* (1943).

For European expatriates, the war movies provided a field day. Here, as in the fields of black cinema and melodrama, they came into their own, not only as performers but also as directors, writers and technicians. Brecht, for example, provided the original story for Fritz Lang's *Hangmen Also Die*, in which Heydrich was played by Hans von Twardowski, a refugee from *The Cabinet of Dr. Caligari*. Dozens of faces familiar from the pre-war Continental stage and screen turned up again in unwonted surroundings, often speaking thickly accented and ungrammatical English. Some of the former leading lights of the Berlin theatre found themselves playing, not Shakespeare or Ibsen, but Nazi officers or partisan leaders, and in John Farrow's *The Hitler Gang* refugee actors impersonated many of the men responsible for their refugee status.

Hollywood studios were already turning out numerous anti-Nazi pictures long before America declared war. The year 1940 alone saw the release of *The Mortal Storm, Four Sons, Foreign Correspondent* and *Escape*, while *Nazi Agent* (1942), *Above Suspicion* (1943) and *Man Hunt* (1941) came in succeeding years. All these films provided a peculiarly

American view of Nazi Germany, fervently "committed", unequivocally anti-Fascist (before that term too became one of abuse), and passionately propagandist.

Perhaps it was sheer coincidence that both Frank Borzage's *The Mortal Storm* (based on Phyllis Bottome's novel) and Archie Mayo's *Four Sons* (suggested by an I. A. R. Wylie story) shared similar themes: the impact of Nazism on a family of European brothers. In Borzage's film they were German (Robert Young, Robert Stack and James Stewart) and in Mayo's Czechoslovakian (Don Ameche, Alan Curtis, Robert Lowery, George Ernst). Each showed the family's coming asunder under the onslaught of Fascism, while the heads of the household (Frank Morgan in Germany, Eugénie Leontovitch in Czechoslovakia) do their best to stem the tide. Though widely admired at the time, *The Mortal Storm* strikes one today as grossly contrived and sentimental, and about as German as blueberry pie. In its crude way, however, it did bring home to U.S. audiences something of the torment through which many Germans went in the Thirties; the casting of top box-office names helped here too.

Escape was equally crude, and even less effective. Directed by Mervyn LeRoy, it starred Robert Taylor trying to rescue Norma Shearer from the Nazi clutches of Conrad Veidt (a part he was to play in several films and with minor variations before his untimely death in 1943). Hitchcock's *Foreign Correspondent* is on an altogether different level, and is still arguably the director's best American film. A dazzling directorial *tour de force*, it recreated the look and "feel" of Europe (London in the Blitz, Amsterdam and its environs) with uncanny verisimilitude, although entirely made in Hollywood; its art direction in fact is one of William Cameron Menzies's greatest triumphs. Hitchcock has seldom equalled its parade of brilliantly inventive set-pieces: the famous assassination of the phony diplomat in Holland with a gun hidden in a camera; the sinister windmill, its sails revolving as a signal to a 'plane in an opposite direction from those around them; the death of Edmund Gwenn, falling to his doom in an attempt to push Joel McCrea off Westminster Cathedral; the climactic plane crash, a marvel of special effects. The heavies, as so often in this *genre*, are English, led by Herbert Marshall. In later films, Nazis were to be impersonated by Sir Cedric Hardwicke, George Sanders and others more likely, one would have thought, to be on our side. *Foreign Correspondent* ends with a broadcast to America from the height of the Blitz: this was still the time when the U.S. was an interested spectator of, not a participant in the European conflict.

Fritz Lang's *Man Hunt*, based on Geoffrey Household's *Rogue Male*, is also set chiefly in London, a very peculiar London, having affinities — as has often been pointed out — with Brecht's *Dreigroschenoper*: the foggy, cobbled streets, the casually menacing figures lurking in the shadows, the whole reminiscent too of the Jack the Ripper legend, a favourite preoccupation of the German cinema. Here, as in Hitchcock's film, the hero's would-be murderer is himself sent to eternity when John Carradine's sword-umbrella provides the means to electrocute him in the Underground. But the scenes set in Germany stay most in the memory: Hitler glimpsed in the lair of Berchtesgaden, the interrogation of the hero (Walter Pidgeon) by George Sanders, the latter speaking perfectly acceptable German, and especially Ludwig Stossel's diabolically sadistic little giggle as he pushes Pidgeon over a precipice to what he supposes will be his death.

Man Hunt, The Mortal Storm, Foreign Correspondent: what all these had in common was their depiction of a set designer's Europe, an art director's Germany, Hollywood's idea of the Old World. Reaching perhaps its wildest flights of fancy in William Cameron Menzies's *Address Unknown* (1944), it showed the offices of top Nazis as something like converted ballrooms, dwarfing their human occupants, with colossal swastikas and Führer-portraits bulking hugely over giant-sized desks, and enormous french windows invariably giving on to immense public squares. Goose-stepping over polished floors, the denizens of these establishments forever threatened to lapse into self-parody, and when they did — as in *A Yank in Dutch* or *Reunion in France* — one could never be quite sure whether the results were intentional or not.

Top Nazis were usually cultured swine. Conrad Veidt's Major Strasser in *Casablanca* ordering caviar and champagne, Basil Rathbone in *Above Suspicion* and *Paris Calling*, Cedric Hardwicke's commandant in *The Moon is Down*, von Stroheim's impeccably accoutred general in *North Star*, all conformed to this pattern. They knew what vintage to order, relished Goethe and Wagner, but didn't hesitate to shoot hostages or torture prisoners whenever it suited their purposes. The conquered, too, belonged to a readily recognisable cinematic stereotype. The towns and villages of France (*This Land is Mine*), Czechoslovakia (*Hostages*) and Norway (*Edge of Darkness*) all harboured their cowled peasant women, their Bronx-accented patriots, their smooth stoolies, their shifty collaborators and their square-jawed Resistance leaders, generally listening furtively to BBC broadcasts or conspiring by night in some cellar to blow up a bridge or liquidate a particularly odious member of the Master Race. The villages they inhabited did movie duty over and over again: for *The Moon is Down*, Fox simply whitewashed the sets built for *How Green Was My Valley*.

Hitler and his colleagues received very special attention in John Farrow's *The Hitler Gang* (1944), a bitingly intelligent and impressively mounted version of the Nazi rise to power. Incisively written by Frances Goodrich and Albert Hackett, knowingly directed, and atmospherically photographed by Ernest Laszlo, its chief distinction lay in its gallery of masterly émigré performers, playing the very men responsible for their exiled condition. Here were Reinhold Schunzel as Ludendorff, Fritz Kortner as Otto Strasser, Alexander Granach as Julius Streicher and — providing the definitive interpretation of a part he has played on the screen five times — Martin Kosleck as Joseph Goebbels, heartlessly brilliant, reptilian in his cunning. Scene after scene was staged with epic sweep and *panache*: the Munich Beerhall Putsch, the camera surveying the proceedings in a bravura crane shot; the Night of the Long Knives, a virtuoso montage of tortures and violent deaths; the meetings with von Papen and the Prussian Junkers, masterpieces of imaginative historical reconstruction; and the late-night conference at which Goebbels proposes a calculated policy of political anti-Semitism. Unhappily Robert Watson's Hitler was sadly inadequate, an amateur's stab at a portrait of the German dictator redeemed only by his striking physical resemblance to the original.

Heydrich was impersonated by Hans von Twardowski in Lang's *Hangmen Also Die* — a cruelly penetrating vignette, played entirely in German — and by John Carradine in Douglas Sirk's *Hitler's Madman* (1943), a far from accurate turn in a far from truthful film. Eventually the *genre* reached its nadir with James Hogan's *The Strange Death of Adolf Hitler*, a Universal cheapie based on a joint idea by expatriates Fritz Kortner and Joe May. Clearly, there was more movie material to be had in showing practical Nazism operating in the Fatherland, as demonstrated in Herbert Biberman's *The Master Race* (1944), Edward Dmytryk's *Hitler's Children* (1943), and especially in William Cameron Menzies's *Address Unknown* (1944) and Peter Godfrey's *Hotel Berlin* (1945). *Address Unknown* used mannered, stylised sets, offbeat angles and semi-Expressionist effects to tell its story of an anti-Nazi family caught up in national events. Full of bizarre touches, its weirdest moment was perhaps that in which a supposedly "Aryan" stage performer is revealed in mid-performance as having been born into the name of Eisenstein.

Hotel Berlin, yet another of the underrated Peter Godfrey's films (a former actor, his masterpiece is *The Woman in White*), was Vicki Baum's reworking of her *Grand Hotel* formula into a topical drama set in an obvious Adlon. One of the most extravagant of all Hollywood war fantasies, it purported to depict an anti-Nazi underground operating practically right under the noses of the German General Staff. Raymond Massey (as in *Desperate Journey*) was a Nazi general, Helmut Dantine — on our side for once — was an underground leader, and Peter Lorre was a clandestinely anti-Nazi professor, providing the film's best scene as he bitterly ransacked his hotel room — looking under the sofa, into broom closets, etc. — for a hypothetical "good German."

Separated from Europe by thousands of miles, forced to recreate contemporary happenings by conjecture, Hollywood responded with spy melodramas that often bordered on the surreal, spilling over into a comedy that was sometimes intentional, sometimes not. The indomitable Joan Crawford starred in two such efforts at M-G-M, *Reunion in*

France (Jules Dassin, 1942) and *Above Suspicion* (Richard Thorpe, 1943). In the former she was a Paris *couturière*, giving as good as she got to the city's German overlords ("A severe wound, I hope", she remarks acidly to an injured Nazi officer), and suffering stoically in gowns by Adrian.

In the latter film she partnered Fred MacMurray in a harebrained expedition to Southern Germany to discover a magnetic mine formula. He was an Oxford don (!), she was his bride, and there was scarcely a dull moment as their quest took them first to Paris, then to Salzburg, where a classic exchange took place in Felix Bressart's bookstore (always a reliable venue for espionage activity). Nazi soldier to MacMurray: "Heil Hitler!" MacMurray: "Nuts to you, dope." Soldier: "I gave you our German greeting, American!" MacM.: "And I gave you ours, dope!" Soldier (to companions): "Was heisst das 'dope'?"

Later, taken on a tour of the Burgmuseum by impoverished aristo guide Conrad Veidt, they are shown a medieval torture device for extracting fingernails, and are assured it's still in excellent condition. "A totalitarian manicure!" quips Joan. The film's highlight was the assassination of a Nazi colonel (described as the commandant of Dachau concentration camp) at a concert during a particularly noisy moment in the Liszt E-flat Piano Concerto. Lavishly staged, it resulted in MacMurray's reunion with former Oxford colleague Basil Rathbone, now a top Gestapo official (again we find the typically Forties conjunction of Hun perfidy and classical music). When Rathbone in due course applies discreet "persuasion" methods to Joan to force her to reveal MacMurray's whereabouts, she exclaims: "I've already told you I don't know — and if you bring in Goering, Goebbels and Himmler my answer will still be the same!" Where this film and others like it scored was in their art direction, often the work of Hans Peters, which reproduced a pastiche, pasteboard Central Europe with enjoyable flair. In *Above Suspicion* one remembers especially the Schwarze Katze cabaret, *echt*-Deutsch, and the "Salzburg" streets, effortlessly convincing.

Warners contributed to this cycle with Vincent Sherman's *Underground* (1941), which had fish-eyed Mona Maris rifling Goering's private desk for incriminating papers; the same director's *All Through the Night* (1942), featuring Bogie, Veidt, Lorre and Judith Anderson in a sidesplitting domestically located German spy yarn incorporating a brilliant auction scene; and Fritz Lang's *Cloak and Dagger* (1946), in which Gary Cooper was a distinguished U.S. scientist pitting his wits against the Teutons. This had one moment of unusual impact: the brutally casual shooting of captive physicist Helene Thimig by her guard/nurse as she is about to be rescued by Allied agents.

Unconsciously funny, *Underground*, *All Through the Night* and others competed for laughs with deliberate send-ups which ridiculed the Germans — though practically never (strangely enough) the Japanese. *World Première* (1941), an almost forgotten comic master-piece directed by cameraman Ted Tetzlaff, featured Fritz Feld and Sig Rumann as subversives sent to Hollywood by Berlin to disrupt the motion picture industry. Feld, diminutive with toothbrush moustache, and Rumann, a ludicrously fumbling giant, deserved on this showing to become as famous a team as Laurel and Hardy, but alas they never did. Feld's scenes as he subdues a lion by tying a knot in its tail or slips a mad Kraut propaganda film into cans containing producer John Barry-more's latest celluloid sensation had an inspired zaniness.

Chaplin's *The Great Dictator* (1940) should have been the definitive anti-Nazi satire. But in his first all-talking film the former "little man" saw himself as something more than a mere clown, more than a graceful gagster: he became embarrassingly serious, harangued the audience, indulged in passionate but naïve rhetoric. The effect was almost to spoil the wit and point of such clever anti-Hitlerian barbs as the scene which showed Hynkel the dictator toying with a balloon globe of the world: entirely visual, a bitterly funny comment realised with an almost balletic insouciance and elegance, this contrasted ill with the schoolboy humour of the rest, the comic-strip parodies of Mussolini, Goering and Goebbels, the *faux-naif* presentation of Hannah the Jewess (Paulette Goddard), the off-colour music-hall verbal jokes. As Hynkel, Chaplin was admittedly often brilliant, marvellously hitting off some of the Führer's grosser mannerisms, but the film as a whole was an unhappy mixture of the crudely farcical and the hortatory.

Leo McCarey's *Once Upon a Honeymoon* (1942), with Ginger Rogers saved from the clutches of Nazi Walter Slezak by journalist Cary Grant, attempted a *Ninotchka*-style satire with limited success. In the same year, *Ninotchka's* director made *To Be or Not To Be*, probably the most famous anti-Nazi parody of all. Set in occupied Warsaw, it of course had nothing to do with that unhappy city but simply exploited it as a convenient location for its Lubitschian buffoonery. Edwin Justus Mayer's brightly written script used many of the devices of traditional French farce — disguises, mistaken identity, etc. — to unravel its complex plot, which revolved around the alleged Polish equivalent of the Lunts (Jack Benny and Carole Lombard, the latter in her last screen appearance) and their efforts to outwit the conquerors. Chief conqueror was again the delectable Sig Rumann ("So they call me 'Concentration Camp Erhardt'?") and Felix Bressart did his usual turn as a mousy nonentity, Mr. Everyman personified. The film, however, belonged principally to Benny, proving himself again one of the American cinema's most accomplished light comedians. As the ham actor Joseph Tura imagining himself being cuckolded by his actress wife Maria (Lombard), he was memorably ridiculous, especially in his stabs at playing Hamlet. Not far behind him came Allyn Joslyn in *A Yank in Dutch*, as a Nazi officer suffering from a sore arm brought on by too much *heil*ing.

But the majority of Hollywood films set in Europe were concerned mainly with emphasising two things: Nazi cruelty to civilians and the latters' organised clandestine resistance. For this purpose directors of the calibre of Lang (*Hangmen Also Die*), Renoir (*This Land is Mine*) and Milestone (*Edge of Darkness*) chipped in with sterling contributions. Set usually in a small town or village, these films were well-meaning but stereotyped exercises in predictable propaganda. Occasionally, as in Milestone's *Edge of Darkness*, they did achieve eloquence and power, but they suffered from the too frequent casting of Americans as Europeans, and from a certain sameness which ultimately detracted from their propaganda value. In this category belong Zinnemann's *The Seventh Cross* (1944), Frank Tuttle's *Hostages* (1943, featuring a fine performance from Oscar Homolka), and Irving Pichel's *The Moon is Down* (1943).

England was a special case. Unconquered, she was actively resisting Germany long before the U.S. Metro seemed especially (and shrewdly in view of the British market) imbued with Anglophilia. In 1942 it produced *Mrs. Miniver*, with Greer Garson supplying the stiff upper lip in a never-never Albion peopled by such English types as Walter Pidgeon and Teresa Wright. Not long after that came Clarence Brown's *The White Cliffs of Dover* (1943), with Irene Dunne substituting (inadequately) for Garson, and the redoubtable Dame May Whitty. Dame May appeared also in *Forever and a Day* (1943), a combined effort by Hollywood's English colony which traced the successive fortunes of a stately London house. Beautifully made, it was the work of several directorial hands, including Edmund Goulding and René Clair, and of such British writers as Charles Bennett and C. S. Forester, while its cast-list read like a roll call of Anglo-Saxon Californian expatriates.

Hitchcock's *Lifeboat* (1944) — based, like *The Moon is Down*, on a John Steinbeck original — was set not in any European country but on the high seas. A laboured allegory, it contrasted the plump sleek Nazi of Walter Slezak, sustaining himself furtively on vitamin pills, with democracy's comparatively feeble representatives (Tallulah Bankhead, John Hodiak, Henry Hull and others) as they all drift through the Atlantic (actually the Fox studio tank) in the aftermath of a sea disaster. The democrats' behaviour in pushing Slezak over the boat's edge to drown at the end was dramatically sound if morally suspect, while the film's deliberate confinement to a single setting allowed its loquacious puppets full scope to air their views.

As the war progressed, movies purporting to show its actuality in terms of battle began issuing from the studios. A favourite setting was Soviet Russia, for these were the days — between the Nazi invasion of the Soviet Union and the beginning of the Cold War — when differences between East and West were temporarily forgotten, and Russia was naïvely lauded in films that were later to prove embarrassments to their makers. Among the most embarrassing was Gregory Ratoff's *Song of Russia* (1944), which presented Robert Taylor as an American orchestral conductor making a pilgrimage to Tchaikovsky's home town at the height of hostilities.

In the same vein was Jacques Tourneur's *Days of Glory* (1944), written by Casey Robinson from a story by Melchior Lengyel. This marked the screen début of Gregory Peck, fresh from the New York stage. He played a partisan leader who ultimately has a reluctant ballerina (Tamara Toumanova) tossing hand-grenades with enthusiasm. Lewis Milestone's *North Star* (1943) was on a somewhat higher plane. Written by Lillian Hellman and photographed (with his customary expertise) by James Wong Howe, it featured an Aaron Copland score, Ira Gershwin lyrics, and a bevy of simple but noble Russian peasants incarnated by Anne Baxter, Dana Andrews, Farley Granger, Ann Harding and the ubiquitous Walter Huston, without whom no film of this type seemed complete. Milestone's craftsmanship — as in *Edge of Darkness* and *The Purple Heart* — gave the film its characteristic rhythm and momentum, which partly counterbalanced its tendentiousness. Erich von Stroheim and Martin Kosleck contributed the villainy, the former as a kid-gloved German general, the latter as a reptilian doctor who drains Russian children's blood for transfusion into German wounded.

Other films which brought the war to bogus life in the Californian hills were built around those few top male stars not in the armed forces. Errol Flynn blustered his way through Raoul Walsh's *Desperate Journey* (1942), in which he represented the Allies against Raymond Massey's sneering Nazi Intelligence officer; *Edge of Darkness* (1943), another finely made Milestone film — this time set in Norway and containing memorable performances from Nancy Coleman and Charles Dingle; and, most notoriously, Walsh's *Objective Burma* (1945), a Jerry Wald production from an original story by Alvah Bessie which depicted Flynn, an American, winning the Burma campaign practically single-handed, with not a mention of Slim, Wingate or indeed of the British role at all.

Humphrey Bogart, too, wore combat uniform on sound stages only. In Zoltan Korda's *Sahara* (1943) he helped flush the Krauts out of North Africa, in Lloyd Bacon's *Action in the North Atlantic* (1943) he

Humphrey Bogart as Rick, Claude Rains as the prefect of police, Paul Henreid and Ingrid Bergman as the fugitive resistance leader and his wife Ilsa, in CASABLANCA, a film indissolubly linked with the name of its director, Michael Curtiz.

"An unconquerable fortress, the American home, 1943": Monty Woolley in the foreground watched by (left to right) Shirley Temple, Craig Stevens, Joseph Cotten, Jennifer Jones, Alla Nazimova, Claudette Colbert and Keenan Wynn in David O. Selznick's production SINCE YOU WENT AWAY, alarmingly expert schmaltz directed by John Cromwell.

performed a similar chore, and in *Pride of the Marines* (Delmer Daves, 1945) John Garfield, another Warners stalwart, portrayed Marine Sgt. Al Schmidt, a famous war hero blinded in combat. For the same director and studio Garfield appeared in *Destination Tokyo* (1944), set on a submarine, and took to the skies for Howard Hawks's *Air Force* (1943). Warners, indeed, was undoubtedly *the* war propaganda film studio, its output exceeding all others in quantity and (on a craftsmanship basis) quality. Paramount, apart from extravaganzas like *Star Spangled Rhythm* and an occasional Alan Ladd vehicle, made probably the least notable contribution, although DeMille's *Story of Dr. Wassell* (1944) was an ambitious but stolid and overlong exception, and *So Proudly We Hail* (Mark Sandrich, 1943), a tribute to combat nurses with Veronica Lake, Claudette Colbert and Paulette Goddard, was another. *Wake Island* (John Farrow, 1942) had fine moments too.

The North African campaign was responsible for one of Billy Wilder's most puerile efforts, *Five Graves to Cairo* (1943), notable mainly for Erich von Stroheim's Rommel, whom the actor presented as yet another variation on his standard Hun villain. Snapping at Anne Baxter (whom he encountered the same year on the plains of Russia in *North Star*) amid the heat and flies of Egypt, he provided one of the movie's better scenes as he told her testily of his early-morning aversion to women.

Altogether superior was William Wellman's *Story of G.I. Joe* (1945), based on the exploits of war correspondent Ernie Pyle, played in the movie by Burgess Meredith. Sentimental it may have been, but its manifest sincerity, the dignified playing of Meredith, Robert Mitchum and a largely unknown cast, and above all the beautifully sensitive camerawork of the late Franz Planer — which lent such sequences as the German soldier's tolling his own death-knell a special eloquence — gave it a distinction which the director's later *Battleground* (1949), made for Dore Schary, totally lacked.

Milestone's *A Walk in the Sun* (1946) — made for Fox but subsequently repudiated by them — was also set in Italy, and examined the reactions of the members of a Texas Division platoon on their first day in the country after the 1943 Salerno landing. It is at once the most ambitious and least successful of the director's war films. Afflicted with a windy, pretentious script (by Robert Rossen from Harry Brown's novel), and by a strained, self-consciously "poetic" style, it achieves nowhere near the force or fervour of the same director-writer's Warners collaboration *Edge of Darkness*.

With U.S. involvement in the Pacific after Pearl Harbor, the Japanese joined their Aryan colleagues as prime targets for Hollywood's propaganda machine, the main difference being that whereas the moviemakers did have some knowledge of Europe, albeit often second-hand, they were wholly in the dark about Japan, and presented about as authentic a projection of it as "The Mikado" or "Madam Butterfly". Lewis Milestone's *The Purple Heart* (1944), for example, used pure conjecture in showing the supposed treatment of a group of American prisoners of war by the Japanese. In his autobiography, Cedric Hardwicke tells how he and Sir C. Aubrey Smith figured among a group of made-up "Japanese judges" in a courtroom test scene for this picture. The results were so ludicrous that everyone burst out laughing and genuine Oriental players were substituted. The anecdote is instructive, for it indicates just how far Hollywood and its film-makers were removed from the real war. For all that, *The Purple Heart* remains intermittently an extraordinary film, superbly mounted, and in its "Japanese" scenes barbarically exotic and abandoned. Nipponese tormentors rendered Farley Granger, blinded in Milestone's *North Star* the previous year, permanently speechless in this one.

In other movies, mostly B's, the Japs were portrayed as repulsive, sadistic, libidinous little monkeys, grinningly bespectacled, and sporting king-size choppers. An honourable exception was Lewis Seiler's *Guadalcanal Diary* (1943), from the admirable book by Richard Tregaskis, which showed the Pacific war with a degree of authenticity uncommon in films of the time.

While Occupied Europe figured in countless pictures, occupied China had to content itself with M-G-M's *Dragon Seed* (1944), directed (in sepiatone) by Jack Conway from Pearl Buck's novel. Immensely long and costly, its large cast (including the inevitable Walter Huston) all had their eyes appropriately stretched, and its climax — a banqueting-hall of Japanese officers succumbing agonisingly *en masse* to poison placed in their stew by Katharine Hepburn — was well worth waiting over two hours for.

The same year saw the release of M-G-M's *Thirty Seconds Over Tokyo* (Mervyn LeRoy), written by Dalton Trumbo, which dramatised the first U.S. bombing raid on Japan under Lieutenant-Colonel James H. Doolittle, played by Spencer Tracy. A tedious, tendentious affair, its avowed morale-boosting aim was to emphasise the close co-operation between army and navy that made the Tokyo raid possible and — ironically in view of later developments — to foster closer relations "between the American people and their courageous Chinese allies."

Equally soporific was John Ford's *They Were Expendable* (M-G-M, 1945), a confused and scrappily made study of an episode in the Pacific war notable only for Joseph August's distinguished camerawork.

Nazi doings still remained Hollywood's principal preoccupation, both at home and abroad. At home, Lillian Hellman's stage play *Watch on the Rhine* became a film (1943) starring Bette Davis, giving one of the worst performances of her screen career as the American wife of a German anti-Fascist. Saucer-eyed, stagey and overwrought, she indulged her most irritating mannerisms, providing poor support for the expert villainy dispensed by the inimitable Kurt Katch, the smoothly amoral George Coulouris and the thin-lipped, snake-eyed Henry Daniell. This infernal trio, plotting Nazi monstrosities around a table, gave the film its best moments, although they all had to struggle against Herman Shumlin's theatrical direction and the simpleminded symbolism of a script which called the Katch character Herr Brecher ("destroyer") and the chief German anti-Fascist Max Freidank ("freethought").

Tomorrow, The World (Leslie Fenton, 1944), from another stage play, was very similar. Here Fredric March played host to a vicious ex-member of the Hitler Youth (Skip Homeier), brought to the U.S. to live with relatives. A thorough little monster, he insulted Jewess Agnes Moorehead and disrupted an entire household before being shown the errors of his Fascist ways. Tracts for the times, these talkative productions were designed to show the American public how easily the contagion of Nazism could be introduced into even the most seemingly wholesome and respectable U.S. homes.

Those homes, minus their men, were strongholds of motion-picture female fortitude throughout the height of the war. Edward Dmytryk's *Tender Comrade* (1943), written by Dalton Trumbo from his own original story, presented a bevy of war wives, headed by Ginger Rogers, setting up house together while their husbands are away defending Uncle Sam. Factory-workers, they spend their days at the war plant assembly line and their nights mooning over their spouses' photos by their bedsides or listening to the soap-box exhortations of their refugee housekeeper (Mady Christians) in this feebly pro-Communist film.

Flaccid and lacklustre, *Tender Comrade* represented the nadir of home-front films, just as John Cromwell's *Since You Went Away* (1944) represented their apogee. Containing some of the most alarmingly expert schmaltz ever served up by Hollywood, this is a key work among pop movies of the Forties, summing up the essence of its chosen time, place and milieu.

In a Norman Rockwell house live the Hiltons: Claudette Colbert, her daughters Shirley Temple and Jennifer Jones, her maid Hattie MacDaniell and her bulldog, Soda. "This is the story of an unconquerable fortress, the American home, 1943," proclaims an introductory title, as the camera pans slowly across a telegram, a prize fish, a family portrait in a leather foldout, and Soda awaiting his mistress's return in the rain. Everything is good, clean, hygienic, untouched, shining with a soft glow (Lee Garmes and Stanley Cortez are the cameramen). Tim, head of the house of Hilton, has just gone off to the wars, leaving a loyal, broken-hearted wife, the epitome of Mrs. America, 1943, haunted by their tune "Together". She is everything most housewives would like to be: ecstatically married, yet still wholesomely attractive; sweet and patient to a fault, yet capable of giving as good as she gets when her cause is just; brave in adversity and discreetly helpful to those less fortunate than she (which includes just about everybody). Under her pillow is a note: "Wherever I am — always — I'll be kissing you — Tim." (The screenplay is producer David O. Selznick's.)

Unreal and banal, *Since You Went Away* is still one of the Forties' masterpieces because of its ravishing expertise, the marvellous confidence and cinematic know-how with which its idiotic sentiments are put across. Cromwell — like Mitchell Leisen, among the most underrated of Hollywood directors — brings unostentatious mastery to such sequences as the aircraft hangar dance, a dazzling set-piece introduced by the Dixie Doodle, and made even more memorable by Moorehead enthusiastically leading a conga line; Robert Walker and Jennifer Jones's expedition to the country, excitingly shot and featuring a chaste idyll in a barn; the lovers' railway station farewell; the Hiltons' train journey, supposedly to meet their man, with "heart-tugging" vignettes *en route* and Florence Bates glimpsed briefly nibbling on a drumstick; the schoolgirls' graduation ceremony, flag unfurling over Lincoln's statue, America the Beautiful intoned, Claudette, Aggie and the whole town lined up in formation (cf. *Ah, Wilderness!*).

But the film's dexterity reaches its height in the aircraft hangar dance already referred to: a fiercely nostalgic evocation of dancing couples, young men going off to war, a world warm and secure but already threatened by violence. This ambience of threatened comfort, of decent people about to be deprived of their loved ones, is what gives the whole film, at this distance in time, its affectingly poignant flavour. Despite itself, it does catch something of the roused emotion mingled with apprehension and bitterness of a civilian population in a period of war. It is a triumph of pop-art film-making.

So, too, is Curtiz's *Casablanca*. Curtiz and *Casablanca*: the names are indissolubly linked. What Kenneth Tynan called "a masterpiece of light entertainment" has become something of a cult movie, its "Blue Parrot" Café, for instance, popping up in quite recent incarnations on American university campuses. Yet here is one cult movie that does deserve its reputation. It will soon be 30 years old, but it continues to exert an appeal even on those too young to have received its initial impact.

A spinning globe revolves, a doom-laden voice intones an introduction and the globe comes to rest at North Africa, Burbank-style, inhabited by seemingly every expatriate in Hollywood (Bogart and Dooley

Wilson are almost the only Americans in an exceptionally large cast). Philip G. and Julius J. Epstein's script (with Howard Koch) is a small miracle of organisation and construction, expertly juggling enough stories and anecdotes to supply material for half-a-dozen lesser features. The psychology of its main protagonists is hit off with unerring exactitude: Rick Blaine, 36, tough-sentimental, bruised by life but with his ideals still somehow intact; Ilsa Lund (Ingrid Bergman), his former mistress, now the wife of a fugitive Resistance leader, warmly feminine, torn between duty and emotion; Captain Renault (Claude Rains), French police prefect, amiably lecherous and immoral, a charming opportunist ("I'm only a poor corrupt official"); Sam (Dooley Wilson), Rick's Negro aide, loyal and sympathetic to a fault. There are numerous others — Conrad Veidt's Major Strasser, Peter Lorre's sharply drawn, fidgety little Ugarté ("You despise me, Rick, don't you?" "If I gave you any thought I probably would"), Sydney Greenstreet's fezzed, fly-swatting Senor Ferrari, proprietor of the Blue Parrot Café — all essentially stock and two-dimensional yet given an illusion of reality through incisive and witty writing and inspired casting.

All this is put across with some of Warners' most fabulous technique: the exotic setting brings out the virtuoso in Curtiz whose highly individual low-key camera style, catching the razzle-dazzle excitement of Rick's Café, the glare and lattice-work of an Eastern bazaar, or the rain-washed menace of a nocturnal airport, has seldom been more excitingly shown off; in Max Steiner, supplying one of his most characteristically effective scores; in the editor Owen Marks, expertly matching hundreds of complicated shots; and especially in the cameraman Arthur Edeson, surpassing even his own achievement in *The Maltese Falcon* as he runs through practically the entire gamut of black-and-white legerdemain. These combined talents invest such scenes as Dooley Wilson's rendition of "Knock on Wood!", Lorre's frantic flight from the police, or the flashback to Paris ("Was that cannon fire — or is it my heart pounding?" asks Bergman of Bogie, *Perfidia* alternating with *Deutschland über Alles* on the soundtrack) with their uniquely enchanting chemistry.

Curtiz made two other cinematic contributions to the war effort, both in the same year, 1943. *This is the Army* was a musical romp with original music and lyrics by Irving Berlin. *Mission to Moscow*, adapted by Howard Koch from the book by former U.S. ambassador to Russia Joseph E. Davies, was a passionately pro-Stalin apologia. Its politics need not concern us here. What does matter is its epic sweep, its magnificently lavish studio pastiche recreation of Russia, its brilliant, well-nigh irresistible propagandist verve. In this it was the feature-film counterpart of the U.S. Army's *Why We Fight* series, a parallel made all the more forceful by the presence in the leading role of Walter Huston, narrator of the army series.

This masterpiece also used newsreel and actuality clips and a ferociously incisive editing style to bludgeon its audience into agreement. Even more technical wizardry was expended on the semi-fictional episodes: the 1937 Moscow purge trials, staged in a palace of Babylonian proportions; the scenes at the city's railway terminal, among the most splendid of their kind ever filmed; and Huston's exhortation to an American rally, the camera swooping down on him, isolated in the centre of (presumably) Madison Square Garden, in a crane shot of almost incredible virtuosity, rivalled in the cinema only by Capra's similar effects in *Meet John Doe*. Curtiz, working again (as he so often did) with Owen Marks, Max Steiner and other technicians, ensured that the film made a maximum impact. The later troubles it gave rise to are surely an index not only of his own consummate skill but also that of Warners and Hollywood itself. Its makers clearly poured all they knew of their craft into *Mission to Moscow*, only to be censured for their pains when the political winds changed. Surely it is now time for this astonishing film to be accorded its rightful place, with *Triumph of the Will* and *Ten Days That Shook the World*, as one of the great propaganda pieces of the screen.

7. Prestige Pictures: Biographies and Literary Adaptations

SINCE THE days of Bernhardt's *Queen Elizabeth* and Geraldine Farrar's *Carmen*, Hollywood had never been indifferent to Culture. Sneered at by the Establishment, equated with pulp fiction and the music hall by educators and sociologists, it periodically tried to assert its claim to artistic respectability with jumbo-sized adaptations from the classics (Dickens and Dumas were favourites) and lavish pageants masquerading as historical biographies. The Thirties were particularly rich in epics of this kind, with the Muni-Dieterle series, didactic and redolent of the schoolroom, serving as standard models. With *A Midsummer Night's Dream* Dieterle had a fling at Shakespeare too, achieving only slightly more happy results than in his *Madame Dubarry* (1934), which featured Mendelssohn's music as an accompaniment to action taking place 50 years before it was written and Dolores del Rio as a kind of Mexican-spitfire royal mistress.

Such charades may have convinced audiences in the stalls that they were witnessing a culturally edifying spectacle, but they served only to reinforce intellectuals' conviction that Hollywood's product was not worth their attention. The Forties saw more of this sort of thing, yet among the elephantine epics and costume extravaganzas were several films which did in fact reflect little but credit on the film factory. No doubt this was partly because Los Angeles had by then become the refuge of many distinguished literary exiles and expatriates who were not above lending their talents to motion pictures — although, like Brecht, they may have privately bewailed the straitened circumstances which compelled them to do so. Thus Aldous Huxley helped turn *Pride and Prejudice* and *Jane Eyre* into perfectly respectable screen versions, while Isherwood, Faulkner, Leonhard Frank and other more or less eminent writers made similar contributions to often less ambitious films. With money rolling in and attendances at an all-time high, studios in the Forties could afford to indulge "prestige" as perhaps never before. Lives of the great and famous proved, as always, tempting material: authors, saints, politicians, scientists, inventors, and tycoons received solid if none too accurate tributes, ranging from Bergman's St. Joan and Fredric March's Mark Twain to Greer Garson's Mme. Curie and Alexander Knox's Wilson. Big and top-heavy, these productions seemed to proclaim Hollywood's "serious" intentions defiantly and self-consciously to a sceptical intelligentsia. Whenever pulpits or editorials railed against the allegedly low calibre of the studios' standard offerings, the moguls could always point with wounded pride to Jennifer Jones staring transfigured at Linda Darnell's features in *Song of Bernadette* or Robert Walker impersonating Schumann in *Song of Love*. History? The Middle Ages lived again in Walter Wanger's *Joan of Arc*, the Napoleonic Wars and Trafalgar in *Lady Hamilton*, nineteenth-century rural America in *Abe Lincoln in Illinois*. Literature? Had not Republic Studios, home of Roy Rogers and Vera Hruba Ralston, financed Welles's film of *Macbeth*, and had not the works of Dostoievski, Henry James, Gustave Flaubert, Guy de Maupassant, Stefan Zweig, John Galsworthy and many more of the same ilk been tapped for screen material? They had, and the surprising thing throughout the decade is that the classics should have been exploited with so great a measure of artistic success — although the failures, when they occurred, were undeniably colossal.

Set against these we must consider equally undeniable triumphs: the fidelity and cinematic brilliance with which such works as Jack London's *The Sea Wolf* (Curtiz, 1941), Wilkie Collins's *The Woman in White* (Peter Godfrey, 1948), or Charlotte Brontë's *Jane Eyre* (Robert Stevenson, 1944) were brought to the screen, the care, taste and accuracy with which they were mounted, the high standard of literacy — not merely literariness — frequently embodied in their scripts. The role of the producer here was often no less important — perhaps sometimes more so — than that of the director. Henry Blanke at Warners, Zanuck at Fox, Victor Saville and Sidney Franklin at M-G-M, John Houseman at various studios, and independents like Selznick, Korda and Goldwyn ensured that their respective prestige productions looked as solid and authentic as the talents of Hollywood's best art directors and set designers could make them. Seldom giving directors a chance to do more than intelligently guide the proceedings along stylistically orthodox lines, these films focused attention instead on the skills of artisans and decorators, photographers, costume designers and technicians. If the end results were sometimes beautifully dull, vapidly handsome, ploddingly unexceptionable, that was certainly a small price to pay for the exquisite *Letter From an Unknown Woman* (Max Ophüls, 1948), the ample physical splendour of Henry King's *Wilson* (1944), or the lavish production values of Korda's *Lady Hamilton* (1941).

What frequently bemused "serious" critics of the time, and what has since allowed many Forties prestige films to languish in undeserved obscurity, was the casting of inept box office names in key roles. How easy, for example, to deplore the inadequacies of Eleanor Parker and Gig Young in *The Woman in White* and to overlook the superb acting of Sydney Greenstreet, Agnes Moorehead, John Abbott and Curt Bois; to concentrate on that preposterous pair, Robert Cummings and Susan Hayward, in *The Lost Moment*, at the expense of the film's magnificent quasi-Venetian visuals, its sensitively recorded soundtrack. Unqualified successes these films may not have been, but neither were they unqualified failures; and where, as in *Jane Eyre*, the plus and minus elements are about as well balanced as one can reasonably expect, the results are among the most pleasurably civilised films the sound cinema has yet given us.

1940 was M-G-M's Edison year, in which the great inventor received a two-film tribute. *Young Tom Edison*, directed by Norman Taurog, had Mickey Rooney as the youthful scientist, and its sequel, *Edison the Man*, directed by Clarence Brown, featured Spencer Tracy as the adult creator of the talking machine and the motion picture itself. Both produced by John Considine Jr., they had Dore Schary working on their scripts and shared other credits as well.

Young Tom Edison owed more to scriptwriters' invention than to fact, but some of the improbable incidents did actually figure in reliable Edison biographies. Norman Taurog handled it with his accustomed affection, responding warmly to its Michigan small-town setting.

Better still was Clarence Brown's *Edison, The Man,* which traced the inventor's career from the time he arrived penniless in New York at 22 to his triumph with the incandescent electric light in October, 1879. Told in flashback as the elderly Edison, a reluctant guest of honour at the 1929 Golden Jubilee of Light, recounts the vicissitudes of invention to a spellbound audience, it was an admirably straightforward and factually sound production, well mounted and drawing considerable dramatic tension from such episodes as the brainwave which led to the talking machine and the first night New York is lit by electricity. As Edison, Tracy looked remarkably like the Wizard of Menlo Park, particularly when made up as the 82-year-old inventor, and helped to hold the meandering episodic script together by the restraint and sincerity of his performance.

At Warners, William Dieterle, "biopic" specialist of the Thirties, made two further contributions to the genre in 1940, both starring Edward G. Robinson. The first and better film was *Dr. Ehrlich's Magic Bullet,* about the discoverer of Salvarsan, Paul Ehrlich. Written by (among others) John Huston, this displayed considerable daring for the period by considering the hitherto tabu subject of syphilis, which had its first mention by name in a Hollywood film and received sober, dignified treatment, approved not only by the Hays Office (after several weeks of worried deliberation) but also by medical societies and the U.S. Public Health Service.

Dr. Ehrlich was evidently such a *succès d'estime* that Warners, Robinson, and Dieterle went ahead and followed it immediately with *A Dispatch from Reuters,* set also in nineteenth-century Germany and recounting how the founder of the famous news service started out by using carrier pigeons to disseminate news. By now, however, the formula had run dry, and the clichés of innovator-versus-the-world, bolstered by understanding wife and one or two faithful friends, all swathed in an odour of near-sanctity, no longer sufficed to impress critics or public. Despite its excellent cast — Montagu Love, Nigel Bruce, Gene Lockhart, Eddie Albert — *Reuters* flopped.

Over-reverence vitiated much of the merit also of John Cromwell's

Abe Lincoln in Illinois (1940). This followed close on John Ford's *The Young Mr. Lincoln* (1939), with Henry Fonda in the title role. Based by screenwriter Robert E. Sherwood on his own stage play, and starring the Canadian Raymond Massey as Lincoln, it proved a mostly slow-moving and ponderous bore, well-meaning and sincere but painfully naive, with Ruth Gordon as Mary Todd Lincoln shrilly shrewish in her screen acting début. Only towards the end when, aided by a beard and other make-up, Massey bore a striking resemblance to the original, did the film gain stature and momentum, particularly during his speech on a train platform as he leaves, newly elected, for Washington. This achieved an impressive eloquence, stagy perhaps but nevertheless quite moving.

Whereas these 1940 biopics had to struggle sometimes to extract dramatic situations from their generally humdrum material, scenarists Walter Reisch and R. C. Sheriff found themselves confronted with an embarrassment of action and conflict in bringing the story of *Lady Hamilton* (1941) to the screen for producer-director Alexander Korda. They opted for a predominantly intimate, small-scale treatment, stressing the aspects most likely to appeal to a feminine audience: Emma Hamilton's rags-riches-rags progress, her convention-defying love-match, the reactions of their respective spouses to the affair. It became a sentimental true-romance novelette, and Vivien Leigh's Emma a kittenish, slender sprite, quite different from the calculating, plumpish opportunist who stares out at us from the Romney portrait.

Aided by Vincent Korda's sumptuous sets and Rudolph Maté's elegant photography, the film was consistently handsome, while Alan Mowbray as Sir William Hamilton — dying, he stares at blank walls stripped of his sunken art treasures, the collection of a lifetime — and Gladys Cooper as Lady Nelson, conveying generations of straitlaced provincial rectitude, contributed memorable performances. Olivier's Nelson was made the mouthpiece of timely patriotic homilies, stressing for World War II audiences the parallel between Napoleon and Hitler ("You cannot make peace with dictators: you have to destroy them — wipe them out!"), and his death scene, an exact replica of the famous painting, became an excellent *tableau vivant*.

Orson Welles's celebrated *Citizen Kane* (1941) is a depiction of the American Dream gone sour, on a scale commensurate with the dimensions of the dream itself. Starting out as a fresh-cheeked idealist, promulgator of a utopian "Declaration of Principles," Kane is swiftly corrupted by the lure of the Bitch Goddess: he conducts buccaneering forays into journalism and domestic politics, contracts a loveless marriage to a niece of the President of the United States, acquires a mistress whom scandal compels him to marry and whom he in turn compels with ludicrous results to attempt a career in grand opera. Yet still he cannot find whatever it is that he seeks. It is not money: that he has in plenty, sufficient to build Xanadu, a grotesque expensive shambles of a castle stuffed with priceless uncrated antiques and containing "the biggest private zoo since Noah." It is not power: his wealth gives him enough of that to start South American wars, but that bores him, too, after a while. Perhaps it is love: but no love he bears for anyone can equal the love he bears himself. So he sits watching his wife manipulate her giant jigsaw puzzles, oblivious of time, overcome by a monstrous *ennui* that not even an occasional orgiastic picnic, accompanied by the shrill half-scared, half-delighted cries of female guests being raped outside his tent, can entirely dispel. Everything American society considers worth striving for — success, riches, power — is shown as empty, sterile and meaningless.

Finally, Kane's adult career is explained by implication as an unconscious quest to recapture the lost "innocent" world the sled Rosebud represented, but by offering this "explanation" Welles almost destroys the many-layered fabric he has spent the rest of the film so painstakingly building up. If the film's centre proves to be banal, how can we accept the remainder? Fortunately, we can ignore Rosebud: it is not a "key" unlocking the film's mystery but a device obviously designed to impose an arbitrary semblance of order on what would have seemed to 1941 audiences merely chaotic.

Welles's famous battery of Expressionist effects keeps coming between us and Kane, endistancing him, impersonalising him, adding to him a dimension of strangeness and complexity not in the script, although his performance in the central role, encompassing a great range of emotion and almost an entire adult lifetime, is a major acting *tour de force*. Less successful is the film's quasi-musical pace, its allegro-andante-allegro structure, "slow" scenes succeeding "fast" like movements of a grandiose symphony: thus most of the sequences involving Joseph Cotten's Jedediah Leland, inserted between set-pieces of volcanic vitality, are often needlessly heavy, and laboured in their humour. And, after repeated viewings, *Kane's* (at first) dazzling mechanics dazzle rather less: wobbling miniatures, insecure process shots and all too obvious models become distractingly apparent. For all his intoxication with cinema *legerdemain*, Welles was not yet the technical equal of a Capra or Curtiz.

But nothing can detract from the film's vivid Balzacian rendering of a dynamic society, its high-powered American virtuosity: the effect of *Citizen Kane* on the art of film has, as everyone has said, been incalculable.

Scientists, politicians, tycoons, inventors: what of authors? *The Loves of Edgar Allan Poe* (Harry Lachman, 1942), intended as a full-scale biography, dealt only with part of his life, and superficially at that. Shepperd Strudwick (then calling himself John Shepherd) played the writer as a mildly disturbed alcoholic, given to strange turns during which he heard unearthly voices. Linda Darnell was absurdly miscast as Poe's tubercular paramour Virginia Clemm, Jane Darwell only slightly more acceptable as Aunt Clemm, and the handling disappointingly pedestrian and lacklustre.

Warners fared little better with the Brontë sisters, whose story was turned by director Curtis Bernhardt into something called *Devotion* in 1943; the studio withheld it for three years before releasing it in 1946. Their hesitation is understandable: Keith Winter's screenplay makes of the drab sisters' lives a turgid, romanticised, impassioned saga, improbably characterised by glamour and excitement. Opening about 1836 when the Rev. Patrick Brontë moved with his son and three daughters to Haworth, and just a few years before Emily and Charlotte published "Wuthering Heights" and "Jane Eyre", it offered Olivia de Havilland as Charlotte, Ida Lupino as Emily, Nancy Coleman as Anne, Arthur Kennedy as Branwell Brontë, and Montagu Love as their sire.

The Rev. Arthur Nichols, at whom Emily is made to set her cap, becomes in Paul Henreid's performance a Central European *Now Voyager*-style seducer; he ignores her for the beautiful Charlotte, whereupon Emily wastes away with consumptive frustration. The film carried absurdity to preposterous lengths by having Charlotte, after the successful publication of "Jane Eyre", squired around the London salons by a portly, jocular Thackeray (Sydney Greenstreet) encountered in a carriage. From this fiasco we may salvage Arthur Kennedy's excellent performance as Branwell Brontë, disintegrating weakly under alcohol as his sisters' fame overshadows his own.

Undaunted by the failure of *Devotion*, Warners the following year made of another author's life a resplendent grand-manner production when it cast Fredric March in the title role of *The Adventures of Mark Twain*. The director Irving Rapper, aided by the skill of his cameraman Sol Polito and by an eloquent folk-orientated Max Steiner score, created some virtuoso set-pieces: the splendidly vibrant Mississippi riverboat sequences, a gala New York literary dinner attended by Ralph Waldo Emerson and Oliver Wendell Holmes, a superbly staged degree-conferring ceremony at Oxford presided over by Sir C. Aubrey Smith, and particularly Twain's global lecture tour montage which featured an astonishing moment in Allahabad as the camera appeared to withdraw in a dizzying trick "crane" shot to show the author addressing a million-strong multitude. In strikingly faithful makeup, March gave an exceptionally fine performance, helping to make this perhaps the most impressive of all Forties large-scale biopics, sustained throughout its 130-minute length by a marvellous narrative drive and a strong feeling for America's colourful nineteenth-century past.

To those who considered his life ideal potential screen material, the film biography *Jack London* by Alfred Santell for producer Samuel Bronston in 1943 must have come as a cruel disappointment. Ernest Pascal's screenplay deliberately sidestepped the more neurotic aspects of the author's personality, concentrating instead on his Asian adventures, realised in impressive sets and attractive sepiatone images. Michael O'Shea played London as a two-fisted extrovert, obsessed with his mission as a writer, and Susan Hayward was in it somewhere to supply romantic interest. Appearing at the height of World War II, the film in its last third became little more than an anti-Japanese tract. Bronston also turned London's novel "Martin Eden" into an undistinguished programmer for Columbia (1942).

If Hollywood often came to grief with films about authors, it invariably foundered with films about saints. *Song of Bernadette* (Henry King, 1943) was one of the ugliest and most vulgar quasi-religious pictures that has ever disgraced the screen, inexcusably inept in every department. *Joan of Arc*, produced by Walter Wanger and directed by Victor Fleming in 1948, and based by screenwriter Maxwell Anderson on his own play, was an expensive disaster, costing and losing a fortune. Ingrid Bergman repeated the role she had played on the New York stage, reducing the Maid's stature to that of a chain-clad cheer-leader. A tedious, ponderous 2½ hours, the film had perhaps only two points in its favour: the coronation sequence in a magnificently re-created Rheims Cathedral, and José Ferrer impressively making his screen début as the Dauphin.

A year after his *Bernadette* catastrophe, Henry King made a far better showing with *Wilson* (1944), Darryl F. Zanuck's lavish tribute to the World War I President. A prestige production in the grand manner, this took over 2½ hours to trace the rise and decline of Woodrow Wilson, idealised in Lamar Trotti's screenplay and Alexander Knox's performance into a figure of almost saintly rectitude. Zanuck spared no expense to give the film a "big", crowded look, particularly in its superb re-staging of the 1912 Baltimore Democratic Convention: a huge congested auditorium, fans flapping in the heat, the hurly-burly of big-time politics marvellously well suggested. A large cast of players of the calibre of Thomas Mitchell, Cedric Hardwicke, Charles Coburn and Geraldine Fitzgerald contributed markedly to the film's effect, one of solid, unfussy movie-making, conscientious if somewhat bloodless.

American history was rather less well served in Frank Borzage's *The Magnificent Doll* (1946), which featured Ginger Rogers as Dolly Madison, friend of one U.S. President and wife of another. Irving Stone's screenplay ignored history, while David Niven and Burgess Meredith seemed very ill at ease as Mrs. Madison's admirers.

Darryl F. Zanuck's lavish tribute to a former President: WILSON, directed by Henry King with Alexander Knox as Woodrow Wilson, Geraldine Fitzgerald as Edith, Ruth Ford as Margaret, and William Eythe.

Faultless performances marked Michael Curtiz's THE SEA WOLF, gripping version of Jack London's novel with, Edward G. Robinson as the satanic Wolf Larsen and Alexander Knox as the prim Henry van Weyden.

Orson Welles played Roches and clearly influenced the style of JANE EYRE directed by Robert Steven

Arturo de Cordova, Ingr Bergman, Gar Cooper and A Tamiroff in th three-hour blockbuster, S Wood's FOR WHOM THE BELL TOLL based on Hemingway's novel of the Spanish Civil War.

The remaining biopics of the period chose scientific subjects. Mervyn LeRoy's *Madame Curie* (1943) had Greer Garson and Walter Pidgeon, those Forties-M-G-M successors to Eddy and MacDonald as filmdom's favourite married couple, discovering radium; Preston Sturges's uncharacteristic *The Great Moment* (1944), from a book by René Fülöp-Miller, featured Joel McCrea as the discoverer of anaesthesia. Both were worthy, well-intentioned and rather dull examples of the prestige film at its dreariest.

★　　★　　★

It is scarcely surprising that a majority of classic authors' works filmed in the Forties should have been American. A favourite was Jack London, whose eminently cinematic books became all too frequently undistinguished Monogram or Columbia B's. With Michael Curtiz's magnificent 1941 version of *The Sea Wolf*, however — the sixth screen adaptation, incidentally — full justice was for once done to London's text, here adapted by Robert Rossen. With the aid of models, newly introduced fog machines and a studio tank the film hauntingly captured an eerie, malevolent atmosphere, brooding and full of terror. From its economic opening scenes in San Francisco's dockside area in 1900 to its powerful climax aboard the sinking scavenger ship *Ghost*, its blind sadist captain and one of his victims dying together as it goes down, it gripped consistently. Throughout, Curtiz provided object lessons in the use of sound — the groaning timbers of the ship, creaking footsteps, the wind — and close-up, while the art direction of Anton Grot, Sol Polito's bravura low-key camerawork and the masterfully understated music of Erich Wolfgang Korngold helped make *The Sea Wolf* a triumph of Warners craftsmanship.

The performances were faultless: Edward G. Robinson's Wolf Larsen, obsessed, satanic, played to the hilt as a demoniac descendant of the Flying Dutchman and Captain Ahab, a tormented Nietzschean figure who delights equally in inflicting cruelty on his underlings and reading the works of Milton and Shakespeare; Alexander Knox's Henry van Weyden, prim, soft, overcivilised, forced to resort to jungle law and cunning to save his friends, though he cannot save himself;

Barry Fitzgerald's treacherous and spiteful Cooky, an evil leprechaun whose leg is torn off by a shark in an extraordinary scene; Gene Lockhart's "Dr." Lewis Prescott, a drunken sawbones who throws himself to his death from a mast-top rather than face further humiliation from Larsen. Ida Lupino as the reformatory fugitive Ruth Brewster and John Garfield's ex-convict George Leach made a strong unsentimental romantic team: their scenes together had an authentic magic, palpable and electrifying.

Equally distinguished was the same producer Henry Blanke's 1946 production of Wilkie Collins's *The Woman in White*, that intricately plotted nineteenth-century precursor of the *roman policier*. Under Peter Godfrey's fluent direction, which had a stately, measured quality perfectly in keeping with the novel, the story of the wicked Count Fosco (Sydney Greenstreet) and his plot with Sir Percival Glyde (John Emery) to murder one of two twin sisters to gain access to a family fortune of £20,000 became compelling melodrama, brilliantly acted by almost all save Gig Young, Eleanor Parker and Alexis Smith. Greenstreet's Fosco — chucking his pet monkey, Iago, under the chin, peeping at a woman undressing or dwelling with equal lasciviousness on an emerald necklace — was a splendidly lecherous villain. John Abbott as Frederick Fairlie, uncle of the twin sisters, and Curt Bois as his browbeaten manservant, played their scenes together with uncanny rapport, while Agnes Moorehead as Countess Fosco brought her rich presence to a tiny part, especially in the climactic scene in which she silences her husband's insufferable dwelling on some jewels' attractions with a dagger planted deep in his back. Small scenes like Parker's escape from Fosco's private asylum, or a conference between the three chief plotters at the height of a thunderstorm, were admirably directed, while Max Steiner's score — suggesting perhaps more the eighteenth than the nineteenth century — effectively contributed to the fustian mood of the film.

Eugene O'Neill was another major American author whose work Hollywood often adapted. The Thirties had seen screen versions respectively grotesque and masterly of *Strange Interlude* and *Ah, Wilderness!*, and the Forties brought additional adaptations in Dudley

114

Nichols's *Mourning Becomes Electra* (1947) and Alfred Santell's *The Hairy Ape* (1944). Both were disappointing. *Mourning Becomes Electra* ran for 175 minutes and featured Rosalind Russell and Katina Paxinou as distaff members of the Mannon family, with Raymond Massey and Michael Redgrave as their menfolk. Practically a straight photographed play, its bloated mixture of incipient incest, murder, insanity and suicide often proved embarrassingly risible, as when Redgrave and Paxinou as mother and son indulge in a window-seat cuddle or Paxinou sits on the steps of the Mannon mansion moaning noisily with grief. *The Hairy Ape* updated the action of the 1920s stage sensation to the outbreak of World War II, with William Bendix in the part made famous in the theatre by Louis Wolheim. Artily directed by Santell, it had Susan Hayward taking a Dante's Inferno tour of a Lisbon-New York freighter on which she is a rich passenger. Encountering Bendix, sweaty and misshapen, stoking a furnace, she becomes attracted and he follows her in New York. The play's language was considerably modified and its class-conscious emphases played down in this interesting but unsatisfactory filming.

The works of Henry James improbably provided material for two films: Martin Gabel's *The Lost Moment* (1947) and William Wyler's *The Heiress* (1949). *The Lost Moment* was adapted by Leonardo Bercovici from "The Aspern Papers" and became in Walter Wanger's production one of the strangest and one of the most exquisitely made of all Hollywood's misguided forays into "art." In this vulgarised version of the tale, Robert Cummings was a young American publisher masquerading as a callow author to gain access to the love letters of a famous poet written to the lady of an ancient Venetian house. Lovely visuals (Hal Mohr) accompanied a delicately recorded soundtrack that caught perfectly the tinkle of cut-glass chandeliers, the faintest whisper and rustle of the nocturnal household. The early scenes just after Cummings's arrival, sombre and melancholy, achieved an intriguing atmosphere, and a nice touch was the use of a Shelley miniature to represent the late poet Jeffrey Ashton.

The Heiress, adapted by Ruth and Augustus Goetz from James's "Washington Square", came to the screen via their Broadway play.

Ralph Richardson, repeating his stage role of Dr. Sloper, played the father of a repressed, plain virgin, Catherine (Olivia de Havilland) who is courted by a glib, personable fortune-hunter, Maurice Townsend (Montgomery Clift). The setting and situation brought out Wyler's best qualities: a scrupulous regard for vagaries of mood, for inflections in dialogue, and for character relationships, as well as an unerring instinct for placing the camera in precisely the right position to catch his characters' most subtle and yet revealing reactions. Leo Tover's camera recorded dispassionately the Sloper house's stiff Victorian curtains and furnishings, the sliding doors behind which emotions were repressed, the light carried by Catherine as she ascends the stairs in the final sequence, leaving the man who once deserted her beating desperately at her locked door. Disciplined, exceedingly well acted by de Havilland, Richardson and Miriam Hopkins, the film had perhaps one major flaw: Clift's Maurice Townsend, altogether too guileless and open to be a convincing liar and deceiver.

Wyler's other stage adaptation of the Forties, of Lillian Hellman's *The Little Foxes* (1941), was much less satisfying. Cold and mechanical, though technically expert, it achieved a kind of frigid proficiency, acceptable enough as a rendering of the author's lines but emotionally uninvolving. Bette Davis's performance as Regina Giddens was an unhappy one, never bringing the character into clear focus. Only in the famous scene — imaginatively shot by Gregg Toland — in which she deliberately leaves her husband (Herbert Marshall) to die of a heart attack, and in the final showdown between mother and daughter (Teresa Wright), with the rain pattering down as accompaniment, did *The Little Foxes* achieve the force and power it aimed at. With all its inadequacies, however, it still proved superior to Michael Gordon's *Another Part of the Forest* (1948), which, based on a subsequent Hellman play, displayed the Hubbard family at an earlier and no more attractive stage of its career.

F. Scott Fitzgerald and Ernest Hemingway supplied material for a mixed collection of films. Elliot Nugent's 1949 version of *The Great Gatsby* was a travesty of the novel, only Betty Field as Daisy managing to suggest something of the Fitzgerald flavour. Robert Siodmak's *The*

Killers (1946), based loosely on Hemingway's story, is discussed in another chapter. From the author's Spanish Civil War novel *For Whom the Bell Tolls*, Sam Wood made a three-hour Technicolor blockbuster (1943), with Gary Cooper and Ingrid Bergman as the book's ill-fated lovers. Talky and overlong, its best features were the performances of Akim Tamiroff and Katina Paxinou as peasant guerrillas. The true Hemingway ambience, terse and harsh, was captured only once: in Zoltan Korda's 1947 filming of "The Short Happy Life of Francis Macomber", called *The Macomber Affair*. Here Casey Robinson's script, Korda's taut direction, and the concentrated playing of Joan Bennett, Gregory Peck and Robert Preston — as, respectively, wife, big-game-hunter lover, and cuckolded husband — added up to very good cinema. The scenes in which Mrs. Macomber pointedly humiliates her husband by showing her preference for Peck had an animal cruelty, and the African jungle setting, *echt*-Hemingway, provided an ideal background to this tale of honour, bravery, adultery and murder.

Dwight Macdonald has definitively deflated the pretensions of Thornton Wilder's 1938 play "Our Town", its crackerbarrel philosophising uneasily united with some of the more familiar devices of the German Expressionists. In 1940 it became, under Sam Wood's direction, a beautifully executed film, William Cameron Menzies's sets, Bert Glennon's photography and the fine playing of Martha Scott, William Holden, Beulah Bondi, Fay Bainter and Thomas Mitchell helping to distract attention from its intellectually threadbare source material. Another of the author's works came to the screen in 1944 with Rowland V. Lee's undistinguished version of his novel "The Bridge of San Luis Rey".

Far removed from the cosy, condescending Americana of Thornton Wilder was the Buddenbrooks-like social observation of Booth Tarkington's 1918 novel *The Magnificent Ambersons*, which became Orson Welles's second (released) film in 1942. Here the technical fireworks of *Citizen Kane* were replaced by a less showy but perhaps more mature style, scaled down in keeping with the tale's relatively modest scope. Though outwardly faithful to the novel, even to the extent of re-creating the Amberson house in intricate detail, it altered some of its emphases and softened its central irony in presenting its portrait of a solid, aristocratic nineteenth-century family overtaken and destroyed by the crude thrust and vigour of the automobile age. Welles did not appear in it, but his narration, matched to Stanley Cortez's glowing deep-focus visuals, confirmed it as unmistakably his: the famous ball scene, with its "flowers and plants and roped vines brought from afar," the festive sleigh ride, the bold complexity of its compositions, together with the measured, polished playing of his Mercury Theatre cast, could have been engineered by no one else. Small-scale and subdued, *The Magnificent Ambersons* stands almost alone in Welles's *oeuvre*, losing nothing in distinction for lacking his other films' larger-than-life abandon or their melodramatic energy.

With the exception of Mervyn LeRoy's unremarkable re-make of Louisa May Alcott's *Little Women* (1949), the remaining filmed literary classics of the Forties derived from English or Continental originals. Among English authors, Edwardians tended to dominate: Kipling, Conrad, Maugham and Galsworthy were favoured over the richer heritage of the nineteenth century. Zoltan Korda made of Kipling's *Jungle Book* a lavish vehicle for Sabu (1942), with Miklos Rozsa's celebrated score perhaps its most enduring feature, and John Cromwell turned Conrad's much-filmed *Victory* into one of the Forties' neglected masterpieces, a true *film maudit* (1941).

Adapted by John L. Balderston, who added a note of black humour to the novel's tale of Heyst (Fredric March), the lonely introvert who lives in an island estate at Samburan in the Dutch East Indies, and his strange love affair with Alma, a downtrodden pianist in a travelling girls' orchestra, the film memorably introduced its assortment of bizarre characters, centred on the Palace Hotel at Surabaya, in a series of masterly economic strokes: Makanoff (Fritz Feld), the prim, correct and ruthless band-leader, his sadistic harpist wife (Rafaela Ottiano), Schomberg (Sig Rumann), the lecherous hotel owner determined to seduce Alma (Betty Field), and Schomberg's silent wife (Margaret Wycherly), forever staring blindly over the cash register, her perpetual widow's weeds a symbol of her marital plight.

To this outlandish *ménage* come Mr. Jones (Cedric Hardwicke in his greatest screen performance), a soft, white homosexual crook in sunglasses, his companion Martin Ricardo (Jerome Cowan), a sinister Cockney catamite, and the diabolical and simian Colombian alligator hunter, Pedro. Egged on by the jealous Schomberg, this trio tries to upset the relationship between Heyst and Alma, and the film, distinguished by Leo Tover's sun-dappled, luscious photography, Frederick Hollander's subtle music, and above all by Balderston's bitter, cutting dialogue, more heartless than anything in Conrad, becomes in its closing scenes conventionally melodramatic, although still beautifully staged. Harsh and misanthropic, astonishingly explicit (for the period) in its depiction of Mr. Jones's liaison with his "secretary," superlatively rendering the steamy bamboo-and-fern ambience of its tropical hotel, the heavy torpor and exhaustion of Mr. Jones and his companions adrift in a boat for days without water, and wholly consistent in projecting its writer's dark and disenchanted *Weltanschauung*, *Victory* is among those very few filmed classics that bear comparison with their originals.

The following year Albert Lewin filmed the work of another English writer attracted to the exotic South Seas when he made *The Moon and Sixpence* from Somerset Maugham's 1919 novel suggested by the life of Gauguin. George Sanders played Charles Strickland, the middle-aged broker whose passion for painting pulls him from bourgeois respectability to a leper's death in Tahiti. In sepia and colour, and with Herbert Marshall's author-narrator — a part he was to essay again shortly afterwards in *The Razor's Edge* — providing moralistic disapproval of the hero's unconventional behaviour to appease suburban audiences, this was an unorthodox and often beautiful film, finely acted by Sanders, Marshall, Albert Bassermann and several little-known supporting players.

Despite the importation of an English director, Compton Bennett, M-G-M's 1949 version of part of Galsworthy's "The Forsyte Saga" as *That Forsyte Woman* was routine and undistinguished. In Greer Garson it did however have as star a player who had helped to make the same studio's *Pride and Prejudice* in 1940 a thoroughly respectable rendering of Jane Austen's novel. This captured the Austen flavour — dry, ironic yet warm and sympathetic — to a degree, with Laurence Olivier's Mr. Darcy providing a perfect foil for Garson's Elizabeth Bennet.

Aldous Huxley's contribution to the script of *Pride and Prejudice* certainly constituted one of that film's chief merits. He contributed also to *Jane Eyre* (1944), sharing screenplay credit with John Houseman and Robert Stevenson, the last-named credited as the film's director. However, the work clearly bears throughout most of its length the directorial stamp of Orson Welles, who also plays Rochester; this is reinforced by the presence of such Mercury Theatre stalwarts as Houseman and Agnes Moorehead, by Bernard Herrmann's music and by the *Kane*-like ambience of designer William Pereira's Thornfield. Most of all it is present in the film's style, from the opening shot of a candle being borne through the black corridors of Gateshead Hall, through the scenes at Lowood School and particularly at Thornfield, a glowering Xanadu-like structure sheltering a homicidal madwoman whose shrill cackles pierce the night, who perpetrates sudden arson and who claws her half-imbecile brother (John Abbott) almost to death.

The film's first half is especially fine: upside down, Jane is carried asleep into Lowood School, an institution run by Mr. Brocklehurst (Henry Daniell in one of his most malevolently edgy performances), a sadist-cum-religious fanatic. The girls rise, wash and eat like automatons, to the ring of a bell or a snap of the fingers. For a minor transgression Jane is left standing on a stool all day, and another inmate (Elizabeth Taylor) dies from the effects of marching as punishment around the schoolyard in the rain.

These scriptwriters' inventions — and their later elisions, telescopings and even character-interpolations — are so perfectly in keeping with the novel's spirit that, so far from doing it violence, they seem ideal solutions to the problems it poses for screen adaptation. Certainly, the look of the film, its production values, could hardly be bettered: George Barnes's magnificent photography, Pereira's marvellous sets and the splendid miniature work are all beyond praise. So are the performances of most of the cast: if Joan Fontaine, in a part rather too similar to her role in *Rebecca*, plays it all perhaps too much on the one note, this is more than offset by Welles's Rochester, a moody, strong characterisation aided by a rubber nose and layers of make-up, and by Edith Barrett's grey and gentle Mrs. Fairfax.

In 1947, Aldous Huxley adapted his own story "The Gioconda Smile" for producer-director Zoltan Korda. It became *A Woman's Vengeance*, with Jessica Tandy in good form as the frustrated murderess Janet who poisons the wife (Rachel Kempson) of Charles Boyer, improbably cast as an English country squire.

Perhaps the less said about Orson Welles's *Macbeth* (1948) the better. Shot in three weeks for producer Charles K. Feldman, it took place in a series of dank, clammy sets suggesting an amalgam of sewer and refrigerator ("This castle hath a pleasant seat" in this context strained the meaning of language to its limit), and was cursed with some of the most lamentable acting seen anywhere outside high-school dramatics. Welles here offered Shakespeare the supreme insult: he turned the Bard into a bore.

From the Continent, French authors fared more happily than their rivals. Maupassant, Flaubert, Mérimée and Dumas would possibly not have recognised some of their handiwork, but it was undeniably there on the Forties' screens, albeit sometimes strangely metamorphosed. *Madame Bovary*, for instance: what, one wonders, would Flaubert have said (or thought) could he have seen the beautiful Jennifer Jones as his plain, ill-favoured Emma in Vincente Minnelli's 1949 film? Or, for that matter, if he could have seen himself impersonated in the same picture by a walrus-moustached James Mason? From that unhappily mis-guided production — a romantic antithesis of Flaubert's intention — we may salvage only the ball, imaginatively staged by the Minnelli of the film musicals, and a scene in which Emma repulses the advances of a lecherous shopkeeper (Frank Allenby), as approximations of the novel's *moeurs de province*.

Minnelli's Charles Bovary, Van Heflin, appeared also in George Sidney's spoof version of *The Three Musketeers* the previous year, as Athos to Gene Kelly's D'Artagnan and Lana Turner's Milady de Winter; Pandro S. Berman produced and Robert Ardrey wrote both these films. As for Mérimée, what the director Charles Vidor, Rita Hayworth and Glenn Ford and the screenwriter Helen Deutsch did to his "Carmen" (*Loves of Carmen*, 1948) would have dismayed him: the *Gilda* team fumbled badly with this one.

Maupassant was represented by Robert Wise's *Mademoiselle Fifi* (1944), a Val Lewton production with Simone Simon in which the original story was combined with "Boule de Suif" to make a bitingly intelligent parallel with World War II in a Franco-Prussian 1870 war setting. More ambitious, and more expensive, was Albert Lewin's *The Private Affairs of Bel Ami* (1947), with George Sanders as a nineteenth-century Parisian *roué* and Ann Dvorak and Angela Lansbury as his victims. A lavish two-hour affair, it had little to do with Maupassant, but its mounting (Gordon Wiles) and music (Darius Milhaud) did lend it some distinction.

Perhaps because so many French expatriates — director Jean Renoir, composer Michel Michelet, cinematographer Lucien Andriot — were involved in its making, *The Diary of a Chambermaid* (1946) became an extraordinarily provocative and (in spirit) faithful rendering of Octave Mirbeau's novel. Treading a tightrope path between social satire and perverse tragedy, between surface levity and an underlying moralistic tension, Renoir guided a mixed international cast through the dark byways of Mirbeau's world so expertly that the film puzzled many at the time of its release.

Today it may be seen as a key Renoir work, a major clue to his Olympian contemplation of human nature in all its facets. Here, as in *La Bête Humaine* and *La Chienne*, he is concerned with the dark, the sinister, the ugly.

Blacker than Clouzot's *Le Corbeau*, the film has a disturbing, unsettling quality, particularly pronounced in such moments as that in which the captain played by Burgess Meredith unthinkingly crushes his pet squirrel to death or the corrupt man-servant Joseph extinguishes the life of a goose with a long needle. Judith Anderson, trembling with perverse possessiveness for her family silver, and Francis Lederer's Joseph, smouldering, menacing and depraved, are perhaps the most memorable among a generally fine cast. This is unquestionably Renoir's best American film.

Russian authors were treated distinctly less well than French. Based on Chekhov's "The Shooting Party", Douglas Sirk's *Summer Storm* (1944) was a curious piece, ambitious but indifferently realised. Linda Darnell played — as in *Hangover Square* — a heartless *femme fatale* who turns the respective heads of a dissolute Russian count (Edward Everett Horton), a judge (George Sanders) and the cuckolded peasant she marries (Hugo Haas). Sirk conscientiously strove to capture a genuine Russian flavour with authentic-looking sets, costumes and landscapes, but cast and script (on which he collaborated) conspired to defeat him.

Kitsch of a more grandiose order came in Robert Siodmak's *The Great Sinner* (1949), concocted by Ladislas Fodor, René Fülöp-Miller and Christopher Isherwood from the life and works of Dostoievski. Into this *potpourri* went bits of "The Gambler", "Crime and Punishment" and part of the novelist's youth: Fyodor (Gregory Peck) ruins himself gambling at Wiesbaden, 1860, after becoming involved with Ava Gardner's adventuress, Melvyn Douglas's casino operator and Walter Huston's roulette addict. Turgid and self-conscious, the film embodied Midcult at its most madcap: here were Agnes Moorehead as a pawnbroker, peering in bloated close-up through an outsize magnifying glass; Frank Morgan and Ethel Barrymore grandly lending "distinction" to bit parts as compulsive gamblers; and Ava Gardner gathering up "Fyodor's" manuscript from the floor of his cheap lodgings.

By contrast, Max Ophüls's *Letter From an Unknown Woman* (1948) displayed not only sincerity but a still rarer quality: sensitivity. Adapted by Howard Koch from the Stefan Zweig novella, the film, set in the director's native city, Vienna, in the early years of this century, reveals his Central European romanticism at its purest, his almost Mozartian faculty for concealing deep emotion beneath an elegant, decorative surface. Joan Fontaine gave a beautiful performance as the girl hopelessly enamoured of Louis Jourdan's concert pianist, and what could easily have been banal or insipid became instead an expatriate's declaration of love for the vanished culture and environment of his youth. One of its last representatives, Ophüls created in this film a valedictory to Imperial Vienna. The Hollywood system which permitted that could surely not have been entirely bad.

8. Action, Outdoor and Pastoral Films

(i) Swashbucklers

WITH HIS début in *Captain Blood* in 1935 Errol Flynn established himself instantly as Hollywood's King of Buckle and Swash, succeeding to the throne left vacant by Douglas Fairbanks, Sr., who died the following year. Lithe, athletic, quick and graceful in his movements, exuding an air of devil-may-care *joie de vivre*, Flynn wore period clothes well and turned in some very acceptable swordsmanship. By the Forties, though, he was somewhat past his prime, and others — Tyrone Power, Douglas Fairbanks Jr., Cornel Wilde — were rising to challenge him.

Yet the prototype of every swashbuckler of the era can be found in *The Adventures of Robin Hood* and Flynn's other Thirties films, mostly directed by Curtiz. They established a pattern, created a form, perfected a style that Fairbanks Senior had introduced to the cinema in the silent period. Ritualised and formal as a Japanese samurai epic — with which they had much in common — they had also (at their best) a zip and panache, an elegance and dash, that survive the years intact. Flynn's Forties' competitors and successors may have displaced him, but they never surpassed him. Everything they did, and every film they appeared in, proclaimed a debt to him and Curtiz.

The Sea Hawk (1940) was the final Flynn-Curtiz collaboration. Owing nothing to Rafael Sabatini's novel save the title, it was mounted with Warners' customary splendour, rousingly scored by Erich Wolfgang Korngold, and acted by many of those who had appeared in *Robin Hood*. Flynn played Francis Thorpe, dashing courtier to Queen Elizabeth I (Flora Robson), who in Howard Koch and Seton I. Miller's screenplay became a kind of sixteenth-century Churchill (this was 1940, remember), with the Spanish Armada roughly analagous to the Luftwaffe. Often slow and talky, particularly during scenes at Elizabeth's court, the film sprang into life in its action sequences, staged on the newly-built Warners Ocean, an expensive million-gallon sea of warm water capable of responding to waves and storms of assorted size and violence. Best among these episodes was one on board a slave galley, the chained oarsmen stroking to the rhythmic beat of two huge drums at the head of the ship.

The Adventures of Don Juan (1949), directed by Vincent Sherman, represented Flynn's farewell to swashbuckling. If by then he had physically deteriorated, Warners' art and costume departments had not. This was a breathtakingly executed production, its Spanish Court sets the equal of anything in *Robin Hood* and its colour photography discreetly borrowing from seventeenth-century Spanish painting. Its final duel with rapiers and daggers between Flynn and a bewigged Robert Douglas was thrillingly staged on a gigantic staircase, watched by Queen Margaret (Viveca Lindfors) and the assembled Court. Alan Hale's Leporello, Douglas's sneering villain and Lindfors's intelligently played Queen all entered admirably into the film's spirit.

Fatter than Flynn, and shorter, Tyrone Power at Fox was still a worthy successor, and the films into which Darryl F. Zanuck put him were staged no less lavishly and spectacularly than Jack Warner's Flynn projects. Often, in fact, they were straight imitations: they drew on the same source material (Sabatini, etc.), utilised identical villains (Rathbone), and featured similar climactic sword-fights choreographed by Fred Cavens, a former Belgian fencing master who was responsible for staging all major screen sword duels. Even Alfred Newman's music took on a Korngold "sound", with the same brass and percussion effects, the same sonorous bombast.

All these elements came splendidly together in Rouben Mamoulian's *The Mark of Zorro* (1940), a spirited, zestful version of Johnston McCulley's novel *The Curse of Capistrano*. With Rathbone, Montagu Love and Eugene Pallette in the cast to emphasise its Flynn-*Robin Hood* derivations, it had an engaging humour of its own, as when Power disguised as a monk flirts with Linda Darnell or when — like the Scarlet Pimpernel — he affects foppishness as a cover-up for revolutionary activity ("Quiet, you popinjay!" Rathbone snaps at him before being smartly disillusioned in a lengthy sword-fight). Visually,

Mamoulian and his photographer Arthur Miller made much play with the nineteenth-century California setting: a sea of Mexican-style hats around a poster, two blanketed peons dozing by a large cactus.

Mamoulian's visual flair was allowed far greater scope in the following year's *Blood and Sand*, in which, working in colour, he created some magnificent effects. Impossible to forget such scenes as the boy's nocturnal visit to the bullring to practise capework with the prize bull, the sumptuously beautiful church interior — like an El Greco canvas — in which Linda Darnell is seen praying, the tensely erotic dance performed by Rita Hayworth and Anthony Quinn in a smoky Spanish *boite*. Above all, the scenes in the *corrida*, passionately directed and filled with thousands of Mexican extras, are perhaps the most thrilling of their kind ever filmed, with their justly famous shot of the purple contents of a burst wineskin spilling on a white napkin to signal the bull's offscreen death. Mamoulian has seldom equalled his achievements here.

Scarcely less good was John Cromwell's *Son of Fury: The Story of Benjamin Blake* (1942), which had Power — not for the first time — playing hero to George Sanders's villain. Set in eighteenth-century London and also in the South Seas, this was almost perfect entertainment, with everyone giving their best: Philip Dunne's literate screenplay, Alfred Newman's excellent pastiche of a Korngold-Steiner score, Richard Day and James Basevi's resplendent art direction, the ravishing photography of Arthur Miller (particularly in the Pacific Island sequences). Cromwell's discreet yet never showy direction fluently took in ceilinged sets, models and large crowd scenes, keeping the narrative flowing beautifully. Among a large cast of sterling supporting players, Dudley Digges's portrait of the London lawyer Benjamin Pratt was magnificent, giving as memorable a glimpse of grand-manner acting as Constance Collier and Reginald Owen were to do in Mitchell Leisen's *Kitty* (1945), set in the same era. Harry Davenport as Blake's grandfather, Elsa Lanchester's pathetic skivvy and John Carradine's sailor-convict all helped contribute to the film's excellence.

The Black Swan (Henry King, 1942), boasted similar virtues, though not to the same degree. Here Power played Jamie Waring, a seventeenth-century adventurer involved with Sir Henry Morgan (Laird Cregar), newly appointed Governor of Jamaica, and Lady Margaret Derby (Maureen O'Hara, a staple swashbuckle heroine), daughter of the former governor (George Zucco). The villainy was again supplied by Sanders, almost unrecognisable in a thick red wig and beard. Playing Captain Leech, a merciless privateer, he received his come-uppance from Power during an attack on Maracaibo Harbour, staggering around a ship's cabin mortally wounded with a sword protruding from his chest. Beautifully designed (Day and Basevi) and colour-photographed (Leon Shamroy), and graced with a literate and at times surprisingly bawdy script (Ben Hecht, Seton I. Miller), *The Black Swan* suffered from King's relatively lacklustre direction, although Power made of Jamie a dashing, lusty figure, and Laird Cregar, resplendent in vast wig and Charles II costumes, enjoyably delivered some fruity dialogue ("Your fulminations, my hosts and gentlemen, are full of bilge and blather").

A bout of war service interrupted Power's screen swashbuckling. It resumed with two Samuel Shellabarger adaptations, both — like *The Black Swan* — directed by Henry King. *Captain from Castile* (1947) was a dull if lushly handsome adventure about the preliminaries to Cortez's conquest of Mexico, notable mainly for its rich colour and Alfred Newman's martial score. The actor's physical decline, already evident, was even more pronounced in the following year's *Prince of Foxes*, made on location in Italy. This was a curious work, occasionally — as in a flamboyantly staged siege sequence — suggesting the directorial intervention of Orson Welles, who played Cesare Borgia. Apart from Welles and his erstwhile colleague Everett Sloane, almost the only cast member displaying even a faint awareness of the film's historical background was Felix Aylmer. A handsome film, it became ultimately wearisome because of the script's banality and the routine quality of most of the performances.

By this time, Flynn and Power had acquired formidable rivals in the costume action field. Chief among them was Douglas Fairbanks Jr., following none too successfully in his father's footsteps. Agile and dashing enough, he couldn't handle a sword very well and often had to be doubled in duels. Despite these handicaps he still cut a fine figure in such well-mounted pieces as Gregory Ratoff's *The Corsican Brothers* (1941), a free Dumas adaptation in which Akim Tamiroff was the villain, *Sinbad the Sailor* (1947), directed by Richard Wallace and based loosely on the Arabian Nights tales, and even in Max Ophüls's film *The Exile* (1948), which he also wrote very badly and produced. Based on Cosmo Hamilton's novel *His Majesty the King*, this had Fairbanks playing Charles II in Holland prior to the Restoration of 1660, its stylised windmills, garrets and inns looking awkwardly artificial in sepia. Henry Daniell was Fairbanks's main opponent, and his love interest an inept Maria Montez. Ophüls directed the film with endless meaningless tracking shots and it was as gauche and inept as Preminger's *Forever Amber* (1946), which made of a dull book — set in the same era and milieu — an even duller film.

Paul Henreid may have seemed an unlikely contender for swashbuckling honours, but in *The Spanish Main* (Frank Borzage, 1945) he did don doublet and hose and cross swords with Walter Slezak who, in a role similar to his part in Minnelli's *The Pirate*, delivered a brilliant comic performance as the corrupt governor of a West Indies Spanish port. The film was, in fact, an hilarious spoof of the genre, aided by a clever and devastatingly witty script (George Worthington Yates, Herman J. Mankiewicz) and delicious tongue-in-cheek playing from Binnie Barnes (as the pirate Anne Bonney), Curt Bois, Barton MacLane, John Emery, J. M. Kerrigan and even Maureen O'Hara. Henreid occasionally struck a wrong note, and some backdrops and miniatures were distractingly obvious, but it was Slezak's apotheosis: bursting into involuntary guffaws while having a pedicure, being embraced by a tailor ("You were supposed to fit me, not fondle me"), making grotesque love to O'Hara ("If my references to your beloved seem vague, I mean of course myself"), rejecting the counsel of the clergy ("Your advice is sound. However, I will ignore it"), denigrating Henreid ("No one would want to marry a pirate — except maybe another pirate") and generally having a ball.

At Columbia, swordfighting was wisely entrusted to the ex-Olympic champion Cornel Wilde, who in *The Bandit of Sherwood Forest* (George

Errol Flynn's farewell to swashbuckling, breathtakingly executed production THE ADVENTURES OF DON JUAN, directed by Vincent Sherman and co-starring Viveca Lindfors.

A dull but lushly handsome film directed by Henry King: THE CAPTAIN FROM CASTILE, with Jean Peters and Tyrone Power.

Grandiose, elemental, passionate . . . the Forties' most flamboyant Western, DUEL [IN?] THE SUN, a David O. Selznick production mostly directed by King Vidor, which told t[he?] story of Pearl Chavez (Jennifer Jones, here seen with Herbert Marshall).

Sherman and Henry Levin, 1946) made a far better showing as the son of Robin Hood than he had as Chopin two years earlier. The following year, Larry Parks, whose musical sequences for *The Jolson Story* (1946) had been directed by Joseph H. Lewis, starred for the same director at Columbia in *The Swordsman*, a stunningly made Scottish adventure featuring some fine colour and superb Kurosawa-like tracking shots following the hero on horseback through a forest. More modestly budgeted than the best of Curtiz's films, this was nevertheless their equal technically, and in George Macready — sporting, like the rest of the cast, a very acceptable Scottish accent — it had as choice a villain as Rathbone or Henry Daniell.

Rathbone had few opportunities for swordplay during the Forties. One of the best was in Mitchell Leisen's *Frenchman's Creek* (1944), based on Daphne du Maurier's novel, a big, beautifully designed Technicolor costumer in which Joan Fontaine put paid to his lecherous advances — and his life — by hurling a full suit of armour at him. In this film Leisen experimented boldly with perspective and his art directors, Hans Dreier and Ernst Fegte, deservedly won an Academy Award for their efforts. Also at Paramount, Leisen's former mentor Cecil B. DeMille made, in *Reap the Wild Wind* (1942), another elaborate colour costume adventure, its chief attraction being a giant artificial squid, a simulated carnivore rivalling Fritz Lang's dragon in *The Nibelungen* as one of the screen's most convincing studio-made creatures.

In a class by itself was Anthony Mann's *Reign of Terror* (1949), a sombre, broodingly handsome French Revolution melodrama made pictorially compelling by William Cameron Menzies's designs and John Alton's Germanic low-key black-and-white camerawork, which in scenes of underground torture or revolutionary mob hysteria recalled Lubitsch's *Madame Dubarry* and the UFA spectacles of the immediate post-World War I years. Not least of the film's many pleasures were the performances of Richard Basehart, visually perfect in death's head makeup, as Robespierre, and Arnold Moss as the cunning Fouché, both of whom more than compensated for the routine leads, Robert Cummings and Arlene Dahl.

Universal's candidate in the swashbuckling sweepstakes was Jon Hall, whom they cast opposite Maria Montez in one fantasy after another. More at home in swim-trunks than wielding a sword, Hall still made a respectable poor man's Flynn, and in *Ali Baba and the Forty Thieves* (Arthur Lubin, 1943) the parallel with Robin Hood and the Sherwood Forest bandits, as well as a debt to Korda's *Thief of Bagdad*, hardly needed stressing. Altogether better, and more original, was Roy William Neill's *Gypsy Wildcat* (1944), an energetic, good-looking *jeu d'esprit* in which Douglass Dumbrille's villain and enjoyable appearances by Curt Bois, Gale Sondergaard and Nigel Bruce lent Hall and Montez fine support. The picture boasted an exceptionally well-recorded Romany-style score and a whirlwind climactic carriage chase that made *Stagecoach's* seem limp by comparison.

(ii) Westerns, Actioners

The character of Westerns changed little in the Forties: their "adult" phase still to come, they perpetuated the conventions that had accumulated around the genre since the days of Tom Mix and William S. Hart. Part of a tradition and yet grandly independent of it, John Ford, greatest Western director of them all, went on making them his own way, while other film-makers like Wyler, Lang and King Vidor, not primarily identified with horse operas, made significant contributions too.

Although William Wyler began his directorial career in the late 1920s with two-reel oaters, he eschewed the outdoors thereafter until *The Westerner* (1940), a mannered, stylised piece which represented a *tour de force* for the photographer Gregg Toland, who invested its story of a conflict between cattle-men and farmers with a lush pictorial richness. Gary Cooper embodied the forces of good, Walter Brennan as "Judge" Roy Bean the forces of evil: their climactic showdown in an almost empty theatre, the camera rising in a nicely judged crane shot to emphasise Bean's solitude in the deserted auditorium (he has bought out the house to view Lily Langtry undisturbed), showed Wyler's command of tension, atmosphere and timing at its best. Elsewhere, Toland's virtuoso photography sustained the film practically unaided, each beautifully composed shot held just a little longer than necessary. Not until Ford's

My Darling Clementine six years later did a Western offer such artful imagery: a farmers' open-air thanksgiving ceremony, a girl standing over her father's grave turning the scorched pages of a family Bible after a crop fire, a country dance sequence foreshadowing *Clementine* itself. Cold and posed, *The Westerner* was saved from being a mere technical exercise by the warmth of Brennan's Academy Award performance.

The chief attraction of Fritz Lang's first Western, *The Return of Frank James* (1940), is its beautiful feeling for the outdoors, established in a lovely opening sequence showing Henry Fonda ploughing. This celebration of the open air continues in episodes made on location in the Rockies, including a chase and gun duel anticipating Anthony Mann's *Bend of the River* and *Winchester '73*. Sensitive colour photography (George Barnes, William V. Skall) and sound recording enhanced an otherwise fairly routine sequel to Henry King's *Jesse James* (a clip from the latter introduces Lang's film). Its best scene shows a mail train being held up by night at a small siding: here the simulated "night" feeling, the train headlight piercing the darkness, and the thrillingly recorded sound offer a brief but brilliant display of Hollywood craftsmanship.

Competent but uninvolved, Lang's direction kept things moving fairly briskly, as it did the next year in *Western Union*, a Zane Grey story about the laying of telegraph wires from Omaha to Salt Lake City in the 1860s. In colour, this showed Randolph Scott and Robert Young battling the villainy of Barton MacLane in their efforts to get the wires down. That the film perpetuated some staunchly held beliefs about an idealised Old West was subsequently confirmed by survivors of the era who wrote personally to the director.

Equally idealised was Henry Hathaway's Mormon epic, *Brigham Young* (1940), a pedestrian account of the great Mormon Utah trek of the 1840s, and William Wellman's *Buffalo Bill* (1944), with Joel McCrea as the legendary Indian scout and frontiersman. Wellman did little better in another pioneering saga, *The Great Man's Lady* (1942), which featured Barbara Stanwyck as a contemporary centenarian in a cotton-wool wig and rimless specs perfunctorily narrating the story of her youth and womanhood in the early Middle West. Six years later the director made another, no less ambitious Western, *Yellow Sky* (1948), in which Joe MacDonald's brilliant high-key camerawork — especially in the salt flat scenes, hard and white and clear — made something visually compelling out of trite situations, poor scripting and worse acting.

Altogether better was Howard Hawks's 1947 epic *Red River*, written by Charles Schnee and Borden Chase from a Chase story. It depicted the first cattle drive over the Chisholm Trail, from Texas to Kansas, in 1865. John Wayne played Tom Dunson, a tough Texan whose domineering ways cause his adopted son Matthew Garth (Montgomery Clift) to rebel and lead the trek to Abilene instead of to the scheduled Missouri. Not without clichés, and suffering from too many studio-shot, simulated nocturnal campfire scenes, *Red River* was none the less a true successor to *The Covered Wagon* and *Cimarron*, its best passages — the start of the trek, the camera executing a 360-degree turn prior to a montage of yelling cattlemen's faces, a stampede, the finely handled arrival in Abilene on August 14, 1865 — achieving a rhythm, scope and grandeur that many Westerns aim at but few realise.

"Screenplay by the producer, David O. Selznick, suggested by a novel by Niven Busch": the credits for *Duel in the Sun* leave one in no doubt that this is primarily the expression of a single personality, Selznick's. The film was to have been the *Gone With the Wind* of the 1940s, grandiose, elemental, passionate, and it succeeded in being all three. It also succeeded in absorbing the talents of at least three directors (William Dieterle, King Vidor and Josef von Sternberg; Selznick directed none of it himself), three cameramen (Lee Garmes, Ray Rennahan and Harold Rosson) and an army of extras, special-effects men, editors and second-unit directors. As in *Gone With the Wind*, Selznick somehow managed to fuse the work of many hands into an organic, viable whole — although some sequences do betray a noticeable visual and directorial disparity.

Before the credits, shots ring out. After them, Orson Welles's voice introduces this Wagnerian horse opera, this Liebestod among the cactus: "Deep among the lonely sunbaked hills of Texas the great and

132

weatherbeaten stone still stands. The Comanches called it Squaw's Head Rock. Time cannot change its impassive face, nor dim the legend . . . [of] . . . Pearl [Chavez], who was herself a wildflower, sprung from the hard clay, quick to blossom and early to die.'' Pearl's legend is one of unholy love and fratricidal enmity. Most of the action takes place on Spanish Bit, the Texas ranch of Senator McCanles (Lionel Barrymore) and his wife Laurabelle (Lillian Gish). Their two sons, Lewt (Gregory Peck) and Jesse (Joseph Cotten) are a Western Cain and Abel: Lewt, amoral, attractive, seduces Pearl (Jennifer Jones), a half-breed relative of Laurabelle's. Eventually, to save the upright Jesse from Lewt's murderous designs, Pearl shoots her lover during a protracted encounter in which she is also killed; they die in each other's arms.

Large of gesture, florid and monumental, *Duel in the Sun* had an almost operatic quality, each bravura set-piece shot, edited and scored for maximum kinetic effect: Pearl's runaway horse, exhilaratingly filmed as it canters unrestrained across the Texan landscape; the celebrated summoning of the station-hands, a tremendous montage of galloping horses and riders massing to the accompaniment of reverberating bells; the subsequent confrontation between Lionel Barrymore and Harry Carey at the barbed-wire fence, a mob of Chinese coolies trembling at the expectation of violent death; and the final duel, preceded by Jones's desert trek, a wordless chorus accompanying her as the inescapable sun shines full into the camera. This was film-making in the grand manner, utterly self-confident and self-sufficient, its plastic splendour ultimately cancelling out its colossal lack of taste.

Although Vidor directed most of the picture, with some sequences done by Sidney Franklin and Otto Brower, William Dieterle was responsible for possibly its greatest scene, Tilly Losch's dance: on a raised platform in the centre of the gigantic Presidio Saloon, Losch as a wanton Indian gyrated to throbbing drums and screeching brass, while all around her milled the pleasure-seekers of the West. Here, and throughout the film, Dimitri Tiomkin's pulsating score added immeasurably to the excitement: martial, sentimental or sensual, it was exotically orchestrated and played under the composer's direction with impassioned intensity.

If *Duel in the Sun* was the Forties' most flamboyant and inflated Western, Ford's *My Darling Clementine* (1946) was indisputably the purest, most classically executed and proportioned. Here Ford combined formal beauty with a celebration of the triumph of good over evil, an idealised, poetically reinterpreted Old West with an admiration for human dignity and the simple manly virtues. After the wonderful signpost credits, we plunge straight into the action: an encounter between the Earp brothers (led by Henry Fonda as Wyatt) and the Clanton clan (led by Walter Brennan) results in the cold-blooded murder of the youngest Earp. Later, when Wyatt has become marshal of Tombstone, he joins "Doc" Holliday (Victor Mature) at the O.K. Corral in a gunfight in which the last of the Clantons meet justice.

Some of *My Darling Clementine* is very ponderous, particularly the interiors, but whenever it goes outdoors Joe MacDonald's photography and Ford's direction combine to raise it to the heights. (It was largely shot in Monument Valley.) Its most lyrical sequence is the dedication of the Tombstone church: Earp, newly barbered and pomaded, escorting "Doc" Holliday's former fiancée Clementine to the platform, Russell Simpson playing fiddle in the square-dance band, and everyone gaping as Earp treads a clumsy yet beautiful measure with his partner. This passage, the church bells tolling, two U.S. flags fluttering, the townsfolk merrymaking, has a mythical, archetypal quality, among the greatest Ford has created. And the film's last scene — Earp farewelling Clementine, his figure disappearing down the road, hers almost a part of the landscape, both posed in long shot — excels anything Wyler and Toland achieved in *The Westerner*.

The other side of the Ford sensibility — boisterous, loud and infantile — tended to dominate *Fort Apache* (1948), in which Fonda played a martinet colonel of the 1870s who knowingly leads his men into a hopeless engagement against the Indians, and *She Wore a Yellow Ribbon* (1949), a Technicolor oater with John Wayne and Ward Bond at their most knockabout. Neither picture represented Ford at his best. Wayne also appeared, with Pedro Armendariz and Harry Carey Jr., in *Three Godfathers* (1948), in which Ford, aided by Winton Hoch's warmly glowing colour photography of Arizona, attempted a laboured quasi-religious allegory in a story of a fugitive bank robber trio who seek a haven for an abandoned baby born in the desert. Its parallel with the Wise Men's journey to Bethlehem could hardly have been more mawkish or banal, but this was still a very characteristic Ford piece, visually eloquent and illuminated throughout by a genuine feeling for its people and landscapes.

Of the general run of Forties saddle sagas little need be said. Roy Rogers and George "Gabby" Hayes at Republic represented one end of the spectrum, a big Technicolor Western like John Farrow's *California* (1947), with Ray Milland and Barbara Stanwyck, the other. In between came competent grade-A movies like George Marshall's *Texas* (1941), with Glenn Ford, or David Butler's *San Antonio* (1946), with Errol Flynn, all rather nondescript and predictable. Raoul Walsh's "psychological" Western *Pursued* (1947) had some striking photography, sombre and eloquent, by James Wong Howe, and excellent playing by Robert Mitchum, Teresa Wright and Judith Anderson.

That America's pioneering past had its roots planted perhaps even more firmly in the eighteenth than the nineteenth century was suggested by King Vidor's *Northwest Passage* (1940), which presented Spencer Tracy as Major Robert Rogers, leader of the 200-strong Rogers' Rangers in New England in 1759. Shot in colour on location at McCall, Idaho, the film was solidly realistic, almost documentary in tone, its most elaborate sequence being an attack on the Indian village of St. Francis, which came over very effectively in muted Technicolor and with a fine use of natural sound. The same era and milieu figure in Cecil B. DeMille's *Unconquered* (1947), set in the area near Fort Pitt in 1763, and featuring Paulette Goddard as a slave rescued from bondage by Gary Cooper in superbly shot colour exteriors.

DeMille used Miss Goddard also in his *North West Mounted Police* (1940), dyeing her face nut brown for her role as an Indian wench who seduces Robert Preston in this Canadian-based adventure, spiritedly staged in C.B.'s most punchy manner. The following year Canada provided another setting for period conflict in Irving Pichel's *Hudson's Bay*, with Paul Muni, bearded and French-accented, as Pierre Esprit Radisson, and Vincent Price, breeched and bewigged, as Charles II.

While Paulette Goddard graced most of Paramount's grade-A actioners, Marlene Dietrich performed similar chores at Universal and — once — Warners. Her role as Frenchy in *Destry Rides Again* (1939) had changed her image from one of aloof mystery to one of hard-boiled, wisecracking camaraderie, a pose she sustained through *Seven Sinners* (Tay Garnett, 1940), *Manpower* (Raoul Walsh, 1941), *Pittsburgh* (Lewis Seiler, 1942) and *The Spoilers* (Ray Enright, 1942). Mostly co-starred with John Wayne, Dietrich played her molls, saloon hostesses and bar-room floozies with an amusing, and amused, *Weltschmerz*, her best effort in this line being as Cherry Malotte, proprietress of an Alaskan gin-palace, in *The Spoilers*. Gutsy, fast-paced, funny, the film was irresistibly energetic, while *Manpower's* Zolaesque story-line had the erstwhile Lola Lola fought over by Edward G. Robinson and George Raft as a pair of electricity linesmen. These were all well-mounted programme pictures, tough, colourful, rousingly put together.

More ambitious was John Huston's *Treasure of Sierra Madre*, from B. Traven's novel about the effects of greed and the lure of sudden wealth on three penniless prospectors (Humphrey Bogart, Walter Huston, Tim Holt). Set in Mexico in 1920, it attempted to be a morality play within an adventure setting and only partly succeeded. Physically, it was often superb, with Ted McCord's harsh, grainy images lending the early Mexican scenes — with Huston himself in a bit part — a striking, seemingly casual immediacy, and the action sequences, such as a bandit raid led by the unforgettably evil-looking Alfonso Bedoya, were excitingly managed. But when Bogart as the mentally unstable Dobbs went melodramatically to pieces, so did the film, with its jarring studio "exteriors," its heavy-handed symbolism and glib irony, the gold-dust blowing among the cactus in the final shot as toothless Walter Huston laughs bitterly at the wilfulness of fate. The director, one felt, had really little to say and was not especially involved with his characters or their predicaments.

(iii) Pastoral, Animal and Children's Films

That the outdoors could also be gentle, a setting for childhood joys or bucolic pleasures as well as for battles and adventure, was demonstrated in films laid among primitive or rural communities, centring on the struggle for existence, cornbelt melodrama or the love of a child for a favourite dog or horse.

With *Une Partie de Campagne* and *La Règle du Jeu* behind him, it was perhaps quite natural that Jean Renoir should have been attracted to the picturesque Deep South, going there on location to film *Swamp Water* (1941) at a time when location shooting — save for Westerns — was practically unheard of. Despite a Dudley Nichols screenplay and good performances from Walter Huston, Dana Andrews and Walter Brennan, the film emerged as an indifferently made rustic tale, with Brennan hiding out in the Okefenokee Swamp for a crime he didn't commit, Andrews establishing his innocence, and the real culprits being lured to grisly ends in the bayou. Peverell Marley's camera, gliding through foliage and sinister waterways, occasionally offered hints of style and atmosphere, but players like Anne Baxter and Eugene Pallette never for a moment convinced as hillbillies, their urban faces imperfectly concealed beneath applied artificial dirt.

Similar faults vitiated Renoir's *The Southerner* (1945), ostensibly a lyrical hymn to the indomitable spirit of man. It charted the fortunes of the Tuckers, Sam and Nona, their children and granny, as they battle poverty, the elements, disease and neighbours' hostility in their efforts to set up a farm in the South. Everything goes wrong: a storm wrecks their crops, a malicious neighbour sends a cow to ruin their vegetable patch, one of their children falls sick from malnutrition. Renoir's sincerity was not in question, nor his faculty for sympathetically rendering the Tuckers' milieu, but it was impossible to accept so urban a personality as Zachary Scott as Sam, catching a fish with his bare hands, offering up a hillbilly prayer to the Almighty, or Betty Field as his wife, or for that matter Beulah Bondi as Granny. These were all too obviously sophisticated masqueraders, quite different from Ford's people in *The Grapes of Wrath*. The effect was to falsify and sentimentalise a perfectly valid and manifestly deeply felt conception.

The same thing happened in Clarence Brown's *The Yearling* (1946), an elaborate, lengthy, handsomely produced version of Marjorie Kinnan Rawlings's novel about a boy's love for a faun. Claude Jarman

Jr. as the boy was acceptable, but Gregory Peck and Jane Wyman as his parents, adopting cornpoke accents and trying to pass as yokels, were not. Nevertheless, the film, in colour, was often attractive to look at, especially the magnificent bear hunt in a forest, alive with a warm feeling for nature and shot, edited and recorded with admirable expertise. Expert, too, were Brown's *National Velvet* (1944), with Mickey Rooney and Elizabeth Taylor entering a cherished horse in the Grand National, and Fred M. Wilcox's *Lassie, Come Home* (1943), with Roddy McDowall slobbering all over a collie.

Master McDowall's affinity with the animal kingdom was further demonstrated the same year in *My Friend Flicka*, directed at Fox by Harold Schuster. Like its M-G-M counterparts, this boasted fine colour and spawned sequels: *Thunderhead, Son of Flicka* (1945) and *Green Grass of Wyoming* (1948), both directed by Louis King. Zanuck's apparent weakness for horse-racing yarns was also indulged when he put top stars and production values into such accomplished programmers as *Home in Indiana* (Henry Hathaway, 1944) and *Homestretch* (Bruce Humberstone, 1947).

A film of higher calibre was Lewis Milestone's version of John Steinbeck's *The Red Pony* (1949), from a screenplay by Steinbeck himself. This entered with sensitivity and imagination into the world of childhood as it told the story of the affection of Tom Tifling (Peter Miles), a rancher's schoolboy son, for his pony Galiban.

Shot mainly on location, the film was part of Republic Studios' bid for "prestige" that had also resulted in Welles's *Macbeth*. Its score by Aaron Copland, its attractively restrained colour, and the charm of scenes like the one in which Tom imagines himself leading a magical procession along a country road, fully realised the studio's prestigious aspirations. The film's prevailing pastoral mood was almost shattered, however, by a cruel and terrifying fight between Tom and a buzzard he finds feeding on Galiban's corpse: this struck a note of savagery and bloodshed quite out of keeping with the rest.

No such lapse marred Stuart Heisler's *The Biscuit Eater* (1940), a classic among films about children and the finest of all screen stories of youngsters' attachments to animals. From its evocative credits — a series of shots of hunting dogs, the panels appearing as they freeze in point — to its vigorously staged climax, the film never faltered. Made almost entirely in Albany, Georgia, it owed much of its effect to Leo Tover's *plein air* photography, which glowingly captured the fields, forests and bayou swamp country of that state. It owed even more to Heisler's direction of the child actor Billy Lee, a "natural" performer and prototype of every boy that ever owned a dog. The dream sequence as he laughs in delight while ghostly phantom-puppies frolic all over him was marvellous; so was a sequence of Lee and a young Negro companion braving an excursion into the swamps to retrieve their bird-dog, Promise, from the mysterious zombie-like negro recluse Echo, the creepers and vines and peculiar fauna all building up an aura of the horrid and unknown. The climactic show-dog trials, making fine use of natural sound, were ingeniously shot and cut, and the fade-out — Promise shot dead, his pups on hand to continue his line — was calculated to bring a lump to even the most sophisticated throat.

Whereas in all the foregoing films human cast members outnumbered animals, in *Bill and Coo* (1948) 273 love birds and a crow occupied almost its entire running time of 61 minutes. Set in the "bird village" of Chirpendale, it seems in retrospect a benign precursor of Hitchcock's *The Birds*, a celluloid aviary full of merry feathered friends. Only the world of the animated cartoon offered *Bill and Coo* rivalry: it remains perhaps the only live-action feature drama issued by a commercial studio with a predominantly non-human cast.

9. Women's Pictures

THE THIRTIES had seen the establishment of an extraordinary number of gifted women stars: Claudette Colbert, Carole Lombard, Rosalind Russell, Katharine Hepburn, Ginger Rogers, Bette Davis and Joan Crawford, to name only some of the most outstanding. Most were cast in comedy or broad melodrama, and the idea of constructing a full-scale dramatic vehicle around a specific performer had largely been restricted to Garbo, and, on a more minor scale late in the period, Crawford and Davis. With the advent of *Gone With the Wind*, and its more modest black-and-white rival, *Jezebel*, studio heads began to see how a lavish production built around a female character could ensure box-office returns. In the Forties, with the vast audience of lonely women left behind by their soldier husbands, lovers and sons, the need for escapist vehicles of this kind became clearly pressing.

M-G-M decided to meet the need by mounting a succession of films that reflected the shrewdly sentimental mind of Louis B. Mayer, starring the radiantly genteel Greer Garson and Walter Pidgeon. Theirs were the "nice", safe, films in which middle-aged women could find solace, a sense that, amid restrictions and shopping queues and the long wait for letters from the fronts, Life after all could be Beautiful. Self-sacrifice and a search for happiness were the themes of these productions, mounted with tasteful luxury, photographed with immaculate cleanliness and gloss.

At Warners, formerly a stronghold of the male starring vehicle, the mood was different. The brothers evidently decided that as well as an escape into a world of beauty almost untouched by any reference to war, the female fans also required emotional catharsis. They were to achieve it through Bette Davis, Joan Crawford (after her period at M-G-M), Ann Sheridan and Barbara Stanwyck, the studio's chief stars playing the roles of women mixed up in mayhem, battling against mishaps to build decent lives for themselves in a world run by men. All-American — sometimes wicked, sometimes good — they typified the emancipated woman fighting for love and security. And usually in settings so grand, so Home Beautiful, photographed with such elegance, so cosily shut off from reality, that wish-fulfilment could be indulged along with emotional empathy. One day, perhaps, when the war was over and rationing at an end, a rich husband might be captured, a mansion obtained: such was the substance of celluloid dreams.

Bette Davis, for instance, was always earthy enough for women to identify with her, but her circumstances were never less than dazzling; in *The Great Lie* she had a "little country place" that boasted a private landing-field, a stable of horses, two servants, and a drawing room in New England modern complete with grand piano; her income was sufficient for her to offer world-famous pianist Mary Astor enough money to live on permanently in return for a baby's custody. In *A Stolen Life* she had a New England house in Norman Rockwell contemporary and a mansion in Boston the size of the White House with a curving marble staircase, chandeliers, and priceless French furniture everywhere. In *Deception* she had the alternatives of a baroque New York house owned by Alexander Hollenius, greatest of American composers, or a studio apartment modelled on Leonard Bernstein's, T'ang vases fit for a museum used as lamp-stands, a cupboard stocked with chinchillas and two dozen cocktail creations, and a very well-filled icebox ("How about some pâté? — Chock-full of vitamins.")

The other characters could not, of course, be permitted to entertain the central figure in a manner to which she was not accustomed. In *A Stolen Life*, Charlie Ruggles, the heroine's friend and adviser, is given a Cape Cod brick-and-clapboard cottage full of wing-chairs covered in expensive chintz, a fire crackling in a king-size grate, a white mantelpiece decorated with sporting trophies and china animals, and upstairs a fairy-tale bedroom again in chintz and maplewood, a four-poster bed, softly glowing standard lamps, and a gleam of good cheer.

When suffering became unbearable, escape could always be found to satisfy the patrons; in *All This and Heaven, Too*, a French country mansion with Charles Boyer to speak Casey Robinson crackermottoes in silhouette across a fire; in *Now, Voyager*, a luxury cruise that took in Nassau and Rio ("the only sight that doesn't disappoint you after the picture postcards") with a foreign gentleman in a white tuxedo; in *A Stolen Life* a lighthouse refuge done out in French provincial. She was often given "cultural" overtones, ranging from doing some expert embroidery in *The Letter*, to painting in *A Stolen Life*, poetry in *Winter Meeting*, concert pianism in *Deception* and novel-writing in *Old Acquaintance*.

Bette Davis moved through her dream world with an air of absolute conviction. Her brisk, no-nonsense look, tight voice, crisp urgent gestures were very much those of a New Englander, brought up in a tradition of disciplined puritanism; and several of her pictures had a New English or even British air that helped secure her a huge and devoted following in the United Kingdom. Most intelligent and likeable of the stars, she seized each part courageously for what it could yield her; and of all her parts the most rewarding was William Wyler's *The Letter*, made at the outset of the period in 1940.

The film opens with a series of bold dramatic strokes, setting an atmosphere of tropical tension and violence. We are in a plantation somewhere near Singapore: rubber drips from a tree, the moon scuds behind palms, coolies toss restlessly in hammocks. Suddenly, shots echo from the plantation house veranda; a white cockatoo flaps from a fence; and Leslie Crosbie (Davis) walks out firing and firing. The white-coated figure of her lover slumps forward, filled with bullets. Leslie looks up at the moon, her eyes haunted, shining with its light.

From this opening sequence on, the direction is masterly, expertly blending theatre and film techniques. Maugham's true-life story of a planter's wife who kills her lover and is saved from death by a tormented counsel had already made a vehicle for Gladys Cooper on the stage and for Jeanne Eagels in an early sound film; here it is reworked in vivid detail by Howard Koch. Two motifs bind the work together: the moon, which holds an intense fascination for the murderess, who returns to look at it again and again through the blinds of her room, who gazes up at it every time she undertakes a nocturnal journey and in the end seems driven by it to her death; and her lace, stitched oval by tiny oval through trial and subsequent confession, at once a symbol of her amazing will-power — her ability to build piece by piece a complex pattern of deceit — and a method by which she steadies her nerves to face the ordeal. At the end, when she goes to her death in the moonlit garden — looking at her shadow advancing ahead of her, stabbed to death by her lover's wife — the completed lace is left behind, drifting in a breeze from the chair where she sat.

The *mise en scène*, photographed in torrid dark images by Tony Gaudio, is made up of exotic details: whirling fans, gin slings clinking in tall glasses, palm-leaves, a complex pattern of shadows, pools of moonlight, white faces and burning lamps at dusk. Max Steiner's score conveys the anguish of the heroine as she lies and lies, pretending to her interlocutors that she killed only to save herself from rape. Bette Davis and James Stephenson as the trial lawyer act together with extra-ordinary intensity: she flinging herself on his mercy, he fighting against his conscience. In one fine scene, he accompanies her to a Chinese shop to obtain a letter which alone can save her; here, as the wife in her white mantilla moves to her car from the ornamental garden, as the car-lights throw up mysterious faces, as a tinkler jangles through clouds of opium smoke to announce the owner of the letter (Gale Sonder-gaard, gilded and slit-eyed), Wyler's direction and the playing of the stars are at their most accomplished.

The Little Foxes (1941), dealt with in another chapter, and *In This Our Life* (1941), feebly directed by John Huston, showed Bette Davis's talent off less well in the role of malefactor. In *The Great Lie* (1941) she was out-acted by Mary Astor as a temperamental pianist. But it was as Charlotte Vale in Irving Rapper's *Now, Voyager* (1942), a triumph of Forties *Kitsch*, that audiences liked her best. Casey Robinson's script, based on a novel by Olive Higgins Prouty, is a very clever wish-fulfil-ment fantasy. Charlotte is ugly in pebble-glasses, dominated by her autocratic mother (Gladys Cooper in fine form) in a Boston Back Bay mansion; she finally collapses into a nervous breakdown. She finds a friend and *confidant* in America's foremost psychiatrist, Dr. Jacquith, played with knowing owlishness by Claude Rains. He suggests a spell at his private sanatorium in the country, Cascade ("As people go to the seashore, they come there"). Later, presenting Charlotte with a phrase from Whitman ("Now voyager, sail thou forth to seek and find"), Jacquith orders her off on a luxury pleasure cruise of the Caribbean and Latin American waters. On board she meets Jerry (Paul Henreid), an unhappily married architect who has the habit of putting two cigarettes in his mouth at once, lighting them simultaneously and passing one to his partner. While touring the environs of Rio, their taxi crashes and they "bundle" for the night — Charlotte is released from her inhibitions and re-emerges in Boston as near to beautiful as the skills of Orry-Kelly and Sol Polito in the wardrobe and camera departments can make her. But there is a long road before the climax, in which she agrees to occupy permanently a Back Street role as the Other Woman, with occasional access to Jerry and his teenage daughter Tina, whom Charlotte and Dr. Jacquith have together cured of her neurosis.

This piffle is directed by Rapper with mesmerising skill. Max Steiner's hypnotic variations on a series of cellophane love-themes ("Wrong, could it be wrong to kiss?" is the most famous of these) underline every scene and give the film a strong romantic coherence. Sol Polito's glamorous photography evokes the shimmering paradise of the Bahamas, the Boston mansion, the soft moonlight of the African coast. Writer and director do well by the rituals — quasi-English and formal — of Back Bay high-life. An opening tea party is very well handled, Jacquith arriving at the Vale house ("Please don't call him *Doctor* Jacquith in front of Charlotte") and the plump spinster descending the stairs, shot from below; later, in a repeat of the same shot, the camera moves up her now slim figure standing on the gangway of a ship, transformed into a fashion-plate from high-heeled pumps to smart hat (the fashions were made deliberately timeless). Jacquith is a pure Forties creation: all-knowing, worldly wise, every woman's dream of fatherly understanding, yet no intellectual, of course ("I don't believe in scientific terms, I leave those to the fakers and writers of books"). Equally woman's magazine is Paul Henreid's Jerry, vaguely Continental, suave, full of homilies, creator for all time of the two cigarettes routine.

Vincent Sherman's *Mr. Skeffington* (1944), was good too: in this, Davis was a woman so beautiful that she could bring a swarm of men to the foot of a staircase whenever she descended it; married to a Jewish bank-broker (Claude Rains) who in a concentration camp loses his sight, she in turn loses her beauty through diphtheria. Since he can no longer see her, to him she is always beautiful.

More fanciful still was Irving Rapper's *Deception* (1946), an *echt-*Forties creation, with a 'cello concerto written by a composer of genius (Alexander Hollenius, played with shock hair and a velvet jacket by Claude Rains), a 'cellist Paul Novak (Paul Henreid) and a pianist (Bette Davis) torn between and lying to both men. John Collier's script is very pretentious. Outside a New York hall after playing (rather indifferently) a Haydn 'cello concerto, the 'cellist is greeted by the

Bette Davis in William Wyler's THE LETTER, in which she had her most rewarding part as the planter's wife who kills her lover. James Stephenson and Herbert Marshall are also seen.

A more pretentious Bette Davis picture was Irving Rapper's DECEPTION in which she portrayed a pianist torn between Paul Henreid (at right) as a 'cellist and Claude Rains as a brilliant composer.

Joan Crawford as a woman driven to a life of crime in George Cukor's A WOMAN'S FACE, a well-made film despite absurd plot and dialogue. Conrad Veidt and Melvyn Douglas also starred.

music editor of the *Bugle*. The conversation goes as follows. "Mr. Novak, which of the living composers do you think I ought to admire?" "Well, er, there is no greatest among the really great." "Whom do you like best, Hollenius—Shostakovich?" "Let's see. Stravinsky when I think of the present. Richard Strauss when I think of the past. And of course Hollenius, who combines the rhythm of today with the melody of yesterday."

We are thus early made aware of the huge reputation of Hollenius. Totally of his period, he lives in a mansion as big as Bette Davis's in *A Stolen Life*, staffed only by one thin Chinaman. Fantastically rude and egotistical, but desperate for his former mistress's love, he offers to continue their relationship even after her marriage to Paul Novak ("Alex, what *are* you?" "What you *made* me!"). She rejects Hollenius, whereupon the great man pours all his vitriol on the name Paul Novak. ("This gutscraper, this puppet of people like myself, who when I write *ffp!* writes *ffp!* And when I write *pff!* writes *pff!*") Memorable scenes include a quarrel between Davis and Rains while Rains sits up in bed reading the funnies, and a splendid dinner-party at which Rains orders more and more bizarre dishes, constantly changing the order until he has reduced his guests, Mr. and Mrs. Paul Novak, to nervous exhaustion. Korngold's hideous 'cello concerto, photography by Ernest Haller, and the all-out performances of the stars can still provide a *frisson* today.

But it is *A Stolen Life*, made in the same year, that remains the most enjoyable of Bette Davis's vehicles of the early Forties. The star plays twins à la Maria Montez in *Cobra Woman* and Olivia de Havilland in *Dark Mirror*, one twin mousy and good, the other mean, hard and almost glamorous. Once more, the film has cultural overtones: the good twin is a painter, who has a tormented love affair with another, more *avant-garde* artist, played with unshaven chin and bad manners by Dane Clark ("Man needs woman, that's basic."). The script is full of the usual Warners cultural talk: attending an exhibition of the good girl's work, Sylvester Pringle, New England's greatest art critic, says: "Excellent . . . a touch of Rousseau?" Both sisters are in love with the same man (Glenn Ford); the bad one is drowned and the good one, whom he has always really loved more, comes into a clinch with him at the finish.

The film presents a typically Forties contrast between an inane story (originally filmed by Paul Czinner with Elisabeth Bergner and a score by Benjamin Britten) and an exhilaratingly alive and dynamic physical presentation. The setting is the rocks and mists of Maine, home and passion of Bette Davis herself for many years, and it is re-created with loving care in California (the star had a hand in the production herself). The effervescent score of Max Steiner with its hornpipes and jolly extrovert string themes, the direction of Curtis Bernhardt, create a strong maritime flavour that pervades the whole production. It is a work of ebullient American energy and zest, filled with the tang and salt of a good nor'wester off the Atlantic.

By contrast, King Vidor's *Beyond the Forest* (1949), represented the apogee of Forties madness and the end of Bette Davis's career at Warners. As Rosa Moline ("You're something for the birds, Rosa," an aged fisherman tells her, "You're something for the birds") she is tired of life in Loyalton, Wisc., with her dull, worthy doctor husband (Joseph Cotten). With long black tresses, print frocks and garishly lipsticked face, she pursues a reluctant beefy lover (David Brian) to Chicago, the Big City of which she dreams in her small town setting. He rejects her, she stages a tantrum, and later she involves herself in murder and miscarriage through her frustrated passion for him. Directed at a feverish pace, accompanied by Max Steiner's high-pressure variations on *Chicago*, the picture has a hot, sweaty eroticism and violence that are very watchable. Rosa careering round the office demanding to see her lover, brushed off by a snooty secretary, or charging down a storm-swept Chicago street to argue with him in a car, seducing him by a beckoning toe round a settee in his log house or marching off to the Loyalton railway tracks at the end, to die of peritonitis on the wrong side of them at last — Bette Davis has seldom had such a chance.

If Davis seized parts on their own level, milking them of every drop, Joan Crawford always walked through hers with an extraordinary air of grandeur. Here was a star to her fingertips: fully conscious of her rather horsy glamour, using her big eyes, her wide gash mouth to splendid effect. Her acting range was limited, but she conveyed an agreeable energy and dash, a hardness and determination, that ensured one's attention for the whole length of a performance. No one could weep like her — hoarse whimpers under fur hats, tears trickling in black mascara rivers down those gaunt cheeks — or smile like her, as though someone had cut her face from ear to ear. Her beauty had a massive quality, baroque and onyx-hard.

She opened the period inauspiciously in George Cukor's comedy about an Oxford Grouper, *Susan and God* (1940), a stage-play shot without flair and featuring a settee in the middle of almost every shot. But in *A Woman's Face* (1941), her personality emerged very fully. As a nursemaid scarred in childhood, embittered and determined to avenge herself on a heartless world, she played with sombre intensity under the direction of George Cukor. Set in Sweden, based by Donald Ogden Stewart, Isherwood and Elliot Paul (among others) on a French play, this was the story of Anna Holm, whose traumatic childhood injury drives her to a lifetime of crime. Her accomplices, a group of petty Stockholm criminals, torment her and she finds a rather prickly solace in the arms of Torsten Barring (Conrad Veidt), uncle of Lars-Erik, a delicate boy whose death will ensure Barring's inheritance of the family fortune. Anna does her best to follow Barring's wishes and dispose of the child, but her better nature overcomes her, and she shoots her lover during a climactic chase on sleighs.

A plot and dialogue of rare absurdity (Barring: "Do you like music? Symphonies? Concertos?" Anna: "Some Symphonies. Most Concertos"); but still a very well-made film. The opening is tersely cut: Anna hurried down a prison corridor, an iron door clanging shut behind her as she is thrust into the glare of a court-room's lights. Her statement to the judge — and the statements, too, of several witnesses — carry the spectator in flashback to the story of Anna's past. Torsten Barring's introduction, in a restaurant deep in pinewoods, applauding two Lesbians dancing together, is memorably decadent. Anna's search for a job, her black-hatted face reflected in mirrors laid along the pavements of Stockholm, and her attempt to murder her infant charge while crossing a waterfall, are excellently realised. A half-sinister, half-jocular little party, candles flickering on a cake, the guests jigging to an eerie spinning tune, the final chase, a torch flung into the night, sleighs whirling with bright bells through dunes of snow, furs sparkling with frost — these scenes have the quality of an evil Scandinavian fairy tale.

It was not until *Mildred Pierce* (1945), that Crawford again had an equal opportunity to show her paces. *Mildred Pierce* reconfirmed a career that had begun to flag with some ludicrous adventures into war resistance melodrama; her next film, *Humoresque* (1947), directed by Jean Negulesco, really ensured her as a great star.

Clifford Odets's script reworked his *Golden Boy* theme of a violinist forcing his way to the top, aided in this version by Helen Wright (Crawford), wealthy alcoholic wife of a neglectful husband, patroness of the arts and collector of handsome, gifted young men. Paul Boray (John Garfield) is the strong, intense object of her affections, treating her roughly, alternating between love-making on bridle path or in beach-house with playing (Isaac Stern did the dubbing) some virtuoso works in the concert halls of America. Finally, unable to compete with the demands of his work, Helen turns on the radio, hears him play the *Liebestod* from *Tristan and Isolde*, and, in a black, sequined dress, walks into the Pacific Ocean and drowns. In a memorable shot, we see the bubbles that announce her doom as she sinks through a shoal of understandably startled-looking fish.

Once again, an idiotic story gets the full Warner Brothers treatment. Crawford's first appearance is in the grand manner: she stands near a fireplace in her mansion, surrounded by admirers, each offering a light for her cigarette. Ernest Haller's photography fills her face with rich, deep shadows as she moves from her first, nervous encounter with Garfield ("Bad manners, Mr. Boray. The infallible sign of talent") to brooding over martinis in panelled cocktail bars ("Let me alone, Paul, I'm a lost crusade") to the last, dazzlingly shot scene when through a chiaroscuro of shining tables, lamps, statues and swaying curtains Helen drifts out towards the beach. She gives conviction even to the script's unusually high-flown musical references: "She's as complex as a Bach fugue." "Martinis . . . an acquired taste, like Ravel."

Negulesco's direction and Jerry Wald's production are at all times enjoyably ritzy: a snapped-up blind roll fading into a piano keyboard, a china figurine on a piano dissolving into the Rockefeller Centre Atlas figure, a party shot through a brandy glass, a track-in to the skating rink at Rockefeller Centre, the skaters reflected upside down in the mirrored ceiling of a restaurant as the sound-track records the opening bars of "Zing went the strings of my heart." This is a film of prodigious energy, with a succession of beautifully edited flowing dark images which shows the Warner magic at its peak.

Possessed (1947), was fine, too, and in its best passages almost as skilfully directed (Curtis Bernhardt). As in *A Woman's Face*, Crawford plays a nurse, this time trapped into a loveless marriage with a wealthy man (Raymond Massey) after his wife's mysterious suicide; her marriage, and her frustrated love for a scoundrel (Van Heflin) drive her to murder and schizophrenia. The opening scenes in Los Angeles, Joan wandering distractedly past a clanking tram in the small hours crying her lover's name, are beautifully shot and recorded, and throughout almost its whole length this cold and clinical film is very watchable.

Where Joan Crawford's presence was regal, Barbara Stanwyck's was briskly energetic and hearty. She always seemed to be involved in cross-country excursions, wearing a high-necked pullover, skirts which always had pockets, and tough walking shoes (in *My Reputation* — a very well-made soap opera — she even ski-ed). She strode about, skirts swinging, in *The Gay Sisters* (1942), a story of three heiresses of a man who died in the *Lusitania*, most of which consisted of a series of wranglings in boardrooms (a monocled Geraldine Fitzgerald and an intense Nancy Coleman played the other sisters). In *Christmas in Connecticut* (1945), she was a journalist, typing out articles for a women's magazine about a chintzy life in the country with a husband and children while she was really living as a bachelor girl in a New York walkup. She played with engaging energy the role of a woman forced to convince her publisher (Sydney Greenstreet) that she was genuine by faking home, family and friends in the Connecticut bankers' belt. In *The Two Mrs. Carrolls* (1947), she was chased murderously up and down stairs by Humphrey Bogart in an English cathedral town where the bells never stopped ringing.

Apart from her major classics of the period dealt with elsewhere — *The Lady Eve, Double Indemnity* and *Sorry, Wrong Number,* — Stanwyck's best remains *Cry Wolf* (1947), beautifully directed by the neglected Peter Godfrey. She played Sandra Demarest, a geologist arriving at the mansion of her late husband, who is supposedly dead but is in fact incarcerated in a private lunatic asylum in the grounds. Convinced that evil things are afoot, Sandra suspects the chemist custodian of the house (Errol Flynn, equipped with pipe and spectacles) of murder. Enterprisingly — this was a part "made" for Stanwyck — she clambers over roofs in the middle of the night or even essays a journey by dumbwaiter, to spy on Flynn in his laboratory (he rudely orders her out the same way). Screams in the night, creaking stairs, two death-falls from balcony to patio, and sinister journeys through woods make up a rich melodramatic brew.

All of this is done with a great deal of sophisticated flair, and Franz Waxman's score is brilliantly menacing. Sandra Demarest's first arrival at the mansion on a storm-swept afternoon, a mysterious girl on horseback galloping past her car, thunder gathering over brooding trees, is marvellously shot and cut. And even better is Sandra's long hunt through the woods for her lost husband, crickets ringing deafeningly in the underbrush, the camera tracking *Rashomon*-like through trees and scrub, birds flapping startled from beneath her feet.

Ann Sheridan, too, had a pleasantly charming and direct personality. Introduced as the "Oomph Girl," she quickly (and all too briefly) developed into a dramatic actress. In *Nora Prentiss* (1947), she wore a memorable succession of pill-box hats as the lover of a man (well played by Kent Smith) who departs his life of drab domesticity for another less respectable after his face is altered by plastic surgery. But it was in Vincent Sherman's *The Unfaithful* (also 1947) that she had her best vehicle.

This finely made film opened outside a house in Beverly Hills. (Although its owner's income is said to be modest, the exterior of Jerry Wald's house was used and the living room was about five times larger than his own.) The story is reminiscent of *The Letter*; a woman (Sheridan) murders a man who appears to be a rapacious prowler, but it later emerges that he was her lover; a counsellor (Lew Ayres) grudgingly acts in her defence. The handling is very smooth, and the use of San Francisco locations complex and vivid; one striking scene shows the dead man's widow climbing onto a cable car, opening a newspaper, and seeing the account of her husband's death, all brilliantly shot by Ernest Haller through the windows of the descending car, her eyes suddenly starting with tears.

At 20th Century-Fox, Gene Tierney made two impressive appearances in women's pictures: *Leave Her to Heaven* (1945) and *The Razor's Edge* (1947). Lushly photographed by Leon Shamroy in rich *Saturday Evening Post* cover colours, its art direction Home Beautiful, *Leave Her to Heaven* is the story of Ellen, a woman driven to madness and murder because of her possessive desire for her husband, author of novels called *Time without End* and *The Deep Well* (Cornel Wilde, having another fling at culture in the wake of *A Song to Remember*). Frustrated by his addiction to the typewriter and his obtrusive family, Ellen drowns his younger brother (Darryl Hickman) in a lake and brings on a miscarriage of her child, finally taking her life with poison. Gene Tierney plays the leading role with a weirdly flat, expressionless stare, like someone driven by fate, blood-sister to Joan Fontaine in *Ivy* and Merle Oberon in *Temptation*. John M. Stahl's direction is smoothly static, while the settings, ranging from the New Mexico deserts to the icy lakes and fir forests of the American North, are very glossy. Ellen riding along a mountain top scattering her father's ashes from an urn; putting on evil-looking dark glasses while her crippled brother-in-law tries to swim across a lake, his cries growing fainter and fainter; her jade eyes flickering open before death on a white pillow: this is a film of the greatest visual fascination, distinguished by the powerfully menacing drumbeats and strings of Alfred Newman's score.

In *The Razor's Edge* (1946), directed by Edmund Goulding, based by Lamar Trotti on the Maugham novel, Gene Tierney was again admirable as Isabel Maturin, rich and heartless prototype of the American woman of the Twenties. If Maugham's novel was very much a book for

151

men, the film version was very much a *Kitsch* picture for women. Maugham's idealistic hero Larry Darrell (said to have been suggested by Gerald Heard) is glamorised out of recognition in the starry-eyed person of Tyrone Power. The settings are made as lavish as possible — Elliott Templeton's Paris apartment now features an *echt*-Forties marble staircase with a crystal chandelier at the top, while his house on the Riviera is a miracle of marble and gilt that would not disgrace Kane's Xanadu. An unreal Paris is used as the setting of the action, clean, incomparably *grande luxe*, full of fountains and jewelled women and exotic Algerian dives.

Despite these improbable décors, the film succeeds. Edmund Goulding's work is immaculate. Each performance reflects the suave intelligence of a director whose sophistication matches Maugham's own. Elliott Templeton — the brittle Twenties snob whose greatest boast is that he has lured two ex-kings to lunch — is brought faultlessly to life by Clifton Webb, Herbert Marshall plays with beautiful discretion as Maugham, and Anne Baxter, though not quite sympathetic enough for the part, captures the agony and confusion of the pathetic Sophie. In a film full of carefully balanced and tailored scenes, one stands out: the death of Elliott Templeton, directed to perfection from the opening shot of a nurse reading a phrase of Vigny to the demise of the arch-snob, his mouth falling open after declining an invitation to the biggest party of the season.

When it came to weepies, Ginger Rogers in Sam Wood's *Kitty Foyle* (1940) and Olivia de Havilland in Mitchell Leisen's *To Each His Own* (1946) vied with each other in wringing the last tear-drop from stories of wronged women.

Of the other female stars of the Forties, Ida Lupino remains the most appealing. Tough, intelligent and always on the go, she was at her best in *The Hard Way* (1942), directed by Vincent Sherman: as a Pennsylvania mill-town girl with a talented younger sister (Joan Leslie), she pushes her way up and up until she discovers that the Big Time is as ashes in the mouth: Sherman's powerful direction, and James Wong Howe's sombre photography, gripped the attention throughout. In *Deep Valley* (1947), she played a stammering, unhappy girl in a family of poor whites; once again, her performance in a film beautifully directed on Big Sur locations by Jean Negulesco was urgent and sympathetic; and she was in splendid form in Negulesco's *Roadhouse* (1949), as a singer croaking *One for My Baby* at a piano, the top of which is scarred by her cigarette butts.

Similar in tone to *Deep Valley* was *Johnny Belinda* (1948), a sentimental triumph under the production aegis of Jerry Wald and the direction of Negulesco. In this story of a Nova Scotia deaf-mute made the victim of rape, a vivid impressionist picture of the life of the fisher-folk was created, and as the girl Jane Wyman gave the performance of her career.

By contrast with the Warners films — all of which had a strong feeling of life in the big city or by the sea, a powerful sense of the American locale — the Metro women's pictures of the decade were heavy, lifeless, trapped forever indoors.

Nearly all of Greer Garson's pictures were unbearably glutinous. *Mrs. Miniver* (1942) was a false and sentimental portrait of the English woman at war, *Random Harvest* (1942) a limp yarn about Ronald Colman's amnesia, all too knowingly aimed at its audience, *Madame Curie* (1943) a preposterous version of the great scientist's life story. Neither *Mrs. Parkington* (1944), despite its skilled direction by Tay Garnett, nor *The Valley of Decision* (1945) was really worthy of remark, and with *Adventure* (1945), which brought back Clark Gable from the war ("Gable's back and Garson's got him" was its nauseous slogan) the star's career reached its nadir.

Together with Greer Garson's *Blossoms in the Dust*, *Waterloo Bridge* (1940), also directed by Mervyn LeRoy, deserves to be recalled. The leading players (Robert Taylor and Vivien Leigh) are appalling, but the film has considerable visual charm: in this story of the love affair of an aristocrat and an ill-fated ballet dancer, the handling is very adroit. The lovers' candlelit dance in a blacked-out restaurant, the candles snuffed out one by one as the band plays *Auld Lang Syne*; the girl running out to meet her man in the rain, her boarding house and its *petit-bourgeois* furnishings expertly realised in excellent sets; the descent of the dancer into prostitution, all UFA gas-jets and shadowy dives, photographed elegantly by Joseph Ruttenberg: these are notable sequences in a conscientiously mounted "big" film of a kind that has vanished forever.

By the decade's close, women's pictures were on their way out as a *genre*. With the war's end, and the upsurge of neo-realist crime films, the beginning of a new need for true-life stories, soap-operas began to lose their appeal. By 1950, Bette Davis and Joan Crawford, Ann Sheridan and Ida Lupino, had left Warner Brothers and Greer Garson was almost finished at Metro. They went their separate ways, to cheaper and cheaper vehicles, until they wound up in crude B-quickies (Crawford), death or retirement (Sheridan and Garson) or a new and more modest career as director (Lupino). Only Bette Davis has managed to hang on, with increasing insecurity, as a star of, at least, minor-A productions.

10. Comedy

BY 1940, American comedy had reached its peak of shrewdness and sophistication. Lubitsch, Mitchell Leisen and George Cukor had been only three of a distinguished group of directors who had worked in the mode. Essentially theatrical — the origins of many of these films had been Broadway successes — talky, composed largely in medium shot, devoid of cinematic trickiness, Hollywood comedy depended almost entirely on the handling of the players, on the expert timing of the dialogue.

Its world was made deliberately artificial and high-toned, so as to release the mass audience into an atmosphere unrelated to war. Almost everyone in these films was rich or was about to be rich: money, furs and diamonds were the objectives of the smart women who so often dominated these fables. And their targets were disclosed with a vulgarity which art directors like Hans Dreier at Paramount and Cedric Gibbons at M-G-M made internationally synonymous with Hollywood. Weekenders were apt to be "little" places on Long Island with drawing-rooms whose french windows opened on to patios where breakfast was served in eternal sunshine, where the heroine could select a favourite horse from two dozen in a well-stocked stable, where there were flocks of funny servants dominated by a monolithic butler with a British accent.

The New York, Paris or London residences of these creatures were apt to boast such horrors as doors with zig-zag patterns in the wood, glass screens embellished with flights of doves or angels, pianos with glass sylphs or nude girls clasping the crescent moon. Hotel suites had seven or eight rooms and a piano (someone, sooner or later, was sure to sit down at it and play a few bars). Ships were white, with dining-rooms and dance-floors open to the stars. They floated across the Atlantic as though on a windless lake, apparently quite free of vibration, and had public rooms so vast they made the Queen Mary's look small. The sea itself was seldom seen, except when two of the characters took a late night stroll, to gaze in each other's eyes and perhaps croon a current tune.

Nobody in this artificial world ever owned a book, a painting worth looking at, or could play anything more inventive than the first few bars of *Liebestraum*. They talked of nothing save sex and money, horses, the Season and the current scandal. Brilliant inventions like Lubitsch's *Trouble in Paradise* and *Ninotchka* had formerly dominated the genre, but no single director had emerged in the Thirties to out-dazzle his competitors. The Forties, though, were to offer a director who emerged above a whole period: Preston Sturges.

Son of a rich stockbroker, Philistine, heartless and bent on success, Sturges was very much the kind of person his films dealt with. In the Broadway-Hollywood tradition, his world was mostly set indoors — in trains, ships, hotels, white houses — peopled with eccentric butlers, clerks, mayors, ship's officers, Rotarians and Lions, dominated by smart women in pursuit of Sucker Sapiens. Pure Hollywood was Sturges's determination to achieve a happy ending the gullible public would swallow like ice-cream: woman not only gets man, but millions; not only sex, but sex with someone who has a handsome face. It was a formula Sturges sold easily to Paramount, and to the Americans: for four years — 1940 to 1944 — he was Box Office in spades; and Paramount, which had given him his first job of directing with *The Great McGinty*, was proud to call him its resident genius, to announce with wonder in its publicity releases that he was the man who wrote the pictures he directed.

Sturges, who had joined Paramount in the Thirties as a script-writer (*Easy Living*, *If I Were King*), after writing a Broadway success in the Philip Barry manner (*Strictly Dishonourable*), resembled in his use of cinematic technique Mitchell Leisen, sophisticated master of the Paramount comedies of the time. *The Great McGinty* and *Christmas in July* (both 1940), Sturges's first two pictures at the studio, were experiments, chances to find his feet: the first a story about political corruption, the second about a young couple and a lottery. Both films let the public have its cake and eat it by at once trouncing and condoning graft and extravagance. With *The Lady Eve* (1941) Sturges really succeeded: this brilliant comedy of manners, heartlessly artificial and gay, showed his flair for timing, for editing a scene so that every shot told, at its best. Like so many of his films, it is the story of a ruthless woman hell-bent on the ruin of a helpless and innocent male.

The film opens with a safari up the Amazon: an explorer's farewell for Charlie Pike (Henry Fonda), young brewery heir ("Pike's Pale, the Ale That Won For Yale") and snake-fancier, who has just captured a rare serpent; on board a liner anchored off the delta society women cluster to see Pike climb the gangway, card-sharper Jean Harrington (Barbara Stanwyck) beating all comers to his attention by adventurously dropping an apple on his head. Later, at dinner in the saloon, Jean watches, maliciously commenting as a succession of gold-diggers, seen in her compact mirror, tries desperately to attract Charlie's attention, at present concentrated on a book called *Are Snakes Necessary?* Finally, she brings him flying with a well-placed foot, expertly luring him to her cabin for repairs on her shoe; she is determined to fleece him, with the aid of her crooked father, of every cent she can get.

From then on, the film perfectly sustains a malicious and witty tone. The big scenes are brilliantly done. A card-game, won hands down by

Jean's father "Handsome Harry" Harrington, flicking aces out of his sleeve to bring about Charlie Pike's defeat ("This is very embarrassing, just make it out to cash" he says as he collects $32,000); Jean's descent on the Pike estate at Bridgeport, Conn., to seduce Charlie all over again, disguised as the Lady Eve Sidwich, scion of an English noble family; their honeymoon on a storm-swept train, "Eve" telling her horrified husband about a series of seductions by grooms, lackeys, etc., on the family estate before sending him flying into the night. The final cheating of the audience is characteristic: Charlie and Jean reunited on board another liner for a happy ending, the cabin door closing and a cartoon snake (which has embellished the opening credits, perkily brandishing an apple in its mouth under a top hat) shown replete and exhausted on the end-title: Eve has got Adam at last.

Stanwyck's full scale star performance, subtly sophisticated, hard-as-diamonds, is at its best in her impersonation of the lady Eve ("I've been British before") complete with fake accent and ostrich feathers and a story of crossing the Atlantic by submarine, telling a series of *risqué* stories at the Pike cocktail bar to a group of socialites, shrieking with laughter at her own jokes while subjecting Charlie to a succession of indignities. Splendid, too, are Charles Coburn as "Handsome Harry", almost lecherously contemplating his victories at cards, Eric Blore as "Sir Alfred McGlennon Keith", fake English baronet and master of invented titles, beady-eyed as he contemplates the spoils of the Connecticut contract bridge belt ("Simply *oozing* with millionaires!") and Eugene Pallette as Pike Senior, clashing together the breakfast dish-covers like cymbals, howling for his food like a spoilt child.

The Lady Eve remains Sturges's masterpiece because its artificiality and lack of seriousness are never flawed by "deeper" significances or emphases, and the breakneck pace, the slapstick, are controlled. *Sullivan's Travels* (1941) is less successful because its intentions are fake-serious.

Its initial premise is that a high-brow director, Sullivan (Joel McCrea) wants to make a story of poverty, *Brother, Where Art Thou?*, at Paramount, while the studio bosses want him to make *Ants in Their Pants of 1939*. Sullivan is told by his butler that his understanding of poverty is non-existent, so he sets out to discover its meaning. Everything he runs into in the sticks is Hollywood's idea of poverty: a hostel for the downtrodden straight out of *My Man Godfrey* and *Man's Castle*, a chain gang straight out of Mervyn LeRoy. It is an unintentional irony of the film that its portrait of reality is as artificially glossed as its portrait of the enclosed life of Hollywood. At the end, after seeing the poor laugh at a Mickey Mouse comedy, Sullivan heads back for Hollywood to feed the public comedy and forget schemes for *Brother, Where Art Thou?* — a cynical piece of self-justification if ever there was one.

In *The Palm Beach Story* (1942), Sturges returned to less "cerebral" subject matter. The film goes along at a pace so frantic that every line of dialogue seems to be delivered like machine-gun bullets: this is, with the single exception of Howard Hawks's *His Girl Friday*, made two years earlier, the fastest-spoken dialogue picture in screen history. Behind the credits, a wedding goes wildly wrong; a couple squabble away for a whole reel in medium-shot; the wife (Claudette Colbert) hies herself off to Palm Beach with divorce and a rich husband in mind. Like the heroines of Walter Lang's *Moon over Miami*, made the year before, she swoops on the wealthy colony like a bird of prey, meeting *en route* Hackensacker III (Rudy Vallee), a mean, purse-lipped, yacht-crazy millionaire and his dizzy blonde sister, a chatterbox bent on men (Mary Astor). As in his two preceding films, Sturges sets a major sequence aboard a train: taken under the wing of the Ale and Quail Club, a cross between the Lions and the Bears, full of eccentric millionaires charging down the Pullmans with guns and dogs in full cry, Colbert is danced off her feet before the carriage is finally uncoupled and abandoned in a siding.

Sturges's next picture, *The Miracle of Morgan's Creek* (1944), was even more frantic, the pace more grimly sustained. A girl in a small town, jazz-mad and soldier-crazy, dodges her father, local police constable William Demarest, and embarks for a night of fun, winding up with a fake marriage complete with curtain ring on her left hand, a pregnancy and no husband. The classic Sturges *sucker sapiens* (Eddie Bracken, stammering incessantly) falls for her sudden protestations of love after years of refusal; he marries her, she delivers sextuplets after their shotgun wedding, and America is thrown into turmoil. Witless, insufferably talky, played without charm by its stars, this is Sturges's unhappiest film. And one uses the word advisedly: the gaiety, lightness and charm of *The Lady Eve* have altogether vanished, to be replaced by a feeling of desperation, of a desire to lode every rift with ore, to keep the rabbits coming out at such a pace that no one will notice there is no longer a hat.

Hail the Conquering Hero (1944) was Sturges's last film of consequence: once again, the unsympathetic Eddie Bracken disfigured the work, and his lack of charm and grace disqualified him as a successor to Harold Lloyd or Buster Keaton. But much of the film is excitingly directed, organised with flair: in this story of a marine of unheroic proportions and a perpetual sneeze, invalided out of the army, greeted at home as though he were a Purple Heart winner, the portrait of small town life is vividly drawn.

The rest of this gifted but erratic director's career makes depressing reading: an ill-advised venture with Harold Lloyd, *Mad Wednesday* (1946), an unfunny if glossily mounted story about a conductor's jealousy, *Unfaithfully Yours* (1947), a Betty Grable vehicle, *The Beautiful Blonde from Bashful Bend* (1949), and the tragic final fiasco of *Major Thompson* in the Fifties. Confidence had slipped away, leaving only a determined showman's grin. Preston Sturges has been overrated; but the dazzling *Lady Eve* remains a permanent monument to his skill.

Also at Paramount, Mitchell Leisen, who had directed Sturges's scripts in the Thirties, was pursuing a more modest and self-effacing career as the studio's other chief comedy director. A man of refinement — expert in historical costume design, art director for many years, creator of the Thirties triumphs *Easy Living* and *Midnight* — Leisen has been a neglected figure. His *Arise My Love* (1940) and *Hold Back the Dawn* (1941) were quite agreeable and smartly paced, successes of direction over scripts by Charles Brackett and Billy Wilder that scarcely showed a trace of their later talents, notably displayed in the charming *The Major and the Minor* (1942). But it was in *Kitty* (1945)

that Leisen really came into his own: this 18th century *Pygmalion* was the story of a gutter waif (Paulette Goddard) picked up by an impoverished fop (Ray Milland) and trained as a lady for marriage with an aged nobleman (Reginald Owen); a direct steal from Shaw has her blurting out some distinctly non-U words at an elegant tea party.

Leisen's knowledge of the period (he designed the costumes) is revealed in the sequences of the street doxies, a visit to Sir Joshua Reynolds's latest exhibition, a debtors' prison observed with the skill of a Rowlandson. The training of the slattern — with a tippling dowager, played in the grandest manner by the magnificent Constance Collier as a kind of Professor Higgins in skirts — in the ways of the fine world is very cleverly scripted and directed. Paulette Goddard, despite equally insecure Cockney and high-class accents, makes a wry, amusing heroine, and Reginald Owen — tottering up flights of stairs in a memorable sequence to learn of the birth of his supposed child — is a portrait of gross venality that is perfectly in period.

Alas, Lubitsch — once the *doyen* of Paramount comedy directors, creator of the dazzling *Trouble in Paradise*, most enchanting of Thirties amusements — was very much in decline in the Forties. *Shop Around the Corner* (1940) was flawed by the sentimentality that at all times threatened *Ninotchka*'s brittle charm; *That Uncertain Feeling* (1941) had one very funny Hungarian dinner party, a living embodiment of the famous saying "If you've a Hungarian for a friend you don't need an enemy", but little else worth remembering; *Heaven Can Wait* (1943) did show traces of the old skill. This period film, charmingly dressed and staged in the best 20th Century-Fox style, opened in hell, where the King of Darkness, plumply impersonated by Laird Cregar, coolly drops a bitchy society lady (Florence Bates) through a trap-door into the inferno before giving Don Ameche a second chance on earth. And *To Be or Not To Be* (1941), also discussed in another chapter, showed much of the old irony and sharp satire in its picture of a Warsaw actors' troupe in Hitler's Poland.

One group of comedies had strong theatrical origins — Broadway successes transferred more or less intact to the screen. *Charley's Aunt* (1941) went at a brisk pace under the direction of Archie Mayo; John

Peter Lorre, Raymond Massey, Josephine Hull, Cary Grant, Priscilla Lane and Jean Adair in Frank Capra's ARSENIC AND OLD LACE, based on the stage play.

Henry, Barbara (Stanwyck), and Preston on the set of THE LADY EVE, *a film of gaiety, lightness and charm, and its director's masterpiece.*

The opening scene in George Cukor's ADAM'S RIB *with Jean Hagen and Tom Ewell cowering before Judy Holliday.*

van Druten's *Old Acquaintance* (1943) and *The Voice of the Turtle* (1947) were smoothly directed by Vincent Sherman and Irving Rapper respectively; Frank Capra provided a rather overstated and strained version of *Arsenic and Old Lace* (1944); Allan Dwan re-created the celebrated bedroom farces *Up in Mabel's Room* (1944), with a funny Charlotte Greenwood and the bug-eyed, spindle-shanked Mischa Auer, and *Getting Gertie's Garter* (1945).

On a higher level than most of these was William Keighley's *The Man Who Came to Dinner* (1941), a sparkling version of the play about an Alexander Woollcott-like columnist, Sheridan Whiteside (played with bristling beard and viper-tongued irascibility by Monty Woolley), his secretary Maggie Cutler (Bette Davis), and their irruption into a typical middle-class household when the columnist slips up on the icy steps of his hosts' home. Incarcerated there for weeks, they drop names furiously and send up Middle Western *mores*. There are many amusing scenes: a fat and inane local doctor presenting his unreadable memoirs to an appalled Sheridan Whiteside; the nurse (marvellously funny playing by the irreplaceable Mary Wickes) encountering a captive penguin, an explorer's present to Whiteside; Beverly Carlton, the Noël Coward-like playwright played to perfection by Reginald Gardiner imprisoning the film star Lorraine Sheldon (Ann Sheridan as herself) in an Egyptian sarcophagus by convincing her she should play the role of a Queen of Egypt and try the coffin on for size. Twenty-seven years after it was made, *The Man Who Came to Dinner* shines as brightly as ever.

Monty Woolley also appeared in *Holy Matrimony* (1943), John M. Stahl's and Nunnally Johnson's version of Arnold Bennett's *Buried Alive*, with a distinguished performance by Laird Cregar as the effeminate art dealer Clive Oxford; and in Irving Pichel's *Life Begins at 8.30* (1945), a pleasant and neglected film about life backstage. Period comedies were many in the decade: *Life With Father* (1947), lavishly presented by Curtiz, with a nice jogtrot score by Max Steiner; George Stevens's *I Remember Mama* (1948), RKO's less satisfactory answer; René Clair's delectable comedy of manners *The Flame of New Orleans* (1941), an impersonation story with Dietrich at her most captivating.

In this story of Claire Ledeux, who swoops on New Orleans in 1841 to trap Charles Giraud, the city's wealthiest bachelor (Roland Young) into marriage by imitating a rich noblewoman, Dietrich was about as French as *Apfelstrudel*, but her exquisitely witty playing, the frilly, flouncy décors ravishingly photographed by Rudolph Maté, and particularly the direction of the last scene — a bold roughneck (Bruce Cabot) snatching her from the altar and making off with her by ship, the wedding-dress flung out of a port-hole in the stern as she settles down for a bout of love — ensured a great deal of civilised amusement.

Nostalgic comedies also included the Paramount versions of Cornelia Otis Skinner's consecutive memoirs, *Our Hearts Were Young and Gay* (1944), and *Our Hearts Were Growing Up* (1946), and Fox's *Margie* (1946), directed by Henry King, in which Jeanne Crain as a middle-aged housewife recalls her youth in the Twenties. In iridescent, beautifully designed colour (the cameraman is Charles G. Clarke), a formal abstract is given of the period, as idealised and stylised as that of another time in *Summer Holiday* and *Meet Me in St. Louis*. Ragtime, Charlestons, a college debate (brilliantly accurate), a skating outing, the helter-skelter atmosphere of young people in a carefree American era, are lovingly re-created. Henry King's direction, far lighter and more dexterous than usual, is at its best as the camera glides like a skater in effortless three hundred and sixty degree pans round a rink, catching the flash of light on steel blades, the whirling of paper lanterns and the sparkle of ice, in the scene when Jeanne Crain takes a bubble-bath, each bubble turned into a prism as the rainbow colours dance, and in the wordless sequence when the young girl lies in a counterpaned bed and the camera moves very slowly towards her as she sleeps, to the gently played strains of "I'll See You in My Dreams." Here, as elsewhere, the combination of the soft-textured colour, the perfect cutting, and the arrangements of Alfred Newman recorded to perfection in the best Fox style, ensure a consummate pleasure.

At the beginning and end of the period, George Cukor, director of the Thirties triumphs *Dinner at Eight*, *David Copperfield*, *Camille* and *The Women*, made two famous comedies: *The Philadelphia Story* (1940) and *Adam's Rib* (1949). *The Philadelphia Story*, adapted from the play by Philip Barry, was set in a familiar world of gracious Long Island living, breakfasts on the sunlit patio, french windows, lawns, dogs and horses and smart people talking incessantly across cocktails. Much admired for Katharine Hepburn's performance as Tracey Lord, brittle heiress, hoverer between divorced husband (Cary Grant) and social gossip reporter (James Stewart), the film today seems empty, a cellophane wrapping containing nothing. *Adam's Rib*, though, is good fun: Judy Holliday shoots and injures her mate; rival counsel, a warring married couple, Spencer Tracy and Katharine Hepburn, battle over her in court. The opening, a stylised quarrel ending up in the firing of the shot, is wittily done; the dialogue (by Garson Kanin and Ruth Gordon) is full of alert comment on the American battle of the sexes; and the unusually long takes — sometimes the camera does not move at all for several minutes while the principals argue in front of it — work cleverly in the context. If Cukor's command of lighting, of ingenious camera movements showed up more clearly in his melodramas — notably *A Woman's Face* and *Gaslight* — his comedies disclose his mastery of timing, of pacing and emphases in dialogue scenes, and the players — Hepburn and Tracy, Stewart and Grant — respond with performances of expert professionalism and grace.

In a category by itself was Chaplin's masterpiece of the Forties: *Monsieur Verdoux* (1947). Verdoux, a story of a Landru-like Bluebeard — impeccably dapper in cutaway coat and top-hat and waxed moustache, coolly disposing of a succession of ill-favoured widows to support his family — remains perhaps the most remarkable of Chaplin's films. The opening, shot in an exquisite range of greys by Rollie Totheroh, takes the viewer into a graveyard, cool and pebbly against sad shrubs, to Verdoux's grave, and his elegant voice on the soundtrack says to the audience "Good evening". From then on, the film combines a subdued lyricism, a strong sense of melancholy, with some of Chaplin's most beguiling comic invention. This combination of sadness and wit is best seen in the episode of Verdoux's seduction of a fruithatted moron played by Martha Raye, and in their last, quiet boating expedition on a lake, shot from a variety of angles, as he tries — à la *An American Tragedy* — to bring about her death. Excellent, too, are

163

the last scenes of Verdoux's downfall, refusing a final drink in the prison, walking almost daintily to his death. The whole work has an impeccable ironic wit, a perfect tightrope-walker's sense of balance.

A world away from the measured civilised intelligence of Chaplin's film were the slapstick, "wild" and far-out farces of the period directed and played with frenzied energy and pace, aimed straight at a fun-hungry homebound populace, at the vast audience of G.I.'s. Of these, the most brilliant was George Marshall's *Murder, He Says* (1945), a neglected masterpiece and perhaps the Forties' funniest farce.

Wittily written by Lou Breslow, this triumphant piece of nonsense satirised both *Tobacco Road*-like "realistic" melodramas and ghost movies like the same studio's (Paramount) *The Cat and the Canary* and *The Ghost Breakers*, a film which is actually referred to at one stage in the dialogue. Fred MacMurray arrives in the heart of the hillbilly belt looking for a missing gangster's moll, Bonnie Fleagle; he lights upon a mad *ménage* living in a ramshackle house in the middle of the wilderness. Mistress of the house is a whip-cracking, bird's-nest-haired termagant given to shrill feral cries of rage (Marjorie Main), a Ma Barker of the sticks; her pair of half-witted twins, one with a crick in his back which can only be cured by a ferocious thwack of his mother's hand; her mousy but deadly little husband (Porter Hall) and a ninny of a niece, mooning around singing a mad song and twining flowers through her hair (Mr. Breslow is not averse even to parodying *Hamlet*). Disguised as Bonnie Fleagle, Helen Walker — trousered and gun-toting — arrives in the *ménage* looking for a hidden treasure. There follows one of the screen's most hilarious comedy sequences as Marjorie Main serves her guests a dinner so loaded with phosphorescent poison that the dishes glow eerily when the lights are turned out. The circular dinner table is whirled round and round as each guest in turn tries to push the fatal dish on to someone else. Finally, Porter Hall appears to die from the poison, and his brightly glowing "corpse" is laid out in an upstairs room.

A hunt begins for the treasure, MacMurray and Walker combing through corridors behind forever moving book-cases while a sinister shadowy figure flees them. Eventually, a piece of embroidery with some words stitched on it, a wheezy old harmonium and the niece's mad refrain give them the clue they need: the tune, stitched on the embroidery and picked out on the harmonium, causes the door of a secret passage to open, and the mysterious, shadowy stranger turns out to be the not really dead Porter Hall. The climax takes place in a barn: brilliantly timed, it shows the entire cast involved in the machinery of a hay-baling apparatus, the mad family emerging trussed up in bundles with metronomic precision.

Murder, He Says was very much in the Thirties mould of zany comedies, a *genre* which had many entertaining descendants in the next decade. Madcap humour, situations of the wildest improbability, fast-moving dialogue and the presence of knockabout clowns were the main features of the mode. Most of these films were aimed directly at the lowest common denominator of the public, but a few did succeed in being sophisticated and sharp-witted at the same time. Andrew Stone's *Hi Diddle Diddle* (1943) was among the best of these: Frederick Jackson's script had an unusual surrealist inventiveness; at the end, there is even an animation effect in which the wallpaper comes to life. A sailor (Dennis O'Keefe), whose ship is delayed long enough to cause hysteria among the guests gathered for his on-shore wedding, finally sets off with his bride for a 48-hour honeymoon, only to be perpetually frustrated by the interruption of a number of bizarre characters. Most notable of these are Genya Smetana, a temperamental opera star played to the manner born by Pola Negri, and Leslie Quayle, a Dietrichesque nightclub entertainer (June Havoc). There are engaging running gags (Sample: after a long night club tour, one of the characters says of a waitress who crops up each time: "I've seen that girl before." Answer: "She's a friend of the director's"). One very well directed scene shows June Havoc moaning a Marlene-like number called "Loved a Little Too Late" while her own image is played back to her on a Slottie Movie (precursor of Scopitones) on the wall. The expression on Pola Negri's face when at the end of a performance she is presented with a bunch of withered roses is priceless.

Many of the wildest comedies of the period were set in Hollywood itself. Olsen and Johnson, fat and funny stage stars of the period, specialised in a brand of slapstick in which unusual violence was administered to the participants and the audience was frequently shown movies within the movie, thus parodying the cinema as a medium itself. Their most famous film, *Hellzapoppin* (1941), the story of an attempt to make a movie called *Hellzapoppin*, features several sequences in the projection booth, the projectionist and his fat usherette girl friend tangled in reels of film. When people rise to leave the theatre, their shadows are shown on the screen we are watching. Many of the gags are very funny: one of the comedians shows a hideous mask to a woman in the theatre and she displays no alarm; when he removes it and reveals his own face, she screams hysterically. But much of the picture is heavy-handed, sadly devoid of wit.

Not so its successor, *Crazy House* (1943), directed by W. C. Fields's director Edward Cline, a triumph of knockabout reminiscent of the best silent gag comedies. Olsen and Johnson arrive at Miracle Pictures (a sign outside carries the studio's proud motto: "If it's worth seeing it's a Miracle") to make a movie, but nobody wants them to do it. Finally they rent a lot, shoot the production using stars' stand-ins, stage a full-scale parade for themselves along Hollywood Boulevard and launch the picture before the creditors can seize the negative. The film's greatest revelation among a shoal of good things was the slapstick comedienne Cass Daley, who plays both herself and her stand-in Sadie Silverfish. Buck-toothed, with a protruding rear like a Sherman tank, she vamps a tepid, timid Percy Kilbride in one scene or flings herself with remarkable energy into a madcap song: "My boss Mr. Finch/He likes to pinch/He likes to pinch/My boss Mr. Finch. . . ."

Variety Girl (1947), wittiest of the all-star movies which pretended to show the inside of the "real" Hollywood to an eager public, similarly features an attempt to crash the strongholds of the studios. Catherine Brown (Mary Hatcher) is a hopeful from the sticks, bent on invading the Big Time. She meets a brassy would-be star (Olga San Juan), disguised under the *nom-de-film* of Amber La Vonne, talks Bing Crosby into a singing test, has her audition ruined by Spike Jones and his City

Slickers, upsets DeMille by invading a set of one of his pictures, and loses a job as dub-singer for George Pal's Puppetoons. Funniest of the film's many funny scenes shows Olga San Juan, determined to be noticed in Hollywood, brashly having herself paged in a restaurant, conducting a high-powered conversation on the telephone for all to hear, then addressing all and sundry on the paging system as though she were already a star. In *Star Spangled Rhythm* (1942), also made by Paramount, Alan Ladd emerges in his usual trench-coat, but instead of drawing a gun from it produces a bow and arrow. And in *Thank Your Lucky Stars* (1943), *Hollywood Canteen* (1944) and *Follow the Boys* (1944) the humour springs from famous stars behaving in manners opposite to those normally associated with their screen personalities: Bette Davis is seen jitterbugging, Orson Welles saws Marlene Dietrich in half.

Slapstick, too, were the films of Danny Kaye, made by Goldwyn, mounted with ripe vulgarity, and featuring the Goldwyn Girls. *Up in Arms* (1944) teamed Kaye with Dinah Shore in a story of a hypochondriac draftee whose girl-friend (Constance Dowling) smuggles herself abroad his troopship disguised as a G.I. in an oilskin. In a dream, he sees himself as a Casanova; this sequence is a precursor of *The Secret Life of Walter Mitty* (1947), an overrated and feebly directed (by Norman Z. McLeod) version of Thurber in which Kaye takes the roles of various heroic figures. *Wonder Man* (1945), Kaye's best picture, shows him as a nervous librarian, haunted by the spirit of his dead brother, night-club star Buzzy Bellew, who has been murdered by gangsters (the same name was given to the character of a band-leader played by Fred MacMurray in *Champagne Waltz*). A very funny climax shows the librarian forced to imitate an opera star in a performance at the Met.

The Forties also saw the last of the Marx Brothers films and of W. C. Fields's famous series of comedies, most notably *The Bank Dick* and *My Little Chickadee* (both 1940): but these were creations that really belonged to an earlier decade, as did William Wellman's incongruously Thirties-style, crude "Twenties" comedy *Roxie Hart* (1942). Far more typical of the Forties were the films of Bud Abbott and Lou Costello, and the countless B-comedies of such groups as The Three Stooges, the bellicose humour of a Judy Canova. In these films, aimed directly at the G.I. and at adolescents and children at home, the fun sprang from seeing various characters subjected to tortures, placed in perilous situations — a car swinging on the edge of a cliff, a wicked sultan about to impale a victim on spikes — and the pace was as frantic as the traffic would allow.

Costello, tubby and cowardly, letting out a series of nervous beeps and quivering like blubber at every successive crisis, and Abbott, talentless, nondescript straight man endlessly worried or bullying his hapless companion, were enormously successful, and some of their films, most notably *Lost in a Harem* (1944), were extremely funny. The Three Stooges, anarchistic, brutally savage to each other, administering nose-tweaks and forehead-knocks that sounded as loud as gun reports, dealing lethally in paint pots, brooms and brushes — they seemed often to be engaged improbably as interior decorators — were on an even cruder level of humour, but much more amusing. In one film, they appeared memorably as the Hitler gang; in another, they were involved with a mad scientist and an ape in an hilarious parody of horror pictures. Their comedic style was reminiscent of Olsen and Johnson's, noisily and totally of its time.

Slightly less frenetic were the "Road" films of Dorothy Lamour, Bob Hope and Bing Crosby, which combined Don Hartman's rather feebly written gag routines with glamorous "locations" — back-projected exotica from Alaska to Zanzibar — a standard presentation of Bob as cowardly if brash, Bing as coolly contemptuous, almost always stealing the girl, and Dottie as a succession of princesses, sarong-clad and delectably dusky. Although these films seem sadly unfunny today, they have a fascination as guides to the taste of a period: it was, for instance, entirely typical that while the trio is crossing the Alaskan wastes by sleigh in *Road to Utopia* (1945) the Paramount mountain should loom into view, complete with crown of cardboard stars: "Ah, there's our bread and butter!" Bob exclaims as he sees it.

These, then, were the assembly line, immensely popular films for the comedy-hungry masses, but other directors were allowed to create farce on a somewhat higher level: among them Sam Wood, whose *The Devil and Miss Jones* (1941) was an engaging trifle, George Stevens and Edmund Goulding, all three directors whose chief reputation now rests on their more serious films. In *Talk of the Town* (1942), Stevens showed an escaped suspected arsonist (Cary Grant) arriving at the home of an over-age, bearded jurist (Ronald Colman) and his housekeeper-landlady (Jean Arthur): the comedy springs initially from Arthur's attempts to keep Grant's supposed guilt from Colman—at one stage, she is forced to slide a breakfast fried egg onto Colman's morning paper to conceal a picture of Grant on the front page. In *The More the Merrier* (1943), recently remade as *Walk, Don't Run*, Charles Coburn, Jean Arthur and Joel McCrea are involved in a story about housing shortages in Washington: although neatly and attractively made, both films suffered from Stevens's directorial anaemia, from a pace that went altogether too deliberately for high comedy.

Edmund Goulding's *Everybody Does It* (1949) was far better. Paul Douglas plays a long-suffering businessman who cultivates a proud opera star Louise Carver (Linda Darnell) to the neglect of his wife, wittily played by Celeste Holm, a shower-room soprano who insists on appearing, like a small-time Mrs. Charles Foster Kane, in a specially hired Carnegie Hall to the distress of her family and friends. While in the bathroom one day, Douglas lets out a baritone yell that shatters brandy-glasses, mirrors and lighting fixture crystals, and convinces Louise Carver she has a potential genius of song on her hands. A very funny finale — reminiscent of *Wonder Man* and *A Night at the Opera* — shows Douglas in a hideous Viking outfit careering around the stage in a sub-Wagner opus, tangled in a six-foot chain and finally brought crashing down a flight of steps to land with a clunk at the horrified Louise Carver's feet. Direction and writing expertly parody opera's fatuous conventions, and the playing is very sophisticated throughout.

The same players also appeared in a film which, made as it was at the end of the Forties, bridged the gap to the artificial comedies made at Fox in the early Fifties: *All About Eve* and *People Will Talk*. This was *A Letter to Three Wives* (1948), also directed by Joseph L. Mankiewicz, a former producer whose unusually literate and intelligent scripts were to build for him a major reputation in the decade that followed. *A Letter to Three Wives* showed the effects of an unseen woman, a catty and notorious local gossip (the part is spoken by Celeste Holm), who writes a malicious letter to three suburban women: the effect is to threaten the security of their marriages. The first episode, involving a gauche suburban housewife (Jeanne Crain) and her social *gaffes* is indifferently done, but the second, with Kirk Douglas and Ann Sothern as a couple involved in radio writing, descended on at one stage by a ferocious sponsor (brilliantly played by Florence Bates) and the third, in which a gold-digger (Linda Darnell) from the wrong side of the tracks enslaves a befuddled business man (Paul Douglas) have a tough, Lubitsch-like sophistication and wit, with an extra edge in the handling: the playing of Darnell and Douglas in particular is wonderfully acid and observant.

A Letter to Three Wives and minor divertissements like Clifton Webb's Belvedere comedies and Richard Haydn's *Miss Tatlock's Millions* (1948) marked, alas, the end of an era. Comedies grew more and more gross, and not only physically, with the onset of the wide screen. Only the very occasional farce of quality — Billy Wilder's *Some Like it Hot*, or Frank Tashlin's *Will Success Spoil Rock Hunter?* (*Oh, For a Man!*) — reminded one, in an admittedly more vulgar spirit, of the charm and skill of that long-vanished mode.

11. Musicals

SINCE ITS RESPLENDENT début with *The Jazz Singer* in 1927 and *The Broadway Melody* in 1929, the American film musical had been dominated by two strains: backstage themes, dealing with the struggles of young and talented entertainers fighting their way to the top, and stories of singers and dancers pitched in exotic locations: Canada,

Vienna, Rio, Berlin. The Forties saw the continuation of both kinds: at M-G-M Judy Garland and Mickey Rooney made a series of films about attempts to put on stage shows by brave, poor and talented youngsters; at Fox, the Betty Grable series, directed by Irving Cumings, Bruce Humberstone or Walter Lang, was pitched in exciting places like Miami, the Rockies, Buenos Aires. But it was a decade in which an entirely new mode emerged: the musical of nostalgia, the evocation — sentimental and handsomely glossed — of a vanished America: *Meet Me in St. Louis* and *Centennial Summer* were both set around cities where famous world's fairs had taken place, and *The Harvey Girls, Coney Island, Hello 'Frisco Hello, State Fair, My Gal Sal, Little Old New York* and *Greenwich Village* also evoked a romantically imagined beautiful past, far from the America of sweat shops and steel jungles, and from the contemporary realities of war.

Typical of the period, too, were the "classical" musicals: *Song of Love*, which glorified Brahms and the Schumanns, *A Song to Remember*, with a Chopin like a champion quarterback. And the "light" musical biographies: Warners spent heavily on lavish tributes to Gershwin and Cole Porter, M-G-M celebrated Jerome Kern and Rodgers and Hart. It was not, though, till the very end of the period that a masterpiece of the musical, comparable with the very best work of Astaire and Rogers and *42nd Street* in the Thirties, emerged: the dazzling *On the Town*, in which Arthur Freed, released from the airless artifices of Minnelli's world, created with Gene Kelly and Stanley Donen a new kind of film, the musical which was sung and danced all over a city, which almost never stopped to indulge the audience with trite and romantic padding.

Freed remains the best-known figure of the Forties musical, producer of 23 major films in the *genre* during the period, from *Strike Up The Band* to *On The Town*. A former singer with the Marx Brothers' stage act, theatre owner (The Orange Grove, in Los Angeles), co-author with Nacio Herb Brown of the songs for *Broadway Melody*, creator of the celebrated numbers "Singin' in the Rain", "I've Got a Feelin' You're Foolin'" and "You Are My Lucky Star" among many other hits, Freed assisted Mervyn LeRoy as producer of Victor Fleming's *The*

171

Wizard of Oz in 1939 before becoming full producer with *Babes in Arms* in the same year, a charming Rooney-Garland backstage fable featuring a baby orchestra. His contribution to the decade lay chiefly in giving freedom to the men who worked for him; a team organiser rather than a specifically creative genius on his own.

Strike Up The Band (1940), his first film of the decade, was directed by the great Busby Berkeley, creator of the bizarre surrealist ballets of the Thirties, and one number — the "La Conga" — a song-and-dance routine lasting five minutes and shot from a bewildering variety of camera angles, was scintillating. *Little Nellie Kelly* (1940), a sentimental Irish story, was less successful, *Lady be Good* (1941) suffered from Norman Z. McLeod's lame direction, but *Babes on Broadway* (1942), with wholehearted performances by Garland and Rooney and a brisk pace under Busby Berkeley, was an engaging piece of backstage nonsense. It was this film that introduced Vincente Minnelli to Hollywood: he directed Judy Garland's big solo numbers.

Minnelli, destined to be the most famous of musical directors, had begun in the Twenties as a photographer's assistant, one of a troupe of travelling entertainers, and an assistant stage manager and designer to the Balaban and Katz theatre chain. Earl Carroll discovered Minnelli and engaged him for work on his vulgar *Vanities* series of stage shows. He designed stage settings for the New York Paramount à la Ziegfeld, scenery and costumes for Grace Moore's production of *The Du Barry*, and the famous Broadway revues *At Home Abroad* and *The Show is On*. He brought to Hollywood his designer's flair, and Arthur Freed gave him two years of intensive training in film direction. The first result of the collaboration was *Cabin in the Sky* (1942), a film that established Minnelli's highly artificial, tasteful, but rather bloodless visual style.

The film's fantastic and bizarre elements were very popular with wartime audiences already pleased by films like *The Thief of Bagdad* and *The Blue Bird*. All-Negro, showing the existence of a black Heaven and Hell in the milieu of a slum in the Deep South, this elaborate curio was chiefly notable for its handsome sepiatone surface, Ethel Waters's rendition of "Happiness is Just a Thing Called Joe", and the splendid Lena Horne's every scene, as a siren sent by the devil to tempt Little

172

Joe (Eddie "Rochester" Anderson). The duet between Horne and Anderson, "That Ole Debbil Consequence", was very engaging.

Minnelli worked on a special number, "Jericho", in *I Dood It* (1943), a Red Skelton comedy officially credited to him in its entirety but in fact made by another. In "Jericho", Hazel Scott, unforgettably on display in Irving Rapper's *Rhapsody in Blue*, rehearses a number backstage with a group of Negro singers; gradually they get worked into a frenzy, a revivalist ecstasy.

Meet Me in St. Louis (1944) followed, and established Minnelli's reputation: it was based on the celebrated "New Yorker" reminiscences — nostalgic, romantic, and smoothly told — of Sally Benson, about a family which learns, in the St. Louis of 1903, and on the brink of the World's Fair, that father is to be transferred to New York and a whole world of peaceful provincial happiness is going to be shattered. The parallel with the disappearance of an innocent America is carefully stressed, and the film — photographed in chocolate-box colours, pretty, cluttered and a trifle airless — is as formally nostalgic as a cameo brooch. The score by Ralph Blaine and Hugh Martin is attractive and catchy — "The Trolley Song", vigorously sung by Judy Garland, is still fresh today — and the Halloween sequence, in which the little girl played by Margaret O'Brien is frightened, has a deliberately artificial charm, a studio-made period glow, that is very appealing.

Minnelli's next film, *Yolanda and the Thief* (1945), was in many ways a revolutionary work, a baroque extravaganza in which the story was almost entirely danced. Fred Astaire played a gambler whose purpose was to persuade Lucille Bremer that he had been sent to earth as a *Here Comes Mr. Jordan*-like heavenly emissary. The design and costumes re-created much of the flavour of Ludwig Bemelmans's illustrations to his own fable, and two numbers, "Coffee Time" and a dream ballet, were executed with considerable verve. This remains an eccentric, agreeable oddity, commercially disastrous at the time.

Also in 1945, Minnelli directed some sequences of *Ziegfeld Follies*, and his work on the picture conveys a sense of strain, of a brittle nervous talent stretched to the limit; this time there was no visual appeal. This hideous revue, rivalled only in ugliness by Mitchell Leisen's *Lady in the Dark*, was dressed without distinction and played without more than a modicum of talent by a formidable array of Metro stars. Only intermittently in the "Limehouse Blues" number, admirably danced by Fred Astaire and Lucille Bremer, and sung by the short-lived Pamela Britton, were there traces of originality and style; but these stemmed largely from Hans Peters's inspired sets for Blue Gate Fields on *The Picture of Dorian Gray*, adapted to create the sequence's fantasy London.

Minnelli's last Forties musical, *The Pirate* (1947), had been a comic vehicle for Lynn Fontanne and Alfred Lunt on the New York stage, and S. N. Behrman's story of the love affair of a well brought up West Indian girl and a strolling player had evidently benefited from their accomplished light playing. Unhappily, neither Judy Garland nor Gene Kelly had the requisite delicacy and humour for comedy, and both acted with noisy charmlessness the roles of seduced and seducer. A hideous dream ballet involved Kelly dancing amid billowing mauve and crimson clouds; dances all over the large harbour sets were deafeningly and luridly staged. The whole film had an air of desperation and strain, of an attempt at gaiety that neither director nor stars could manage. It remains to admire only the opulent colour photography of Harry Stradling and the costumes — brilliantly decorative and fanciful — of Tom Keogh and Karinska.

Similar to *Meet Me in St. Louis* in mode, again produced by Arthur Freed, Rouben Mamoulian's *Summer Holiday* (1948) was a masterpiece of nostalgic charm and appeal, a triumph of Americana. A musical version of Clarence Brown's exquisite *Ah, Wilderness!*, adapted from O'Neill's play, it featured much of the same script by Albert Hackett and Frances Goodrich, although Ralph Blaine added some brilliantly successful rhyming dialogue to the original. Eugene O'Neill's warmly felt evocation of small-town childhood is wonderfully captured in songs (by Blaine and Ralph Martin) and dances of an extraordinary delicacy and gaiety and in family scenes acted and directed to perfection. Highlights were the Stanley Steamer number, with the entire family mounted for a country outing on an exciting new car, spinster aunt Agnes Moorehead joining irresistibly in the fun; the huge open-air party, women with cakes and jams and jellies counter-chorusing men swigging tankards of ale; the lyrical polka of the young lovers across a bright green expanse of lawn; the 4th of July scenes and the graduation ceremony, beautifully authentic and apt; the adolescent boy (Mickey Rooney) growing drunk in a saloon, seeing a floozie (Marilyn Maxwell) grow larger and redder and more alarming with every successive drink. The film was a formal abstract of American youth and the beauty of a family life gone forever, tenderly done, photographed in rich colours by Charles Schoenbaum.

But Freed's greatest triumph of all was *On the Town*, made a year later, directed by Gene Kelly and Stanley Donen from Leonard Bernstein's Broadway musical. A wharf labourer wanders onto the New York waterfront, singing an early morning song; three sailors (Frank Sinatra, Jules Munshin and Gene Kelly) dance gleefully across the pier, singing "New York! New York! It's a Wonderful Town!" — from this exhilarating opening, the film never ceases to sparkle. It moves all over the city, to the top of the Empire State, to the Bronx and the Battery, to the Public Library and the back streets of Greenwich Village. Harold Rosson's bright primary-coloured camerawork pans and swoops dizzyingly as the sailors with their three girl friends (Ann Miller, Betty Garrett, Vera-Ellen) Kick Back The Traces and go On The Town, bantering, bickering, laughing and finally kissing goodbye.

Notable among the film's many wonderful numbers are "Prehistoric Man", led by an exuberant Ann Miller, healthiest of American dancers, dazzlingly tap danced by the cast through the ancient creatures of a museum; Frank Sinatra's duet with Betty Garrett as a predatory taxi driver ("Come up to my Place") with its excellent use of the New York guide book as a basis for the lyrics; the Miss Turnstiles ballet, in which Kelly sees Vera-Ellen in a subway advertisement which comes to life, sung and danced in spare impressionist sets suggesting the imagined life of a successful city girl; and the tour of the nightclubs in montage, featuring Alice Pearce, gloriously funny throughout as an ugly, adenoidal girl whom nobody wants ("I'm just a Streetcar named Impulsive"). Best of all is the effervescent gaiety of the scene when the cast dance out of the Empire State Building and through Manhattan, singing the title song ("We're Really Living, Jack, We're Going on the Town!").

Similar and perhaps influential in mood and pace was the earlier *Anchors Aweigh* (1945), directed by George Sidney, starring Gene Kelly and Frank Sinatra, and also dealing with a story of sailors on leave. Elaborately staged on Californian locations, the film — full of daring crane-shots, studded with memorable dances including Gene Kelly's duo with a little girl (Sharon McManus) and another cleverly combining live action and animation — suffered from Sidney's vulgarity and an overall crudity of presentation not wholly compensated for by the opulent scale of the images.

On an altogether lower level were Paramount's *Blue Skies* and *Holiday Inn* and many M-G-M musicals featuring Esther Williams, Jane Powell, Kathryn Grayson, Jose Iturbi, Lauritz Melchior and other light or "serious" performers, all blended together to show that even the great could let their hair down when the lion roared. Vulgar, inept and lifeless, these films were worlds removed from the sophistication of Freed's better efforts.

At Columbia, Charles Vidor's *Cover Girl* (1944) was certainly one of the best musicals of the period. It combined two elements: a light-hearted examination of the world of fashion, dealt with in a vein of purest fantasy — the heroine, Rusty Parker (Rita Hayworth) is translated from Brooklyn singer to cover girl for the Golden Wedding issue of *Vanity Magazine* — and an evocation of back-stage life, observed with equal non-realism. It was ideal escapist fare for G.I's and those at home in the last year but one of the war.

The best numbers rise above the rest: in "Make Way for Tomorrow", written, like the rest of the excellent score, by Ira Gershwin and Jerome Kern, the stars — Rita Hayworth, Gene Kelly and Phil Silvers — dance in a burst of optimistic exuberance out of a restaurant and down a street, using dustbins, a milkman and a drunk as part of the routine, prancing up and down steps; the number was nicely designed by Kelly himself. The stagier numbers, set in Danny McGuire's Nightclub in Brooklyn, are less pleasing, but Kelly's dance with his *Doppelgänger*

The film that established its director's reputation: Vincente Minnelli's MEET ME IN ST. LOUIS, with a dreamy Judy Garland (at right) being watched by her mother (Mary Astor) and sister (Lucille Bremer).

The cast of SUMMER HOLIDAY, Rouben Mamoulian's masterpiece of Americana: Agnes Moorehead, Frank Morgan, Gloria De Haven, Butch Jenkins, Mickey Rooney, Marilyn Maxwell and Walter Huston.

The greatest triumph of producer Arthur Freed: ON THE TOWN, co-directed by Stanley Donen and Gene Kelly. Betty Garrett, Ann Miller and Vera-Ellen are backed by Frank Sinatra, Jules Munshin and Gene Kelly.

Hazel Scott sings "The Man I Love" in Warners' life of Gershwin, RHAPSODY IN BLUE, adroitly directed by Irving Rapper.

through the Brooklyn streets at 3 a.m., the figure arguing with him from shop windows, finally dancing down to join him in a duet, is justly famous.

Of other Columbia musicals of the time, *Down to Earth* (1947) was a prettily shot sequel to the same director Alexander Hall's *Here Comes Mr. Jordan*, culminating in a pleasant number in which Rita Hayworth (as the muse Terpsichore, brought to earth) dances with the sensationally talented Mark Platt across a playground filled with whirling autumn leaves. The accompanying song has arguably the silliest lyrics in screen history ("People have more fun than anyone"), but the pastel-coloured visuals are very pleasing.

At 20th Century-Fox, the period was launched with enormous *élan*. Irving Cummings, former actor-cum-gifted craftsman who had made the excellent *Hollywood Cavalcade* in 1939, Walter Lang, accomplished director of Shirley Temple's classic children's film *The Little Princess*, the great art directors Wiard Ihnen, Richard Day and James Basevi and the famous cameramen Ernest Palmer and J. Peverell Marley threw a remarkable amount of expertise into the creation of a vividly exciting series of films unjustly eclipsed (historically) by their Metro counterparts. The studio commanded the talents of Betty Grable, Alice Faye, Carmen Miranda, Jack Haley, Jack Oakie, Phil Silvers, June Haver and many other musical stars. Its colour processing was easily the best in Hollywood, its tones astonishingly vivid and immediate. These razor-sharp images, reds glowing as from the heart of a furnace, greens more brilliant than any seen on the motion picture screen, created a hallucinatory effect like those seen under psychedelic drugs.

Best of all these surrealistic, high-powered Fox films was *The Gang's All Here* (1943), directed by Busby Berkeley, on loan from M-G-M. He re-created with an added touch of brilliance the fantasy world of his best films at Warners in the Thirties: a world of kaleidoscopic patterns of female flesh, dissolving into artichokes, exploding stars, snowflakes and the expanding leaves of water-lilies. With Fox's matchless technical resources he had a field-day, and his talents have never been so totally unleashed before or since. The story is piffle, about a girl in pursuit of a handsome soldier, but this is just a thin excuse for Busby Berkeley's string of tropically rich and exotic kinaesthetic effects.

From the opening, the film is electrifyingly staged. At the top left-hand corner of a dark screen, a Latin American tenor in cameo cut-out sings "Brazil". The circular image, in a more sophisticated development of a technique first worked out in *Gold Diggers of 1935*, moves round the frame and across a diagonal series of bamboo canes. The camera swings up in a gigantic and exhilarating crane-shot over the S.S. Brazil, arriving in New York harbour. Passengers bustle down the gangway; the camera swoops down a huge bunch of fruit to take in the fruit salad hat of Carmen Miranda. In a later number, she sings *The Lady in the Tutti Frutti Hat*: organ grinders' monkeys crawl through artificial palm-trees at the Club New Yorker, the camera moves across a tropical island set, covered in yellow-clad girls who whirl gigantic phallic bananas or turn them into a banana xylophone; finally Carmen Miranda, initially singing the number on top of a waggon in a hat and corsage of bananas and strawberries, is left in an avenue of strawberries five foot high with a cornucopia of bananas sprouting from her head: can surrealism go further?

Perhaps the weirdest of all the film's numbers is the Polka Dot Ballet, introduced by Alice Faye. A child wears a metal sleeve electrically illuminated, which dissolves into a succession of metal hoops, glowing brilliantly as they wind away into a pitch-dark screen, accompanied by a sumptuous and exotic arrangement for strings. Girls in mauve leotards swing the hoops above their heads in an effect of extraordinary daring and beauty; others slowly revolve polka-dots like gambling counters, pink, green, mauve and white. Finally, Busby Berkeley revels in an orgy of bizarre effects as the figure of a blue-skirted girl is split into four, refracted again and again as in the splintered images of a kaleidoscope. Amber and gold, snowdrop and clover-leaf: the colour in its surrealist patterns achieves something of the intensity described by Huxley under mescalin. Finally, the cast emerge from the centre of the kaleidoscope in cut-out, singing *A Journey to a Star* until the whole screen bubbles with tiny heads.

Far simpler, but almost equally diverting, is *Moon Over Miami* (1941), directed by Walter Lang, shot in gaudy peacock colours by Leon Shamroy and J. Peverell Marley, designed by Wiard Ihnen and Richard Day to create a hallucinatory Miami still more extravagantly decorative than the real place. The film opens with a dance, as two singing waitresses, Kay and Barbara Latimer (Betty Grable and Carole Landis), and their cook, the indispensable Charlotte Greenwood, greet guests at their Texas drive-in hamburger stand. They come into a small inheritance, spend the lot on a lavish wardrobe, and head for Miami to capture millionaires: their cheerful American ruthlessness is wittily observed. At Miami, they finally hook "the Miamese twins" — Robert Cummings, heir to 20 million dollars, and Don Ameche, pretending to be rich after the failure of his father's factory. The plot's complications arise from the girls' attempts to pin down their prey.

Perhaps the most striking feature of the film is how much it is ahead of its time, pre-dating *On The Town*, which in many ways resembles it in its use of free dancing through sets and locations. When the three women arrive at their Miami hotel, they dance right across their suite singing with delightful enthusiasm, "Oh me, Oh Mi — ami". The songs flow naturally out of the action, expertly wedded to the dialogue (in particular the Jack Haley-Charlotte Greenwood number "Is That Good?" written with brilliant wit by Leo Robin), and the introduction of Miami is dazzling: shot with iridescent gaiety as director and cameraman create an exciting feeling of discovery, a 'plane flying across a beach past a luxurious hotel, a man swimming across a glowing emerald pool shot from far above, a row of flamingoes, horses spanking down a race-track, accompanied by a male chorus exultantly singing "Miami, Here I Am!" A visit to an underwater aquarium, a motor-boat race shot with great lightness and ease in overhead tracking shots through the everglades; this is a film of irresistible American energy and verve, orchestrated to perfection by Alfred Newman, electrifyingly recorded, especially in the "Conga to a Nursery Rhyme" number expertly danced by Betty Grable and the chorus in an hotel lounge.

Whether in the series of films set in exciting locations — *Springtime in the Rockies, That Night in Rio, Down Argentine Way* — or in their films nostalgic for the past — *State Fair, The Dolly Sisters, Greenwich Village, Coney Island, Hello, 'Frisco, Hello* — the Fox product often shared *Moon Over Miami's* pace and effervescence. Worth remembering, too, is an enchanting minor work, *Young People* (1940), directed by Allan Dwan, with Shirley Temple, Jack Oakie and Charlotte Greenwood in a back-stage story incomparably superior to similar films being done at the time at Metro. The half-sad, half-comical scene when the show business parents and their small daughter execute a dance in a shabby room; the little sequence in the car when they tell her she is an adopted child; a wonderfully realistic storm: here seems full justification for the Gallic passion for Dwan's films.

At Warners, the emphasis was, early in the period, on biographies of light composers: *Rhapsody in Blue* (1945) was the story of Gershwin, *Yankee Doodle Dandy* (1942) of George M. Cohan, *This Is The Army* (1943) was dedicated to Irving Berlin, and *Night and Day* (1946) dealt with a fantasy Cole Porter (M-G-M offered equally fake "lives" of Jerome Kern and Rodgers and Hart). Of these Warner biographies, only the first is really worthy of mention, although the early Christmas scenes and the charming Ginny Simms emerged splendidly from *Night and Day*, uneasily handled by Curtiz. *Rhapsody in Blue*, though, was an entirely different proposition. The second half may have flagged, and the central character of Gershwin was deliberately softened, but Jesse L. Lasky's glittering production values, Irving Rapper's adroit virtuoso direction and the razor-edged photography of Sol Polito with its unusually hard blacks and whites made this a very watchable film.

The schmaltzy story, knowingly written by Howard Koch and Elliott Paul from a treatment by Sonia Levien, probably had little to do with the fiercely ambitious career of the real Gershwin, dead in his thirties, but the direction at all times rose above the script. This is a "big" professional picture from the word go, with the feeling of an entire studio's resources behind it. The presentation is frequently in the grandest manner: the breathtaking slow dolly shot through the french windows of a Parisian salon as Hazel Scott in a white dress at a piano sings *The*

Man I Love magnificently in French, the room glittering with jewels and alive with conversation; the inception of *An American in Paris*, the camera following subjectively the composer's discovery of the city, marred only slightly by the use of stock-shots; the stage performance of *Blue Monday Blues*, sung and danced by a marvellous all-Negro cast, choreographed to perfection by LeRoy Prinz; the big set-piece of the performance of *Rhapsody in Blue*, harking deliberately back to the Thirties in its use of silhouetted instrumentalists and gigantic shadows; the final extraordinary shot at the culmination of the *Concerto in F*, when the camera seems to rise from the keyboard at the Lewisohn Stadium, up, up into the clouds.

Biographies of more "serious" composers were altogether less happy. At Columbia, Charles Vidor directed *A Song to Remember* (1945), a farrago based supposedly on the life of Chopin, who became a strapping athlete to a George Sand of raving beauty, glossy hair and natty suitings. The script, by Sidney Buchman, was a disaster, and the playing by Merle Oberon, Cornel Wilde and Paul Muni dismally inept. As a room is darkened for a recital, a chorus of gardeners, rapt beyond the french windows, hisses one by one, "Sh-hh! Liszt!" George Sand informs her lover with a toothpaste advertisement smile, "You could make miracles of music in Majorca", or instructs him in a much misquoted line: "Discontinue that so-called Polonaise jumble you've been playing for days." Finally, the unfortunate composer is advised that "to make this tour is literally and actually suicide." He undertakes it, coughs photogenic blood on to the piano keys, and dies. George Sand learns of his illness while her portrait is being painted. "Continue, M. Delacroix!" she orders haughtily after this tiresome interruption.

At Universal, Jean-Pierre Aumont played Rimsky-Korsakoff in Walter Reisch's *Song of Scheherezade* (1947), at Metro Katharine Hepburn, Robert Walker and Paul Henreid played feebly the roles of Clara Schumann, Brahms and Robert Schumann in *Song of Love* (1947) — a film so careless of its audience that it squandered the whole of the first reel on a Clara Schumann recital (attended, inevitably, by Liszt) and kept its cast on all fours with babies and the catching of a fowl for dinner for the next two. These are the kinds of movies which Hollywood's enemies like to recall. And so, too, the dreadful *Lady in the Dark* (1944), which, unlike another Weill adaptation, Universal's witty *One Touch of Venus* (1948) with Ava Gardner as a statue that comes to life in a department store, was a vulgar and monstrous betrayal of the composer's genius.

By the middle and late Forties, the musical (away from Metro) had begun a slow decline: Warners were making the slickly empty Doris Day series, Fox had lost its touch and was mounting silly folderols like *Diamond Horseshoe*. Within a few years, the ugliness of DeLuxe Color was to swamp all memories of Fox's brilliant Technicolor heyday in an ocean of feeble blues and pinks and purples. CinemaScope was to come, with all the boring scripts and flat direction and lack of energy that marked its advent. And then, as the Fifties wore on, the musical original virtually died to be replaced in the Sixties by the mammoth recreations of Broadway hits, commercially successful, soulless, and mounted with all the vulgarity of the new decade.

Index *(Major references to films appear in bold type)*

Abbott, Bud 14, 167, 168
Abbott, John 14, 106, 114, 120
Abe Lincoln in Illinois 105, **108**
Above Suspicion 87, 90, 92
Action in the North Atlantic 96
Act of Murder, An 85
Act of Violence 49
Adam's Rib 162, **163**
Address Unknown 89, 91
Adventure 153
Adventures of Don Juan **125**
Adventures of Mark Twain **111**
Adventures of Robin Hood **124, 125**

Ah, Wilderness! 79, 101, 114, 174
Air Force 97
Albert, Eddie 107
Allbritton, Louise 11
Ali Baba and the Forty Thieves 130
All About Eve 169
Allen, Lewis 34, 57
All that Money Can Buy 51, 54
All the King's Men 69, 74, 79
All This and Heaven Too 141
All Through the Night 93
Alton, John 67, 129
Amazing Mr. X, The 52, 66-7
Ameche, Don 88, 140, 179

American in Paris, An 181
Amphitheatrof, Daniele 85
Anchors Aweigh 176
Anderson, Eddie ("Rochester") 56, 173
Anderson, Judith 25, 44, 93, 122, 135
Anderson, Maxwell 112
Andrews, Dana 75, 84, 96, 137
Andrews Sisters, The 11
Andriot, Lucien 122
Angel on My Shoulder 50, 51, 55
Ankers, Evelyn 11
Another Part of the Forest 116
Ape, The 65

Arden, Eve 11, 26
Ardrey, Robert 121
Arise My Love 159
Armendariz, Pedro 134
Arsenic and Old Lace 161
Arthur, Jean 169
Astaire, Fred 171, 173, 174
Asther, Nils 66
Astor, Mary 20, 37, 141, 143, 158
Atlantide, L' 64
Atwill, Lionel 50, 51, 63
Auer, Mischa 161
August, Joseph 57, 99
Aumont, Jean-Pierre 181
Ayres, Lew 151

Babes in Arms 172
Babes on Broadway 172
Bacall, Lauren 9, 38, 39
Bachelin, Franz 75
Bacon, Lloyd 96
Bainter, Fay 43, 117
Balderston, John L. 118, 119
Ballard, Lucien 21, 32, 33
Bambi 12
Bandit of Sherwood Forest, The 128
Bank Dick, The 167
Bankhead, Tallulah 95
Bari, Lynn 11, 66
Barnes, Binnie 128
Barnes, George 120, 131
Barrett, Edith 43, 121
Barrymore, Ethel 75, 123
Barrymore, John 75, 93
Barrymore, Lionel 75, 133
Basehart, Richard 129
Basevi, James 127, 177
Bassermann, Albert 11, 45, 75, 107, 119
Bates, Florence 38, 55, 101, 160, 170
Battleground 97
Battle of San Pietro, The 86
Baxter, Alan 48
Baxter, Anne 10, 96, 97, 137, 152
Beast With Five Fingers, The 51, 58
Beautiful Blonde from Bashful Bend, The 159
Bedlam 61
Bedoya, Alfonso 136
Beebe, Ford 64
Bel Geddes, Barbara 41, 42
Belita 11
Bells of St. Marys, The 55
Bendix, William 115
Bend of the River 131

Bennett, Charles 34, 95
Bennett, Compton 119
Bennett, Joan 24, 42, 117
Benny, Jack 56, 94
Berger, Ludwig 52, 53
Bergman, Ingrid 36, 44, 65, 102, 105, 112, 117
Bergner, Elisabeth 146
Berkeley, Busby 10, 172, 177, 178, 179
Berman, Pandro S. 121
Bernhardt, Curtis 9, 19, 104, 110, 146, 149
Berry, John 41
Bessie, Alvah 96
Best Years of Our Lives, The 84
Bete Humaine, La 122
Beyond the Forest 146
Bey, Turhan 10, 43, 64, 66
Biberman, Herbert 91
Bickford, Charles 70
Big Clock, The 45
Big Sleep, The 38
Bill and Coo 139
Birds, The 139
Birell, Tala 63
Biro, Lajos 52
Biroc, Joseph 56
Biscuit Eater, The 138
Blackboard Jungle, The 69
Black Swan, The 126, 127
Blaine, Ralph 173, 174
Blair, Betsy 83
Blanke, Henry 9, 105, 114
Blondell, Joan 28, 51, 56
Blood and Sand 126
Blore, Eric 44, 157
Blossoms in the Dust 69, 81, 153
Blue Bird, The 51, 52, 53, 54, 172
Blue Dahlia, The 38
Blue Skies 176
Blues in the Night 40
Bodeen, DeWitt 59, 62
Body and Soul 48, 49
Body Snatcher, The 60
Bogart, Humphrey 9, 37, 38, 39, 84, 96, 101, 136, 150
Bois, Curt 41, 106, 114, 128, 130
Bondi, Beulah 117, 137
Boomerang! 68, 80
Borg, Veda Ann 11
Borzage, Frank 88, 112, 128
Boyer, Charles 36, 40, 63, 121, 141
Bracken, Eddie 158, 159
Brackett, Charles 5, 159
Brahm, John 31

Brecht, Bertolt 87, 89, 104
Bredell, Woody 23
Bremer, Lucille 173, 174
Brennan, Walter 130, 131, 134, 137
Breslow, Lou 164
Bressart, Felix 94
Brian, David 146
Bridge of San Luis Rey, The 117
Bridge on the River Kwai 87
Brigham Young 131
Britten, Benjamin 146
Broadway Melody 170, 171
Brodie, Steve 77
Broken Blossoms 31
Bronston, Samuel 111, 112
Brooke, Hillary 62
Brooks, Geraldine 42, 85
Brooks, Jean 60
Brower, Otto 133
Brown, Clarence 69, 79, 95, 106, 137, 138, 174
Brown, Harry 98
Brown, Joe E. 14
Brown, Nacio Herb 171
Bruce, Nigel 54, 107, 130
Brute Force 69, 81
Buchman, Sidney 181
Buckner, Robert 40
Buffalo Bill 131
Bugs Bunny 12
Buried Alive 161
Burke, Billie 56
Busch, Niven 29
Butler, David 135
Byington, Spring 11

Cabinet of Dr. Caligari, The 58, 87
Cabin in the Sky 172
Cabot, Bruce 162
Cagney, James 11
California 135
Call Northside 777 68, 81
Camille 162
Canova, Judy 11
Canterville Ghost, The 51, 56
Capra, Frank 55, 72, 73, 103, 110, 161
Captain Blood 124
Captain from Castile 127
Carey, Harry 133, 134
Carlson, Richard 67
Carradine, John 52, 65, 70, 89, 91, 126
Carrere, Edward 48
Casablanca 19, 44, 86, 89, 101
Cat and the Canary, The 164

Cat People 59, 60, 64
Caught 41
Centennial Summer 171
Chamberlin, Howland 49
Champagne Waltz 167
Champion 48
Chandler, Raymond 36, 37, 38
Chaney, Lon, Jr. 51, 70, 71
Chaplin, Charles 93, 163, 164
Charley's Aunt 160
Chase, Borden 132
Chenal, Pierre 29
Chienne, La 122
Christians, Mady 100
Christie, Audrey 73
Christmas Holiday 23
Christmas in Connecticut 149
Christmas in July 156
Cimarron 132
Citizen Kane 8, 11, 60, 109, 110
Clair, René 9, 56, 67, 95, 161
Clark, Dane 145
Clarke, Charles G. 75, 162
Clift, Montgomery 116, 132
Climax, The 64
Cline, Edward L. 166
Cloak and Dagger 93
Clouzot, Henri-Georges 122
Cobra Woman 145
Coburn, Charles 112, 157, 169
Cohn, Harry 9
Colbert, Claudette 97, 100, 139, 158
Coleman, Nancy 94, 110, 149
Collier, Constance 126, 160
Collier, John 144
Collins, Eddie 54
Colman, Ronald 153, 169
Colmes, Walter 62
Coney Island 171, 180
Confidential Agent 40
Conflict 24
Conte, Richard 24, 81
Conway, Jack 98
Conway, Tom 59, 60
Cook, Elisha, Jr. 38, 43
Cooper, Gary 47, 93, 117, 130, 135
Cooper, Gladys 108, 142, 143
Copland, Aaron 71, 96, 138
Corbeau, Le 122

Corey, Jeff 78
Corey, Wendell 9
Cornell, Katharine 14
Corsican Brothers, The 128
Cortez, Stanley 63, 100, 118
Costello, Lou 167, 168
Cotten, Joseph 21, 57, 110, 133, 146
Coulouris, George 99
Covered Wagon, The 132
Cover Girl 176
Cowan, Jerome 119
Crack-Up 18
Craig, James 54
Crain, Jeanne 78, 162, 170
Crawford, Broderick 69, 74
Crawford, Joan 8, 9, 14, 26, 27, 47, 91, 139, 140, 146, 148, 149, 154
Crazy House 166
Cregar, Laird 11, 32, 33, 39, 51, 54, 55, 127, 160
Crews, Laura Hope 54
Crime Does Not Pay series 13
Criss Cross 24
Cromwell, John 19, 62, 100, 101, 107, 118, 126
Crosby, Bing 166, 168
Crossfire 11, 68, 76, 77
Cry of the City 24
Cry of the Werewolf 64
Cry Wolf 150
Cukor, George 8, 34, 72, 147, 154, 162, 163
Cummings, Irving 10, 171, 177
Cummings, Robert 31, 63, 106, 115, 129, 179
Curse of the Cat People, The 60
Curtis, Alan 88
Curtiz, Michael 9, 19, 20, 26, 101, 102, 105, 110, 113, 124, 129, 161, 180
Czinner, Paul 146

D'Agostino, Albert S. 59
Dahl, Arlene 129
Daley, Cass 166
Dalio, Marcel 45
Dall, John 22
Damned Don't Cry, The 27
Daniell, Henry 23, 61, 99, 120, 128, 129
Daniels, William 39
Dantine, Helmut 91
Dark Mirror, The 24, 145
Dark Passage 20, 39

Dark Past, The 18
Dark Waters 43
Darnell, Linda 67, 105, 110, 123, 125, 126, 169, 170
Darwell, Jane 69, 70, 71
Dassin, Jules 13, 49, 56, 69, 81, 92
Davenport, Harry 126
Daves, Delmer 38, 97
David Copperfield 162
Davis, Bette 8, 9, 11, 47, 99, 116, 139, 140, 141, 142, 143, 144, 145, 146, 154, 161, 167
Davis, Joan 11
Day, Doris 182
Day, Richard 126, 127, 177, 179
Days of Glory 96
Dead End 84
Deception 141, 144
Deep Valley 152, 153
Defiant Ones, The 80
De Havilland, Olivia 83, 84, 110, 116, 145, 152
Dekker, Albert 66
Del Rio, Dolores 104
Del Ruth, Roy 56
Demarest, William 158
DeMille, Cecil B. 97, 129, 135, 167
Derek, John 69, 84
Dernier Tournant, Le 29
De Rochemont, Louis 13, 68, 79, 80
Desert Fox, The 87
Desperate Journey 91, 96
Destination Tokyo 97
Destry Rides Again 136
De Sylva, Buddy 9
De Toth, Andre 43
Deutsch, Helen 121
Devil and Daniel Webster, The—see All That Money Can Buy
Devil and Miss Jones, The 169
Devotion 110
Diamond Horseshoe 182
Diary of a Chambermaid 122
Dieterle, William 54, 57, 74, 75, 104, 107, 132, 133
Dietrich, Marlene 136, 161, 162, 167
Digges, Dudley 75, 126
Dingle, Charles 96
Dinner at Eight 162
Disney, Walt 12, 13
Dispatch from Reuters, A 107

Dmytryk, Edward 38, 76, 77, 91, 100
Dr. Cyclops **66**
Dr. Ehrlich's Magic Bullet **107**
Dr. Jekyll and Mr. Hyde 65
Dolly Sisters, The 180
Donald Duck 12
Donen, Stanley 8, 171, 175
Donlevy, Brian 55
Donnelly, Ruth 83
Double Indemnity 21, **28**, 36, 38, 150
Douglas, Kirk 9, 49, 170
Douglas, Melvyn 123
Douglas, Paul 169, 170
Douglas, Robert 125
Dowling, Constance 167
Down Argentine Way 179
Down to Earth 55, **177**
Dracula 63
Dragon Seed 98
Dratler, Jay 25
Dreier, Hans 75, 129, 154
Dreigroschenoper, Die 63, 89
Duel in the Sun 48, **132**, 133, 134
Dumbo 12
Dumbrille, Douglass 130
Dunne, Irene 56, 95
Dunne, Philip 78, 126
Duprez, June 52
Durbin, Deanna 10, 23
Duryea, Dan 20, 24
Duvivier, Julien 63
Dvorak, Ann 122
Dwan, Allan 180

Eagels, Jeanne 142
Easy Living 156, 159
Edeson, Arthur 37, 102
Edge of Darkness 90, 94, 96, 98
Edison, the Man 106, **107**
Edwards, James 78
Eldridge, Florence 86
Eleventh Hour, The 86
Elsom, Isobel 43
Emerson, Hope 24
Emery, John 55, 114, 128
Enright, Ray 136
Epstein, Julius J. 102
Epstein, Philip G. 102
Ericson, Helen 54
Ernst, George 88
Escape 87, 88
Everybody Does It 19, **169**
Exile, The 128

Face Behind the Mask, The 64
Face of Marble 65
Fairbanks, Douglas, Jr. 124, 127, 128
Fairbanks, Douglas, Sr. 14, 124
Fallen Angel 25
Fantasia 12
Farrar, Geraldine 104
Farrow, John 45, 66, 87, 90, 135
Faulkner, William 69, 79, 104
Faust 54
Faye, Alice 11, 177, 178
Fegte, Ernst 129
Feld, Fritz 11, 93, 118
Feldman, Charles K. 121
Fenton, Leslie 99
Fernandez, Juano 79
Ferrer, Jose 112
Ferrer, Mel 79
Field, Betty 31, 63, 70, 71, 116, 118, 137
Fields, W. C. 166, 167
Fitzgerald, Barry 50, 114
Fitzgerald, Geraldine 24, 40, 112, 149
Fitzpatrick, James A. 13
Five Graves to Cairo 87, 97
Flame of New Orleans, The 8, 161
Fleischer, Max 13
Fleming, Victor 56, 112, 171
Flesh and Fantasy 51, 63, 66
Florey, Robert 58, 64
Flynn, Errol 11, 96, 124, 125, 130, 135, 150
Foch, Nina 64
Fodor, Ladislas 123
Follow the Boys 167
Fonda, Henry 14, 69, 70, 108, 131, 134, 156
Fontaine, Joan 33, 123, 129, 151
Force of Evil **49**
Ford, Glenn 46, 121, 135, 145
Ford, John 8, 69, 70, 71, 99, 108, 130, 134, 135, 137
Foreman, Carl 78
Foreign Correspondent 87, 88, 89
Forever Amber 128
Forever and a Day 95
Fort Apache 134
42nd Street 171
For Whom the Bell Tolls 117
Foster, Susanna, 51, 64

Fountainhead, The **47**
Four Sons 88
Francen, Victor 40
Francis, Kay 14
Frank, Leonhard 104
Frankenstein 63
Franklin, Sidney 105, 133
Freed, Arthur 171, 174, 175, 176
Freeman, Howard 84
Frenchman's Creek 129
Freund, Karl 81
Friedhofer, Hugo 32
Frozen Ghost, The 63
Frye, William 67
Fülöp-Miller, René 113, 123
Furthman, Jules 27
Fury **71**, 79

Gabel, Martin 115
Gable, Clark 8, 14, 153
Gang's All Here, The **177-8**
Garde, Betty 81
Gardiner, Reginald 161
Gardner, Ava 123, 182
Garfield, John 29, **48**, 78, 97, 114, 148
Garland, Judy 171, 172, 173, 174
Garmes, Lee 21, 22, 28, 41, 100, 132
Garnett, Tay 29, 136, 153
Garrett, Betty 175
Garson, Greer 8, 81, 95, 105, 113, 119, 140, 153, 154
Gaslight 21, **34**, 163
Gaudio, Tony 21, 142
Gay Sisters, The 149
Genn, Leo 83
Gentleman's Agreement 68, 77, 78
Gershwin, George 171, 180
Gershwin, Ira 96, 176, 177, 180
Getting Gertie's Garter 161
Ghost and Mrs. Muir, The 51, 56
Ghost Breakers, The 164
Ghost Ship, The 60
Gibbons, Cedric 154
Gilda 10, 45, 46, 122
Gish, Lillian 133
Glass Key, The 38
Gleason, James 55
Glennon, Bert 117
Goddard, Paulette 9, 11, 93, 97, 135, 136, 160
Godfrey, Peter 91, 105, 114, 150

Goetz, Augustus 115
Goetz, Ruth 115
Going My Way 9
Gold Diggers of 1935 178
Goldfinger 61
Goldwyn, Samuel 84, 85, 105
Gomez, Thomas 49, 64
Gone With the Wind 7, 132, 140
Goodman, John 22
Goodrich, Frances 90, 174
Goofy 12
Gordon, Michael 85, 116
Gordon, Ruth 108, 163
Goulding, Edmund 10, 19, 27, 95, 151, 152, 169
Grable, Betty 10, 159, 171, 177, 179, 180
Grahame, Gloria 56, 77
Granach, Alexander 90
Grand Hotel 91
Grapes of Wrath, The 68, 69-70, 137
Grapewin, Charles 69, 71
Grayson, Kathryn 176
Great Dictator, The 93
Great Gatsby, The 116
Great Lie, The 140, 143
Great Man's Lady, The 131
Great McGinty, The 156
Great Moment, The 113
Great Sinner, The 45, **123**
Greene, W. Howard 81
Green Grass of Wyoming 138
Greenstreet, Sydney 37, 40, 102, 106, 111, 114, 149
Greenwich Village 171, 180
Greenwood, Charlotte 161, 179, 180
Grot, Anton 113
Guadalcanal Diary 98
Guest in the House 18
Guffey, Burnett 42
Gulliver's Travels 13
Gun Crazy 18
Guy Named Joe, A 51, 56
Gwenn, Edmund 88
Gypsy Wildcat 130

Haas, Hugo 123
Hackett, Albert 90, 174
Hail the Conquering Hero **159**
Hairy Ape, The 115
Hale, Alan 125
Haley, Jack 177, 179
Hall, Alexander 55, 177
Hall, Jon 10, 130

Hall, Porter 11, 164, 165
Haller, Ernest 9, 21, 145, 148, 151
Hangmen Also Die 87, 91, 94
Hangover Square 31, 33, 123
Hard Way, The 152
Harding, Ann 96
Hardwicke, Sir Cedric 66, 89, 90, 98, 112, 118
Hardy, Oliver 93
Harrison, Joan 22
Harrison, Rex 51, 56
Hart, Moss 77
Hart, William S. 130
Hartman, Don 168
Harvey Girls, The 171
Hatcher, Mary 166
Hatfield, Hurd 66
Hathaway, Henry 80, 81, 131, 138
Haver, June 177
Havoc, June 75, 165
Hawks, Howard 8, 38, 97, 132, 158
Haydn, Richard 170
Hayes, George "Gabby" 135
Hayward, Louis 44
Hayward, Susan 83, 106, 111, 115
Hayworth, Rita 10, 29, 46, 47, 121, 126, 176, 177
Hayakawa, Sessue 87
Heaven Can Wait 51, 55, 160
Heckle and Jeckle 12
Heflin, Van 121, 149
Heiress, The **115**
Heisler, Stuart 54, 83, 138, 139
Hellinger, Mark 69, 81
Hellman, Lillian 74, 75, 96, 99, 116
Hello, 'Frisco, Hello 171, 180
Hellzapoppin **166**
Henreid, Paul 111, 128, 143, 144, 181
Hepburn, Katharine 72, 73, 99, 139, 163, 181
Here Comes Mr. Jordan 50, 55, 173, 177
Herring Murder Mystery, The 12
Herrmann, Bernard 120
Hickman, Darryl 151
Hickox, Sid 39
Hicks, Russell 53
Hi Diddle Diddle **165**
High Wall, The 18

High Window, The 38
His Girl Friday 148
Hitchcock, Alfred 21, 31, 44, 88, 89, 95, 139
Hitler Gang, The 87, **90**
Hitler's Children 91
Hitler's Madman 91
Hoch, Winton 134
Hodiak, John 95
Hoffenstein, Samuel 25
Hoffman, David 63
Hogan, James 91
Hold Back the Dawn 159
Holden, William 55, 117
Holiday Inn 176
Holland, Frederick 42, 119
Holliday, Judy 163
Hollywood Canteen 14, 167
Hollywood Cavalcade 177
Holm, Celeste 77, 83, 169, 170
Holmes, Taylor 27
Holt, Tim 136
Holy Matrimony 161
Home of the Brave 68, **78**
Homeier, Skip 99
Home in Indiana 138
Homestretch 138
Homolka, Oscar 94
Hope, Bob 14, 168
Hopkins, Miriam 116
Hornbeck, William 56
Horn Blows at Midnight, The 56
Horton, Edward Everett 55, 123
Hostages 90, 94
Hot Spot 39
Hotel Berlin 91
Houseman, John 105, 120
House on 92nd Street, The 68, 80
Howe, James Wong 21, 31, 96, 135, 152
How Green Was My Valley 8, 18, 90
Hubbard, John 51, 67
Hudson's Bay 135
Hughes, Howard 17
Hughes, Mary Beth 11
Hull, Henry 47, 71, 95
Human Monster 65
Humberstone, Bruce 39, 138, 171
Humoresque **148**
Hunter, Kim 60
Huston, John 37, 40, 76, 107, 136, 143
Huston, Walter 44, 51, 54, 96, 98, 103, 123, 134, 137
Huxley, Aldous 104, 120, 121, 179

I Dood It 173
I Married A Witch 56
I Remember Mama 161
I Stand Accused—see *An Act of Murder*
I Walked With a Zombie 59
If I Were King 156
Ihnen, Wiard 177, 179
In This Our Life 143
Ingram, Rex 52, 53
Intruder in the Dust 67, 79
Invisible Agent 64
Invisible Man Returns, The 64
Invisible Man's Revenge, The 64
Invisible Woman, The 64
Iron Curtain, The 16, **75**
Isherwood, Christopher 104, 123, 147, 152
Island of Lost Souls 12
Isle of the Dead **61**
It Happened Tomorrow 51, 67
It's A Wonderful Life 51, **55**
Iturbi, Jose 176
Ivan, Rosalind 23, 40
Ivano, Paul 45, 63
Ivy 33, 35, 46, 151

Jack London **111**
Jackson, Frederick 165
Jane Eyre 59, 104, 105, 106, 110, 111, **120**
Jannings, Emil 54
Jarman, Claude, Jr. 137
Jazz Singer, The 170
Jean, Gloria 11
Jesse James 131
Jezebel 140
Joan of Arc 105, 112
Johnny Belinda 153
Johnson, Chic 166, 168
Johnson, Nunnally 69, 71, 161
Johnson, Rita 46, 55
Johnson, Van 56, 73
Jolson, Al 14
Jolson Story, The 128
Jones, Jennifer 57, 76, 100, 101, 105, 121, 133
Jones, Spike 166
Joslyn, Allyn 94
Jourdan, Louis 123
Joyce, Brenda 11
Jungle Book, The 118
Justin, John 52

Kanin, Garson 163

Kaper, Bronislau 21, 36
Karinska 174
Karloff, Boris 50, 52, 60, 61, 64, 65
Katch, Kurt 99
Kaye, Danny 167
Kazan, Elia 78, 80
Keaton, Buster 159
Keeper of the Flame **72**
Keighley, William 81, 161
Keith, Ian 28
Kellaway, Cecil 29, 56, 57
Kelly, Gene 8, 23, 121, 171, 174, 175, 176
Kelly, Nancy 62
Kelly, Patsy 56
Kelly, Paul 77
Kempson, Rachel 121
Kennedy, Arthur 80, 110, 111
Keogh, Tom **174**
Kerrigan, J. M. 128
Keyes, Evelyn 55
Kilbride, Percy 73
Killers, The 117
King, Henry 106, 112, 126, 127, 131, 162
King, Louis 138
King of the Zombies 65
Kings Row **31**
Kinsky, Leonid 44
Kiss of Death 81
Kitty 9, **126**, 159
Kitty Foyle 152
Knock On Any Door 84
Knox, Alexander 105, 112, 113
Koch, Howard 102, 103, 123, 124, 142, 180
Konstantin, Madame 44
Korda, Alexander 52, 53, 105, 106, 108
Korda, Vincent 52, 108
Korda, Zoltan 95, 117, 18, 121, 130
Korngold, Erich Wolfgang 9, 20, 31, 124, 125, 126, 145
Kortner, Fritz 90, 91
Kosleck, Martin 63, 87, 90, 96
Kramer, Stanley 68, 78
Krasner, Milton 48
Kroeger, Berry 24, 75
Kruger, Otto 62

Lachman, Harry 110
Ladd, Alan 8, 38, 39, 97, 167
Ladies in Retirement **43**
Lady and the Monster, The 65

Lady Be Good 172
Lady Eve, The 8, 150, **156**, 157, 159
Lady from Shanghai, The 29
Lady Hamilton 105, 106, 108
Lady in the Dark 173, 174, 182
Lady in the Lake 38
Lake, Veronica 8, 56, 96
Lamour, Dorothy 168
Lancaster, Burt 9, 41
Lancelot, Sir 59
Lanchester, Elsa 43, 46, 126
Landers, Lew 64
Landis, Carole 51, 67, 179
Lang, Fritz 19, 20, 24, 31, 71, 75, 87, 89, 91, 93, 94, 129, 130, 131
Lang, Walter 10, 52, 158, 171, 177, 179
Lansbury, Angela 66, 73, 122
Lasky, Jesse L. 180
Lassie Come Home 138
Latimer, Jonathan 45
Laughton, Charles 22, 23, 45, 51, 56
Laura **25**, 34, 50
Laurel, Stan 93
Laurents, Arthur 32, 78
Lawton, Charles, Jr. 30
Laszlo, Ernest 90
Lean, David 34
Leave Her to Heaven **151**
Lederer, Francis 122
Lee, Billy 139
Lee, Rowland V. 117
Leigh, Janet 75
Leigh, Vivien 153
Leisen, Mitchell 9, 19, 101, 126, 129, 152, 154, 156, 158, 160, 173
Lengyel, Melchior 96
Leontovitch, Eugénie 88
Leopard Man, The **50-60**
LeRoy, Mervyn 59, 71, 81, 88, 99, 113, 118, 153, 171
Leslie, Joan 152
Letter, The 141, **142**, 151
Letter from an Unknown Woman 106, **123**
Letter to Three Wives, A **169**, 170
Levene, Sam 77
Levien, Sonia 180
Levin, Henry 64, 129
Lewin, Albert 65, 119, 122
Lewis, Joseph H. 129
Lewton, Val 11, 52, 58, 59, 60, 61, 122

Life Begins at 8.30 161
Lifeboat 95
Life with Father 161
Lindfors, Viveca 125
Little Foxes, The 8, 116, 143
Little Nelly Kelly 172
Little Old New York 171
Little Princess, The 177
Little Women 118
Litvak, Anatole 7, 40, 83, 84
Live Today for Tomorrow— see *Act of Murder, An*
Lloyd, Doris 11, 63
Lloyd, Harold 159
Locket, The 18
Lockhart, Gene 107, 114
Lodger, The 31-2
Lombard, Carole 94, 139
Lorre, Peter 37, 40, 58, 64, 91, 93, 102
Losch, Tilly 133
Lost Boundaries 79, 80
Lost Horizon 66
Lost in a Harem 168
Lost Moment, The 106, 115
Lost Weekend, The 68, 69, 82
Love, Montagu 107, 110, 125
Loves of Carmen, The 122
Loves of Edgar Allan Poe, The 110
Lowery, Robert 88
Loy, Myrna 85
Lubin, Arthur 64, 130
Lubitsch, Ernst 9, 55, 129, 154, 155, 160, 170
Lugosi, Bela 50, 52, 61, 64
Lupino, Ida 43, 110, 114, 154
Lyndon, Barré 31, 66

Macbeth 105, 121, 138
MacDonald, Joe 78
MacDougall, Ranald 26
MacGill, Moyna 24
MacLane, Barton 128, 131
MacMurray, Fred 28, 92, 164, 167
Macomber Affair, The 117
Macready, George 45, 46, 47, 129
Madame Bovary 121
Madame Curie 105, 113, 153
Madame DuBarry (1919) 129
Madame DuBarry (1934) 104
Madeleine 34

Mademoiselle Fifi 122
Mad Ghoul, The 63
Mad Wednesday 159
Magnificent Ambersons, The 117, 118
Magnificent Doll, The 112
Main, Marjorie 164
Major and the Minor, The 159
Make Mine Music 12
Malleson, Miles 52
Maltese Falcon, The 20, 37, 38, 39, 40, 102
Mamoulian, Rouben 125, 126, 174
Man Hunt 87, 89
Man in Half Moon Street, The 66
Mankiewicz, Herman J. 128
Mankiewicz, Joseph L. 56, 169
Mann, Anthony 50, 129, 131
Manpower 136
Man's Castle 158
Man Who Came to Dinner, The 161
March, Fredric 56, 84, 85, 99, 105, 118
March of the Years series 80
March of Time series 13, 14, 80
Margie 162
Margo 66
Marin, Edwin L. 64
Maris, Mona 92
Mark of Zorro, The 125
Marks, Owen 102, 103
Marley, J. Peverell 137, 177, 179
Marshall, George 38, 135, 164
Marshall, Herbert 10, 62, 89, 116, 119, 152
Marshall, Marion 11
Marshall, Tully 39
Martin, Hugh 173
Marx Brothers, The 167, 171
Mask of Dimitrios, The 40
Mason, James 41, 42, 87, 121
Massey, Raymond 91, 96, 107, 115, 149
Master Race, The 91
Maté, Rudolph 45, 47, 108, 162, 177
Mature, Victor 24, 45, 134
Maxwell, Marilyn 175
May, Joe 64, 91
Mayer, Edwin Justus 94

Mayer, Louis B. 8, 17, 140
Mayfair, Mitzi 14
Mayo, Archie L. 55, 88, 160
McCarey, Leo 93
McCord, Ted 136
McCrea, Joel 88, 113, 131, 157, 169
McDaniell, Hattie 100
McGuire, Dorothy 62, 78
McLeod, Norman Z. 167, 172
McManus, Sharon 176
Meet John Doe 72, 73, 103
Meet Me in St. Louis 162, 171, 173, 174
Melchior, Lauritz 176
Melody Time 12
Memphis Belle, The 86
Menjou, Adolphe 73
Menzies, William Cameron 34, 88, 89, 91, 117, 129
Meredith, Burgess 70, 71, 97, 112
Metty, Russell 33, 42
Michelet, Michel 122
Midnight 159
Midsummer Night's Dream A 104
Mildred Pierce 26, 28, 29, 148
Miles, Peter 138
Milestone, Lewis 27, 70, 94, 96, 98, 138
Milhaud, Darius 122
Milland, Ray 9, 34, 46, 58, 69, 82, 135, 160
Miller, Ann 175
Miller, Arthur 10, 77, 126
Miller, Seton I. 124, 127
Minnelli, Vincente 8, 121, 128, 171, 172, 173, 174
Miracle of Morgan's Creek, The 158
Miranda, Carmen 10, 177
Mission to Moscow 103
Miss Tatlock's Millions 170
Mrs. Miniver 95, 153
Mrs. Parkington 153
Mr. Bug Goes to Town 13
Mr. Deeds Goes to Town 72
Mr. Skeffington 144
Mr. Smith Goes to Washington 72
Mitchell, Thomas 43, 63, 112, 117
Mitchum, Robert 97, 135
Mix, Tom 130
Mohr, Hal 64, 115
Monsieur Verdoux 163, 164
Montez, Maria 10, 51, 64, 128, 130, 145

Montgomery, Robert 14, 38, 55
Moon and Sixpence, The 119
Moon is Down, The 90, 94
Moon Over Miami 10, 158, **179**, 180
Moorehead, Agnes 39, 42, 99, 101, 106, 114, 120, 123, 174
More the Merrier, The 169
Morgan, Frank 88, 123
Morgan, Henry 45
Mortal Storm, The 87, 88, 89
Moss, Arnold 129
Mourning Becomes Electra **115**
Mowbray, Alan 108
Murder in Thornton Square— see *Gaslight*
Mummy, The 63
Muni, Paul 104, 135, 181
Munshin, Jules 175
Munson, Ona 44, 45
Murder, He Says **164**, 165
Murder, My Sweet 38
Murnau, F. W. 54
Musuraca, Nicholas 59
My Darling Clementine 130, **134**
My Friend Flicka 138
My Gal Sal 171
My Little Chickadee 167
My Man Godfrey 158
My Reputation 149

Naked City, The **49**, 69, 81
National Velvet 138
Natwick, Mildred 62
Nazi Agent 87
Nazimova 87
Neal, Patricia 47, 48
Negri, Pola 164
Negulesco, Jean 9, 19, 40, 148, 149, 153
Neill, Roy William 63, 103
Nesbitt, John 13
Newman, Alfred 126, 127, 162, 179
Nibelungen, Die 129
Nichols, Dudley 78
Night and Day 180
Night at the Opera, A 169
Night Has a Thousand Eyes 66
Night in Paradise, A 51, 64
Night Monster 63
Nightmare Alley 19, **27**, 36
Ninotchka 94, 155, 160
Niven, David 112

No Way Out 80
Nora Prentiss 150
North Star 90, **96**, 98
North West Mounted Police 135
Northwest Passage **135**
Notorious 44
Now, Voyager 141, **143**
Nugent, Elliot 116

Oakie, Jack 67, 177, 180
Oberon, Merle 33, 43, 151, 181
Objective Burma 96
O'Brien, Dave 13
O'Brien, Margaret 173
O'Connor, Donald 11
O'Connor, Una 87
Odets, Clifford 148
Of Human Hearts 79
Of Mice and Men 68, **70**
O'Hara, Maureen 127, 128
O'Keefe, Dennis 59, 165
Old Acquaintance 141
Olivier, Laurence 108, 120
Olsen, Ole 166, 168
On the Town 171, **175**, 179
Once Upon a Honeymoon 93
One Touch of Venus 182
Ophuls, Max 41, 42, 106, 123, 128
O'Shea, Michael 111
Ossessione 29
Ottiano, Rafaela 118
Our Hearts Were Growing Up 162
Our Hearts Were Young and Gay 162
Ouspenskaya, Maria 45
Out of the Fog 7, 40
Outlaw, The 18
Owen, Reginald 126, 160
Ox-Bow Incident, The 68, **71**

Pabst, G. W. 63
Pa, George 12, 167
Pallette, Eugene 125, **137**, 157
Palm Beach Story, The **158**
Palmer, Ernest 177
Palmer, Lilli 49
Pangborn, Franklin 11
Paradine Case, The **21-2**
Paris Calling 90
Parker, Eleanor 106, 114
Parks, Larry 129
Parsonnet, Marion 45, 46

Partie de Campagne, Une 137
Pascal, Ernest 111
Passing Parade series 13, 18
Patrick, Lee 11
Paul, Eliott 147, 180
Paxinou, Katina 40
Paxton, John 76
Pearson, Beatrice 49, 79
Peck, Gregory 44, 77, 86, 117, 123, 133, 138
People Will Talk 169
Pereira, William 120
Perinal, George 53
Peters, Hans 65, 92, 174
Pete Smith specialties 13
Phantom Lady 21, **22-3**
Phantom of the Opera 50, 64
Philadelphia Story, The **162**
Pichel, Irving 33, 94, 135, 161
Picture of Dorian Gray, The 65, 174
Pidgeon, Walter 75, 89, 95, 113, 140
Pinky 68, **78**
Pinocchio 12
Pirate, The 128, **174**
Pittsburgh 136
Planer, Franz 97
Platt, Marc 177
Pluto 12
Polito, Sol 9, 21, 113, 143, 144, 180
Polonsky, Abraham 49
Porter, Cole 171, 180
Portrait of Jennie 57
Possessed 149
Postman Always Rings Twice, The 29
Powell, Jane 176
Powell, Michael 52
Power, Tyrone 10, 11, 14, 27, 124, 125, 127, 152
Preminger, Otto 19, 25, 87, 128
Preston, Robert 117, 135
Price, Vincent 25, 64, 135
Pride and Prejudice 104, 119, 120
Pride of the Marines 97
Prince of Foxes 127
Private Affairs of Bel Ami, The 122
Psycho 60
Purple Heart, The 96, **98**
Pursued 135
Pygmalion 160

Quai des Brumes 40

Qualen, John 43
Quinn, Anthony 126

Rafferty, Frances 11
Raft, George 136
Raines, Ella 11, 21, 23
Rains, Claude 11, 26, 31, 44, 50, 54, 55, 64, 102, 143, 144, 145
Ralston, Vera Hruba 11, 65, 105
Rand, Ayn 47
Randolph, Jane 59
Random Harvest 153
Rapper, Irving 9, 143, 144, 161, 173, 180
Rashomon 150
Rathbone, Basil 89, 92, 125, 129
Ratoff, Gregory 95
Ray, Nicholas 84
Raye, Martha 14, 163
Razor's Edge, The 10, 19, 119, **151**
Reap the Wild Wind 129
Rebecca 44, 120
Reckless Moment, The 41, **42**
Red Danube, The 16, 75
Redgrave, Michael 115
Red Menace, The 71, 138
Red Pony, The 71, **138**
Red River **132**
Règle du Jeu, La 137
Reign of Terror **129**
Reisch, Walter 108, 181
Reluctant Dragon, The 12
Remarkable Andrew, The 54
Rennahan, Ray 132
Renoir, Jean 94, 122, 137
Return of Frank James, The 131
Reunion in France 89, 91, 92
Revenge of the Zombies 65
Revere, Anne 78
Rhapsody in Blue 173, **180**, 181
Richards, Ann 41, 75
Richardson, Sir Ralph 116
Ridges, Stanley 23, 85
Ripley, Arthur 64
Riskin, Robert 72
Roach, Hal 56, 67, 70
Road to Utopia 168
Roadhouse 153
Robinson, Casey 31, 96, 117, 141, 143
Robinson, Edward G. 24, **42**, 63, 66, 107, 113, 136

Robson, Flora 124
Robson, Mark 48, 59, 60, 61, 78
Rodgers, Richard 180
Roemheld, Heinz 30
Rogers, Ginger 93, 100, 112, 139, 152
Rogers, Roy 105, 135
Roman, Ruth 49
Rooney, Mickey 8, 11, 106, 138, 171, 172, 175
Rope **21-2**
Rossen, Robert 49, 74, 98, 113
Rosson, Harold 132, 175
Roxie Hart 167
Rozsa, Miklos 20, 29, 53, 82, 118
Ruggles, Charlie 141
Rumann, Sig 67, 93, 94, 118
Ruskin, Harry 29
Russell, Harold 84, 85
Russell, John 53
Russell, Rosalind 115, 139
Ruttenberg, Joseph 35, 154
Ryan, Peggy 11
Ryan, Robert 41, 48, 49, 77

Sabu 10, 52, 118
Sahara 96
San Antonio 135
San Juan, Olga 166, 167
Sanders, George 24, 56, 65, 89, 119, 122, 123
Sandrich, Mark 97
Santell, Alfred 11, 115
Saville, Victor 72, 105
Scarlet Street 20, **25**
Schary, Dore 17, 97, 106
Schnabel, Stefan 75
Schnee, Charles 132
Schoedsack, Ernest B. 66
Schunzel, Reinhold 90
Schuster, Harold 138
Scott, Adrian 69
Scott, Hazel 173, 180
Scott, Lizabeth 9
Scott, Martha 117
Scott, Randolph 131
Scott, Zachary 26, 137
Sea Hawk, The **124**
Sea Wolf, The 105, **113**
Searching Wind, The **74**
Secret Life of Walter Mitty, The 167
Segal, Harry 55
Seiler, Lewis 98, 136
Seitz, John F. 21, 45, 83
Selznick, David O. 17, 57, 58, 100, 105, 132

Sergeant York 8
Set Up, The **48**
Seven Sinners 136
Seventh Cross, The 94
Seventh Victim, The 60
Shadow of a Doubt 21
Shamroy, Leon 127, **151**, 179
Shanghai Gesture, The 8, **44**
Shepperd, John—see Strudwick, Shepperd
Sheridan, Ann 31, 140, 150, 151, 154, 161
Sheriff, R. C. 108
Sherlock Holmes and the Spider Woman 64
Sherman, George 65, 128, 129
Sherwood, Robert E. 108
She Wore a Yellow Ribbon 134
Shop Around the Corner, The 160
Shore, Dinah 167
Shumlin, Herman 75, 121, 175
Sidney, George 13, 75, 121, 176
Sidney, Sylvia 75
Silvers, Phil 176, 177
Simms, Ginny 180
Simon, Simone 59, 122
Simpson, Russell 69
Sinatra, Frank 175
Sinbad the Sailor 128
Since You Went Away 19, **100**, 101
Siodmak, Robert 19, 22, 23, 24, 31, 116, 123
Siren of Atlantis 64
Sirk, Douglas 91, 123
Skall, William V. 131
Skelton, Red 173
Skinner, Cornelia Otis 57, 161
Slezak, Walter 95, 128
Sloane, Everett 29, 127
Smash-Up 83
Smith, Alexis 114
Smith, Sir C. Aubrey 63, 98
Smith, Kent 59, 150
Smith, Thorne 56
Snake Pit, The 68, **83**
Snow White and the Seven Dwarfs 54
So Dear to My Heart 12
So Evil My Love 34, 35
So Proudly We Hail 97
Some Like It Hot 170
Sondergaard, Gale 54, 130, 143
Song of Bernadette, The 105, 112

Song of Love 105, 171, 181
Song of Russia 95
Song of Scheherezade 181
Song to Remember, A 151, 171, **181**
Son of Fury 126
Sorry, Wrong Number 20, 40
Sothern, Ann 170
Southerner, The 137
Spanish Main, The 128
Spellbound 44
Spiral Staircase, The 24
Spiritualist, The—see The Amazing Dr. X
Spoilers, The 136
Springsteen, R. G. 75
Springtime in the Rockies 179
Stack, Robert 88
Stagecoach 130
Stage Door Canteen 14
Stanwyck, Barbara 8, 9, 27, 28, 41, 131, 135, 140, 149, 150, 156, 157
Star Spangled Rhythm 167
State Fair 171, 180
State of the Union 73
Stefano, Joseph 67
Steinbeck, John 95
Steiner, Max 9, 20, 102, 103, 114, 126, 142, 144, 146, 161
Sternberg, Josef von 8, 44, 132
Stevens, George 161, 169
Stevens, Robert 105
Stevenson, Houseley 39, 143
Stewart, Donald Ogden 72, 147
Stewart, James 163
Stolen Life, A 141, **145**
Stone, Andrew 165
Stone, Lewis 165
Stooges, The Three 13
Story of G.I. Joe, The 97
Story of Dr. Wassel, The 97
Stossel, Ludwig 89
Stothart, Herbert 8
Stradling, Harry 75, 174
Strange Affair of Uncle Harry, The 24
Strange Death of Adolph Hitler 91
Strange Interlude 114
Strange Love of Martha Ivers, The 20, 27
Stranger, The 42
Street, The 63
Street With No Name, The 81

Strike Up the Band 171, 172
Strictly Dishonorable 156
Stroheim, Erich von 52, 65, 87, 90, 96, 97
Strudwick, Shepperd 110
Student of Prague, The 63
Sturges, Preston 8, 9, 113, 155, 156, 157, 158, 159
Sullivan's Travels 157, 158
Summer Holiday 162, **174**
Summer Storm 123
Sunday Dinner for a Soldier 18
Susan and God 147
Suspect, The 23
Suspicion 44
Sutherland, A. Edward 64
Swamp Water 137

Tales of Manhattan 18
Talk of the Town 169
Tallas, Gregg 64
Tamiroff, Akim 117, 128
Tandy, Jessica 121
Tashlin, Frank 170
Taurog, Norman 106
Taylor, Elizabeth 138
Taylor, Robert 88, 95, 153
Temple, Shirley 53, 100, 177, 180
Temptation 33, 34, 151
Tender Comrade 100
Terry, Philip 82
Tetzlaff, Ted 44, 93
Texas 135
Thank Your Lucky Stars 167
That Forsyte Woman 119
That Night in Rio 179
That Uncertain Feeling 160
They Live By Night 18
They Were Expendable 99
They Won't Forget 71
Thief of Bagdad, The 65, 120, 172
Thirty Seconds Over Tokyo 99
This Gun for Hire 39
This Is The Army 103, 180
This Land Is Mine 90, 94
Thorpe, Richard 92
Thousand and One Nights, The 53
Three Caballeros 12
Three Godfathers 134
Three Musketeers, The 121
Three Strangers 40
Thunderhead, Son of Flicka 138

Tierney, Gene 10, 25, 44, 45, 51, 56, 71, 75, 151
Tiomkin, Dimitri 133
T Men 50
To Be or Not to Be 94, 150
To Each His Own 152
To Have and Have Not 38
Tobacco Road 68, 71, 164
Todd, Ann 34
Toland, Gregg 70, 116, 130, 134
Tom and Jerry 12
Tomorrow the World 99
Topper 56, 57
Topper Returns 51, 56
Topper Takes a Trip 56
Toth, Andre de 43
Totheroh, Rollie 163
Totter, Audrey 11
Toumanova, Tamara 96
Tourneur, Jacques 59, 96
Tover, Leo 84, 116, 119, 139
Tracy, Spencer 8, 51, 56, 65, 72, 73, 99, 106, 107, 135, 163
Travers, Henry 55, 56
Treasure of Sierra Madre, The 136
Trevor, Claire 38
Trilling, Steve 9
Trotti, Lamar 10, 71, 151
Trouble in Paradise 155, 160
Trumbo, Dalton 55, 99, 100
Tura, Joseph 94
Turnabout 51, 67
Turner, Lana 29, 65, 121
Tuttle, Frank 39, 94
Twardowski, Hans von 87, 91
Two Mrs. Carrolls, The 149
Tynan, Kenneth 101

Unconquered 135
Underground 93
Unfaithful, The 150
Unfaithfully Yours 159
Uninvited, The 51, 57
Unsuspected, The 20, 26
Up in Arms 167
Up in Mabel's Room 161

Vague, Vera 11
Vallee, Rudy 158
Valley of Decision, The 153
Valley of the Zombies 65

Van Druten, John 160, 161
Vansittart, Sir Robert 52
Varden, Evelyn 78
Variety Girl 166
Veidt, Conrad 52, 53, 87, 88, 89, 92, 93
Vera-Ellen 175
Vickers, Martha 38
Victory 19, 118, 119
Vidor, Charles 10, 43, 45, 121, 176, 177, 181
Vidor, King 47, 130, 132, 133, 135, 146

Visconti, Luchino 29
Voice of the Turtle, The 161
Vorhaus, Bernard 66

Waggner, George 64
Wake Island 97
Wald, Jerry 96, 150, 153
Walk, Don't Run 169
Walker, Helen 27, 164
Walker, Joseph 56
Walker, Robert 101, 105, 181
Walk in the Sun, A 97
Wallis, Hal 9, 74
Walsh, Raoul 56, 96, 135, 136
Walton, Douglas 66
Wanger, Walter 105, 112, 115
Warner, Jack 8, 48, 58
Watch on the Rhine, The 99
Waterloo Bridge 153
Waters, Ethel 172
Watson, Lucile 11
Watson, Robert 90
Waxman, Franz 9, 20, 150
Wayne, John 132, 134, 136
Webb, Clifton 10, 25, 152, 170

Welles, Orson 8, 29, 31, 42, 105, 109, 110, 117, 118, 120, 121, 127, 130, 138
Wellman, William A. 71, 75, 97, 131, 167
Werker, Alfred 79
Westerner, The 70, 130, 131, 134
Western Union 130
We Were Strangers 76
Whelan, Tim 52
White Cliffs of Dover, The 95
Whitty, Dame May 63, 95
Whorf, Richard 72, 73
Why We Fight series 18, 86, 103
Wickes, Mary 11, 161
Wilbur, Crane 81
Wilcox, Fred 138
Wilde, Cornel 124, 128, 151, 181
Wilder, Billy 9, 19, 22, 28, 31, 68, 82, 83, 97, 159, 170
Wiles, Gordon 122
Williams, Esther 176
Will Success Spoil Rock Hunter? 170
Wilson 105, 106, 112
Wilson, Dooley 101, 102
Winchester 73 131
Window, The 18
Winnington, Richard 68
Winter, Keith 110
Winter Meeting 141
Wise, Robert 48, 60, 122
Wizard of Oz, The 54, 172
Woman Destroyed, A 83
Woman in the Window, The ~~20, 25~~
Woman in White, The 91, 105, 106, 114
Woman's Face, A 8, 147, 149

Woman's Vengeance, A 121
Woman Who Came Back, The 51, 52, 62
Women, The 162
Wonder Man, The 167, 168
Wood, Sam 31, 33, 34, 117, 152, 169
Woolley, Monty 161
World Premiere 93
Wright, Teresa 85, 95, 116, 135
Wycherley, Margaret 72, 118
Wyler, William 8, 84, 85, 115, 116, 130, 134, 142, 143
Wyman, Jane 82, 138, 153

Yank in Dutch, A 89, 94
Yankee Doodle Dandy 180
Yates, George Worthington 128
Yearling, The 137
Yellow Sky 132
Yolanda and the Thief 173
Young, Gig 106, 114
Young, Harry 63
Young Mr. Lincoln, The 108
Young People 180
Young, Robert 62 74, 77, 88, 131
Young, Roland 56, 162
Young Tom Edison 106

Zanuck, Darryl F. 10, 68, 105, 112, 125, 138
Ziegfeld Follies 173
Zinnemann, Fred 13, 22, 49, 94
Zucco, George 51, 63, 127